Contents

Metric Conversion

	Inches to Millimetres and Centimetres					
	MM—millimetres			CM—centimetres		
Inches	MM	CM	Inches	CM	Inches	CM
1/8	3	0.3	9	22.9	30	76.2
1/4	6	0.6	10	25.4	31	78.7
3/8	10	1.0	11	27.9	32	81.3
1/2	13	1.3	12	30.5	33	83.8
5/8	16	1.6	13	33.0	34	86.4
3/4	19	1.9	14	35.6	35	88.9
7/8	22	2.2	15	38.1	36	91.4
1	25	2.5	16	40.6	37	94.0
1 1/4	32	3.2	17	43.2	38	96.5
1 1/2	38	3.8	18	45.7	39	99.1
1 3/4	44	4.4	19	48.3	40	101.6
2	51	5.1	20	50.8	41	104.1
2 1/2	64	6.4	21	53.3	42	106.7
3	76	7.6	22	55.9	43	109.2
3 1/2	89	8.9	23	58.4	44	111.8
4	102	10.2	24	61.0	45	114.3
4 1/2	114	11.4	25	63.5	46	116.8
5	127	12.7	26	66.0	47	119.4
6	152	15.2	27	68.6	48	121.9
7	178	17.8	28	71.1	49	124.5
8	203	20.3	29	73.7	50	127.0

Movable Storage Projects

Ingenious
Space-Saving Solutions

Charles R. Self

Sterling Publishing Co., Inc. New York

14.95

Library of Congress Cataloging-in-Publication Data

Self, Charles R.
  Movable storage projects : ingenious space-saving solutions /
Charles R. Self.
    p.   cm.
  Includes index.
  ISBN 0-8069-8631-X
  1. Cabinetwork—Amateurs' manuals.   2. Storage in the home—
Amateurs' manuals.   I. Title.
TT197.S52   1993
684.1'6—dc20   92-35847
                                                              CIP

Edited by R. P. Neumann

10 9 8 7 6 5 4 3 2 1

Published in 1993 by Sterling Publishing Company, Inc.
387 Park Avenue South, New York, N.Y. 10016
© 1993 by Charles R. Self
Distributed in Canada by Sterling Publishing
℅ Canadian Manda Group, P.O. Box 920, Station U
Toronto, Ontario, Canada M8Z 5P9
Distributed in Great Britain and Europe by Cassell PLC
Villiers House, 41/47 Strand, London WC2N 5JE, England
Distributed in Australia by Capricorn Link Ltd.
P.O. Box 665, Lane Cove, NSW 2066
Manufactured in the United States of America
All rights reserved

Sterling ISBN 0-8069-8631-X

Introduction

Storage is an often critical need for all but a very few, very fortunate people among us. Well-organized, and well-designed storage makes for a sense of well being: at the very least, the irritation of not having a place to put something is not present, nor is the grumble that comes from not being able to locate anything because everything is crammed into a jumbled pile, in or out of containers.

Movable storage, storage that can be brought from one point to another for any of a number of reasons, is frequently even handier than standard built-in shelves, cabinets and other, stationary, storage. Movable storage, as the name implies, may roll, slide, or be carried from one room, or in some cases, from one country to another. At other times, you may simply want to move it from one spot in a room to another.

In the process of moving from room to room or place to place, the type of material stored may change. Putting wheels or handles on a box and calling the result movable storage, though, doesn't make easy movement true. Boxes, in one style or another, are our main form of storage; we may call them closets; we may call them desks or dressers or bookcases, but they're still basically boxes. What truly makes storage movable, or portable, is adaptability within a fairly decent set of limits.

And easy movement is almost always one criterion.

Careful design makes some types of boxes easier to carry, roll, slide, or otherwise change their shape or position, with or without their contents. Attention needs to be paid to overall size and weight, just as a start. Wobbling around with an 18″-wide toolbox all of 3′ long and 30″ deep, no matter how comfortable the handles, is a chore even when the thing is empty. The chore nearly goes beyond human capacity when the toolbox is filled. Wheels can help, of course. In other cases, movable storage that folds down flat, or nearly so, or disassembles for movement is by far the best for a particular situation. In other instances, wheels and a folding feature may be best; while in still others modular units provide the change to movability, from one type of storage to another that is needed.

I present projects often designed from scratch as movable. The folding projects were designed to fold for simple storage when they're not needed. The rolling projects are designed to fit easily through most standard door passages and move along halls with wheels large enough and strong enough to make getting over household and shop humps and bumps easy.

The cedar-lined walnut hope chest is not easily movable without the addition of wheels. This version is quite large, and may, if you wish, be reduced by one-quarter in height to aid fitting it in small rooms. It should always, though, have a ball-type wheel placed on each corner, or it is not mobile. Larger wheels are visible and ugly, but the ball type is barely discernible, yet provides good mobility.

"Movable Storage" consists of workable woodworking projects, where the primary materials will be one of the oaks, cherry, walnut, pine, plywood or other woods. There is no substitute for wood in a home—or shop. It has marvelous textures, odors, appearance, lustre, works easily, and is durable in the extreme.

In one case, the computer/home office desk, the project is designed as a modular unit, to be useful in a number of different configurations for people with differing needs. After all, not everyone is going to have a home office designed and set up in the same manner, and few other people will even *want* one done so. Thus, the desk, designed to be all-inclusive for a one-person office, needs to be adaptable, which means units need to sit side-by-side and atop one another, and move easily; but they must be stable once in place, with the possibility of being moved from one space to another from time to time.

In some cases, movability isn't the need to wheel or carry something around the home. It is the need to change the configuration of a storage piece so that it can be used either for different items, an expanded job, or a contracted job of storing the same items. Units such as the slide-case stacking drawers take care of that need, as do the stacking bookcases—in a more limited manner. Bookcases primarily store books, but sensible portable bookcases can be made in sizes and arrays that store in many different ways.

Mobility is a feature that needs to be designed into each project; that's what has been done here. At the same time, much of what we store is fairly stable in unit size and shape—records, audio tape cartridges, video cartridges, books (individually, size varies a lot, but the basic shape for most books is still a rectangle)— and where that isn't the case, as with clothing, standards have developed for reasonable space allowances. Sometimes, those space allowances must be modified, upwards or downwards, for more or fewer units; but, here, the modifying has been done so that those units remain full-size.

Curves used are simple. Decorative design features applied are also practical—radiusing of edges and corners helps prevent bruising and lack of comfort.

In addition to general utility and movability, these projects are designed to be interesting to build and use. If decorative accents make you happy, feel free to add wherever, and whatever, you like.

Wood specifications are a matter of personal choice. Some people prefer oak to walnut, while others prefer cherry to anything. Someone working for economy will select pine for all but the members that must be hardwood.

It is *your* project. Do it in the manner and material that makes you happiest.

Charles R. Self

1
Guide to Tools and Materials

■ Tools for Project-Making

Many of these storage projects may be made with portable power tools, or even hand tools. Most are at least a little easier with stationary power tools and some accessories.

Handtools

Handtools needed for storage project construction include the claw hammer, handsaw, screwdrivers of various types, planes, chisels, mitre box, nail sets, measuring tapes and rules, squares, levels, a brace and bit set, and clamps.

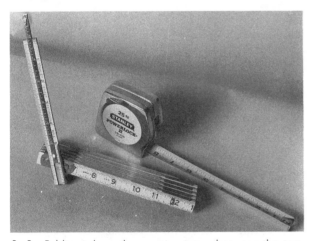

1–1 Folding rule and measuring tape; between the two, most major measuring in the projects is readily done.

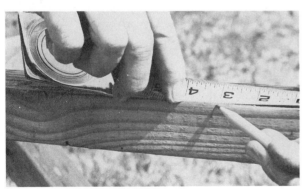

1–2 Tilt tape or rule; mark then is almost on work surface, making for accurate transfer of measurements.

Measuring Tools

Measuring tapes come in many lengths and widths. For storage project purposes, lengths above a dozen feet aren't needed.

Folding rules come in 6′ and 8′ lengths. Flat rules are available in metal and wood.

The basics of measuring include adding a tilt to the tape or rule when a mark is made. Marks may be made with standard pencils, carpenter's pencils or scribes.

1–3 An awl set to be used as a scribe.

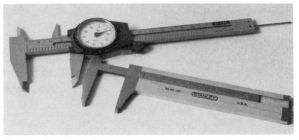

1–4 Calipers work well for many measurements, and are nearly essential for some, especially in lathe work, and where accurate depth and inside-outside measurements are needed.

Squares

Squares for woodworking include the try square, the combination square, the speed square, and the framing square. Squares of two types are essential. The basic, or try, square is a rigid form of metal, or wood and metal. Blade length will be 8″ to 12″, in inch or metric markings.

Combination squares have blades that slide in the handles, offering 90 and 45 degree markings, with slightly less accuracy than a try square.

Framing, carpenter's, and roofing squares are versions of a stamped metal L with a 2″-wide blade and a 1½″-wide tongue.

Handsaws

Saws are the primary cutting tools for woodworking. For our projects a 10-point panel saw or a 12″ or larger backsaw will do. For metal, or harder plastics, get a hacksaw. For rougher cuts, one of the newer hard tooth saws, with eight points per inch, works well. A hand mitre box is a big help.

Hammers

Hammers are available in many styles and sizes, but for our storage projects, a good-quality 16-ounce curved claw is fine as a general hammer. (Head weights vary from 13 ounces to 28 ounces.) For small storage projects, get a 13-ounce model too.

1–5 The combination square works well in setting cutting heights for table saws—and for router bits.

1–7 Fine cuts require dovetail saws.

1–6 The new aggressive tooth design on this saw speeds hand cutting. *(Courtesy of Stanley Tools)*

1–8 The claw hammer may be used to drive chisels. Always wear safety goggles or glasses.

A fibreglass handle is probably the best for most uses, but if you like tubular metal, or wood, go with either.

Soft-faced hammers come in many versions, from rawhide faced to plastic faced. Rubber mallets are also available. For assembly uses with tight fitting joints, any may prove handy. All get frequent use in storage project assembly.

Screwdrivers

Screwdrivers come in all the obvious head styles, to fit old and new head patterns. Select for head style, and for quality. As a basic recommendation, it is wise to go with a reasonable length shank, say 6″ to 8″, as these are the easiest to control.

1–9   A rawhide mallet head will not mar cherry; so it is a great help in driving domed plugs in screw counterbores.

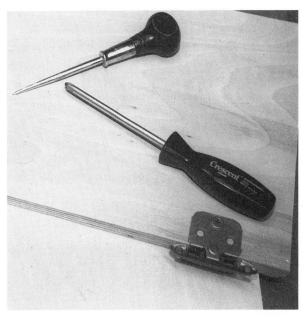

1–11   This and similar Crescent screwdrivers have exceptionally comfortable grips. In this birch plywood, an awl makes a fine center punch and will punch deeply enough to eliminate the need for predrilling of holes for these short hinge screws.

1–10   Rubber mallets are a great assistance in wide-board assembly, even when using biscuit joinery; the rubber tends to allow you to strike a board down and drag it along at the same time.

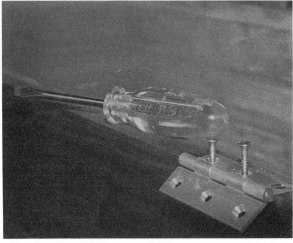

1–12   Slotted head screws work well when hand driven, and hand driving is almost essential in some places, including this solid brass hinge with its solid brass screws.

Electric Drills

Standard corded electric drills come in many versions and chuck sizes. Select for durability as well as power. Drills are one tool where buying cheap can't pay. A ³⁄₈″ chuck drill, with a variable-speed reversible motor drawing 3.5 or more amperes works well for almost all woodworking needs. More power is seldom needed, though on occasion a ½″ chuck is handy.

For driving screws, use a clutched drill. Any variable speed drill will drive screws, but clutched variable speed drill stops driving before it torques the head off.

Cordless electric drills are worth considering as replacements for corded drills. These drills offer the same features found in corded drills, with slightly lower capacities in wood, steel and masonry. If you go cordless, get a drill with a battery pack that charges quickly, and buy a second battery pack. It will also pay to select a two-range model; all the better cordless drills are variable speed, but most also offer two-speed ranges, with the low speed range giving great torque and excellent control of depth. The top speed range provides a good speed for quickly drilling holes.

Drill Bits

For general woodworking, a good quality brad-point drill bit set will do almost all that you need to do. For special requirements, there are other styles available: generally, brad-point bits come in sizes from ³⁄₁₆″ to 1″, though they are also available in larger sizes. Brad points allow easy starting without center punching, and the bits cut a nice, clean hole that is ideal for dowelling.

For very fine work, consider Forstner bits. These bits cut an exceptionally clean hole, and also produce a flat bottom in the hole, making them good for projects that need to have flat bottomed holes that accept dowels, candles, salt and pepper shakers and similar items.

Standard twist drills are what most of us use for most jobs. Good high-speed steel twist drills last a reasonable length of time and are fairly low in cost.

Spade bits are used for rough drilling. Spade bits are cut from flat steel plate about ¹⁄₈″ thick, and have spurs sharpened to give them a good bite. They cut fast, but they cut rough.

There are a great many other bits and bit related drill accessories available, including different kinds of countersink and counterbore and pilot-hole tools.

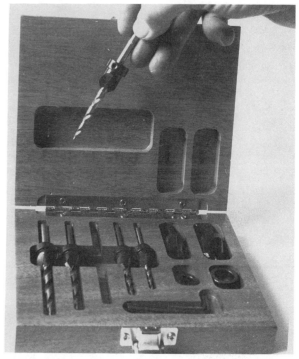

1–14 The Fuller tapered drill bit set includes adjustable countersink/counterbore cutters.

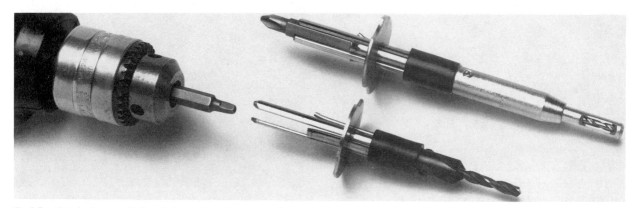

1–13 Quick change drill and driver sets save time when drilling pilot holes and driving screws with a single drill. (Courtesy of The Woodworker's Store)

Power Saws

Selecting a table saw is a moderately simple job even with the wide variety on the market. Blade size may range from 4″ up to 14″, while power can vary from fractional to three phase multi-horsepower. Tight tolerances, tables precisely machined, and well-made adjusters are needed. Mitre slots must be precise, and the rip fence sturdy and accurate. Both mitre gauge and rip fence can be replaced with aftermarket types, but such units are expensive. Several portable saws offer surprising accuracy.

Table saws and radial-arm saws excel at certain jobs: the table saw is best at ripping, grooving, and similar jobs (and moves on to excel at crosscutting when a sliding table is added). Radial-arm saws are excellent at crosscutting, dadoing, compound cutting, cutting dadoes or grooves on the visible side (upper side) of a piece of lumber, and may be fitted with many of the accessories (dado head, moulding head, etc.) that also fit table saws. Radial-arm saws also may be fitted, depending on brand, with rotary shapers, flexible shafts and router bits.

If you have only one major saw in your shop, the table saw is handiest; but if at all possible, have both.

1–16 Finger joints being made on a Delta Unisaw, using an Accujig.

1–15 This lightweight Makita 10″ table saw includes a sliding table. It is mounted on a shop-built cabinet that serves as a cart. For heavy work, it is necessary to block the wheels as well as applying the brakes. The wheels skid on smooth floor surfaces. Otherwise, the combination works fine.

1–17 The Sears Craftsman Electronic radial-arm saw, with the Freud blade, is a great crosscutting and mitring unit.

1–18 This 8" Nicholson dado set would have to be fitted to a 12" table saw to keep from having its use limited–it will strike any standard 10" table saw's dado insert before the set is fully raised. It works beautifully on a 10" radial-arm saw.

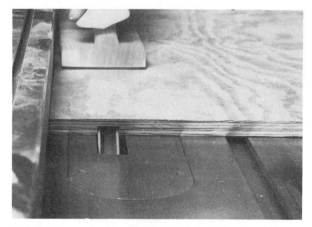

1–19 Use push sticks and push blocks to keep hands from being ahead of work at the start of the cut and behind it at the finish of the cut. Dado blades go invisible when the cut starts, so you must *always* remember to keep your hands clear of their area of blade reappearance.

Grooving and Dadoing

Grooves and dadoes are among the most popular cuts on table saws, and are very handy for storage project building. They differ only slightly: grooves go with the grain of the wood, while dadoes are grooves made across the grain of the wood. Dado sets are used to make both grooves and dadoes, and are stacked blade assemblies that give a wider kerf, or cut. Outer blades are like small diameter-standard saw blades, while inner, or chipper, blades have only two teeth, at opposing sides of the blade. The chipper blades clean out the area between the outer blades, producing a set width groove, or dado.

Single blade dado blades wobble at a maximum specified distance, producing a cut the same size as the wobble. Wobbler dado sets leave more material in the bottom of the grooves than do standard sets, but are faster to set up.

Groove and dado joints are useful for setting in shelves in cabinetry, in cases where shelves and dividers do not need to be adjustable for height. They are much stronger than butt joints, and neater. Dado blades also make rabbet cuts. Rabbets are shelves cut into the wood, into which another piece of wood (or other material) fits.

1–20 Super-cheap gum remover—Easy-Off oven cleaner (or any good brand). Spray on.

1–21 After it sits 3–4 minutes, wipe around a bit. Then, wipe off.

Circular Saws

Circular saws reduce working time and effort over handsaws, and can be more accurate. Blade diameters range from 4″ to 16″; standard is 7¼″.

A circular saw needs a thick base plate, easy to adjust for depth; an 8′ to 10′ long cord; a top handle for easier control; for 7¼″ blade size at least a 10 ampere motor.

Circular saws are used in woodworking to form mitre and butt joints. Their accuracy depends on experience and the jigs used to assist in the cut.

A carbide-tipped blade is best. The blade may be a combination for general use—able to do rip and crosscuts. For the best mitres, use a planer combination blade.

The rip guide helps make long rips and rip bevels. It adjusts to allow the appropriate cutoff with the grain, but is not used for cross-grain cuts. The guide shaft slips into slots on the saw base, and a screw to hold the distance is set. Guide on the outside edge of the work to make the cut.

1–24 DeWalt's Crosscutter makes a clean, accurate cut in walnut.

1–22 Ease of adjustment of blade cut height is essential on a top-grade circular saw. This Black & Decker (now DeWalt) Super Sawcat has a drop foot blade that adjusts quickly and accurately.

1–23 Porter-Cable's Speedtronic here makes a two board cut, with spring clamps providing the holding pressure for the boards. The power of the saw, along with a sharp carbide-tipped blade, means light holding pressure is quite strong enough.

1–25 Skil's 10″ mitre saw is an accurate, relatively low cost tool, and it is shown with work clamp and extensions that add great utility.

1–28 Makita's 3¼ horsepower ½″-collet plunge router is a sturdy beauty. It handles easily for a big, heavy router, and adjust quickly (that's a feature of almost all plunge routers).

1–26 Porter-Cable's Speedmatic 3¼ horsepower five-speed router is one of the most powerful and sturdy production routers available today. It is not cheap, but, as here, it runs forever and cuts beautifully; the router cut all the rabbets for the hope chest and hardly warmed its motor up.

1–27 Porter-Cable's 1½ horsepower model 691 with D handle is a lightweight, easy to use router, but is also exceptionally durable.

1–29 Freud's plunge router is ideal for use on a router table; the adjuster that I am touching makes setting final cut depth very easy, as compared to other router adjustments when on tables. A similar adjuster may be bought for other plunge routers, but adds considerably (about 10 percent) to the cost, where it is included with the Freud.

Routers

If you expect to keep woodworking, get a router. Best use will come from a model of one horsepower or more, with a ½″ collet (the ½″ collet gives both a more accurate cut, and is less likely to allow the bit head to snap off, than a ¼″ collet). A plunge router is sometimes a help, but is not essential.

1–30 Even veining, a fairly delicate operation at some times, is easy with this table and fence combination. The rabbets were also made on the table.

Router Tables

Router tables may be bought or built. Some of the same bits that are useful on a router table may also be used, with great care, freehand, but others are not suitable for freehand use. It is far safer to mount the router in a table.

Other router bits may be used freehand, but do a smoother job on a router table. All safety rules, regardless of bit used, must be observed.

1–32 Note the large fence opening for use with large bits.

1–31 A home-built router table.

Biscuit Joiners

Biscuit joiners are also called plate joiners. These tools have circular blades that cut kerfs 0.156″ thick, to loosely fit biscuits that are flat, football-shaped, and 0.148″ thick. Biscuits come in three widths, No. 0, No. 10, No. 20. The biscuit plates absorb water from the glue and swell past 0.160″.

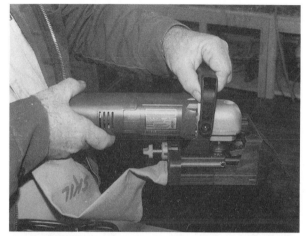

1–33 The Skil is light and handles easily. The dust bag is a boon, too.

1–34 Biscuit joiners easily reinforce mitre joints.

1–35 Porter-Cable has a different, and slightly easier to use, handle design. The adjustable fence is an optional extra that is well worth its cost.

1–36 Porter-Cable joiner working on a mitre.

1–37 End-to-end butt joint layout. (Courtesy of Porter-Cable)

1–38 Mitre layout, step 1. (Courtesy of Porter-Cable)

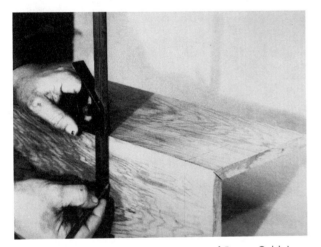

1–39 Mitre layout, step 2. (Courtesy of Porter-Cable)

1–40 Butt joint layout. (Courtesy of Porter-Cable)

Accuracy is easier to get with biscuits than with dowels. The slot cut to accept the plate allows adjustment along the length of the biscuit, while a dowel pegs you to a point and keeps you there. Vertical alignment is maintained, and is exceptionally easy to set. If you've drilled your dowel holes a fraction off, your project will be a fraction off. With plates, you'll never be off because of the way the machines are made. Miss, and you can slip things around until perfect. The biscuits are of solid beech—stamped to size after being sawn into laths.

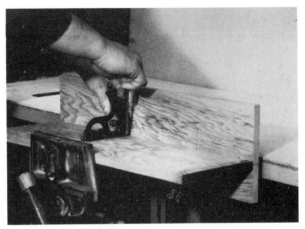

1–41 T joint layout. (Courtesy of Porter-Cable)

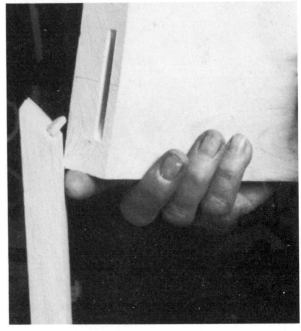

1–42 I've placed the biscuit, and I'm getting ready to add glue and clamp the mitre joint.

Jointers

Jointers are tools that have a flat bed, with at least one part of the bed that may be raised and lowered to determine depth of cut. There is also a back fence against which wood is held while being fed through the blades.

Jointers provide a square, smooth edge that allows us to make good glue joints. A smooth, square edge is the starting point for most projects, and is essential at some point for all.

Planers

Planers do nothing more than smooth the wider flat surfaces of boards. Planers simply smooth boards, but that's saying a lot. For example, the walnut you see used in my storage projects (and the oak and cherry and cedar—I got the redwood already planed) cost about one-fifth of what FAS lumber normally costs. It was then dried and, finally, planed and sorted for use, to give a total cost of under one-third of what FAS walnut costs.

These planers are very-high-speed units that give an exceptionally fine surface finish on planed woods; and you can use wood of any thickness a project requires, producing exactly that thickness in a few minutes in your own shop.

Tool Care

Taking care of tools is nothing more than good common sense. Electrical tools need good cords and unmangled plugs. Keep tools clean, and lubricate those that need it. Use tools for the jobs for which they're made. The screwdriver serves as an example; screwdrivers are to drive screws and for opening paint cans. They are not pry bars, chisels, or levers; probably everyone has used a screwdriver in those ways.

Clean tools after use as a help in keeping them sharp and working for as long as quality allows.

1–44 Some of my home-dried walnut passes into the planer. Note the white sapwood contrasting with the dark heartwood.

1–45 Home-drying and planing allows for the greatest selection of superb grain.

1–43 Wider and thicker boards take larger planers. This 12″ by 2¼″ poplar demanded the 12″ planing width of the Makita.

Tool Safety

Tool safety is also a matter of common sense, combined with some knowledge, especially with power tools, of reactions to force.

Make sure you have a clear cutting line, and that tool cords can't snag as you cut. Snags usually just pull the cut off line, but can be strong enough to yank a tool loose from the cut and the hand. Keep your work area clear. Follow manufacturer's safety instructions for all tools. Always use safety devices.

Wear eye protection, whether safety glasses, goggles or a face shield. Use hearing protection against the cumulative effects of noise. *Think* before you work, and as you're working. Only *you* can assure such safety. If a particular procedure seems unsafe, *do not use it.*

■ Wood and Other Materials for Storage Projects

The projects are relatively small, with a few large enough in size to make the useful array of different woods broad. For larger projects needing wide, flat expanses of wood, plywood is helpful. Solid woods are ideal for areas such as cabinet or door frames.

Plywood

Plywood serves best where panel strength and stability are needed; larger panels (12″ wide and up) are usually best made of plywood, though properly glued-up solid wood is also fairly stable. Plywood panel construction is faster and easier than the use of solid woods.

Hardwood plywood differs in form and intent from softwood plywood. Softwood plywood is lower in cost and often meant for general construction projects; hardwood plywood is usually used for cabinetry and furniture. Face species are usually the attractive hardwoods (white oak, red oak, birch, cherry, walnut, teak, but not alder, aspen, poplar).

Hardwood plywoods come in different types, all meant for interior use. Internal plies may be lumber (lumber core), particle board, or regular plies, based on the intended uses of the plywood. (See the Appendix for Softwood Plywood Grades.)

Edging Plywood

There are many ways to cover edges, some simple, some less easy. Edge-banding of hardwood plywoods is the latest "hot" method, where real wood edge-banding is applied using a machine to glue it in place. The one I use most involves a 250′ coil of real wood, with a glue backing. This is unfurled, placed and cut against the edge to be covered. Then a home flat iron is run over the front of the band, melting the glue and providing a good edge cover. Other types of edge banding use straight strips, with or without glue, installed with any type of adhesive, including contact cement which requires no clamping. If you use regular adhesives, clamping will be needed; you may use 2″-wide masking tape to clamp the edge band to the structure, at 12″ intervals.

Solid wood edging may be used. Wood filler also serves as an edge filler for plywood, when the edges will be painted. It is simple, fast, and low cost.

1–46 Edging plywood with solid wood.

1–47 Solid woods can be glued-up into large panels—here cherry is being butt-jointed to form the ends of a cradle.

1–48 Finger-jointed white oak makes for incredibly strong joints.

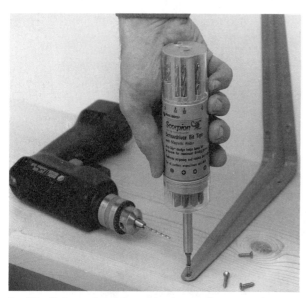

1–49 Softwoods, such as this pine, work very easily, even with hand or light power tools. (Courtesy of Black & Decker)

Solid Woods

Softwoods are generally used as construction lumber, and hardwoods for furniture and cabinetry. As do most generalizations, that falls apart with pine, fir, cedar, redwood, and other softwoods used for furniture as well as general construction.

Whether you choose to use a softwood or hardwood for a project, see if you can pick the wood when buying and laying out the project so there are no wild differences of grain that must appear in nearby panels—unless you *plan* to have such differences appear. Many people like burls, birds-eye maple and similar grains—in fact, with rarity, the desirability of such grain patterns keeps the price high. (See the Appendix for Softwood Lumber Grades.)

1–50 This part of a project is of solid FAS cherry, wood that costs a great deal of money, but was well worth the price.

1–51 This white oak is also FAS, at about ½ the price of the cherry.

Hardwood lumber isn't as easy to come by, or as easy to buy as softwood lumber. The cost ranges from twice as high on up—way, way up in the case of some exotics, but virtually always twice as high as any softwood (with the exception of redwood in the East, where the transportation costs inflate prices).

Hardwood lumber is available in four grades, but there are problems with matching grain, making sure the fault-free cut lengths needed are available in grain matches, and a couple other areas. The four general grades are: FAS (firsts and seconds); Select; No. 1 Common; No. 2 Common. FAS is the best, most expensive, grade. Pieces are no less than 6″ wide and 8′ long. At least $83\frac{1}{3}$ percent of each board has to provide clear cuttings. Selects give the same clear cutting, but boards only 4″ wide and 6′ or longer. One face is allowed more defects than the other. The common grades provide boards at least 3″ wide by 4′ long, with No. 1 Common giving $66\frac{2}{3}$ percent clear, and No. 2 allowing 50 percent.

Mechanical Fasteners

Mechanical fasteners range from screws to nails and back again, with variations. If the variation isn't in the screws or nails, then it is in the devices to be used with them, such as hinges, lid supports, bracing and mending plates.

Boxes sometimes require lid holders. Lid holders may be nothing more than hinges or chains to prevent lids from snapping back too far and breaking hinges. They may also be spring-loaded and balanced types meant for use on large, medium, and small box lids that might otherwise pinch hands (toy storage projects, for instance).

Screws are classified as wood screws, lag screws, or metal screws. Wood screws have round, flat and oval heads, while metal screws use pan, flat, and round heads, in the main. Lag screws generally have square or hexagonal heads, with coarser screw threads than wood screws.

Wood screws come in sizes from ¼″ to 6″ long. For screws to 1″ in length, the step increase in length is ⅛″, while screws from 1″ to 3″ long increase in length by ¼″ at a step. Screws from 3″ to 6″ go up in ½″ increments. Shaft sizes vary with length, with smaller shafts on shorter screws (generally: you can, of course, buy No. 4 ¾″ and on up to No. 10 ¾″).

1–52 The little mini Lignomat is truly pocket-sized, thus easy to keep close by.

1–53 Uncover the probes, push into board, and a light will come on to tell you how dry or wet your wood is, up to 20 percent water content and down to 6 percent. This walnut lit at 10 percent, which was not visible here because the light from the flash over-rode it.

Power drive screws, fine and coarse threaded, come in sizes different than those used for other wood screws. Drive screws are available in longer lengths—up to 3″, for example, with light shanks. Power drive screws have a Phillips head, or a square drive head. They are exceptionally useful for heavier uses, and for general light construction duties like those involved in building some of our larger storage projects.

Drill pilot holes at least one size less than the screw shank in hardwood, and two sizes in softwood. Go half to two-thirds as deep as the screw will sink.

Machine screws are used with nuts and washers to join wood to metal or wood to other materials, including wood. A T nut is a type of nut that drive fits into a drilled hole in a wood surface. They are set in place and then tapped down so teeth in the upper ring grip. The screw is then run into the T nut, so assemblies mate. Ease of disassembly is built in.

Nails are sized by the penny, abbreviated d, a method once used by manufacturers to determine how many cents 100 nails would cost. Sizes range from 2d to 60d. Nails under 2d, or 1″, are classed as brads; over 60d (6″) they're spikes.

Common nails are used for general-purpose nailing from framing work on through some types of flooring installation. Shank styles differ; for greater holding power use deformed shanks such as ring and screw. Coatings are available and nails may be hardened. Common nails come in aluminum and galvanized for outdoor uses.

Box nails are like common nails, differing slightly in head size relative to shank size, with larger head sizes to shank diameters.

Finishing nails are slim, almost headless, in sizes from the 1″ brad finishing nail on up to at least 16d (3½″). In mild steel, galvanized, and hot-dipped galvanized, they are used because small heads set easily (with a nail set) below a board's surface.

■ Glues and Clamps

Wood glues hold wood joints together, making the adhesives essential to much storage projects construction (there are mechanical fasteners and there are joints that do not always require glue—some forms of dovetailing—but for most purposes, joints will be made with one of the wood glues).

Selecting a Woodworking Glue

There aren't as many true woodworking glues as you may be led to believe, but there is a wide enough variety to cover the storage projects maker's need for strong joints. Woodworking adhesives are classed as animal or hide glues and synthetics. Animal glues are less used today because synthetics offer properties they do not. There are properties offered by hide glues that synthetics don't offer, or don't offer as completely.

1–55 Franklin's newly introduced Titebond II is an excellent, low-cost weatherproof glue, suitable for all above-waterline uses.

1–54 T nuts.

Hide Glues

Hide glues are thicker than white or yellow synthetic glues, resist solvents other than water well, and have a pale tan glue line. They sand nicely without gumming, but resist water poorly.

Synthetic Adhesives

By far the greatest percentages of woodworking adhesives are synthetics, made specially for use in woodworking. Some come from other fields. Most are resin glues that gather strength by chemical reaction, or curing. Curing depends on the temperature of the glue.

Polyvinyl Acetate Resins

White glues (polyvinyl acetate resins) come in squeeze bottles on up to gallon and larger jugs. There are many brands, and most are acceptable for general woodworking purposes. They come ready to use, as do the yellow glues.

White glue is a good, inexpensive glue, but requires speed in assembly and clamping, and gums up sandpaper during sanding. Poor heat resistance also means white glues are best not used during hot summer days. The glue line is almost invisible.

Liquid Yellow Glues (Aliphatic Resin)

Liquid yellow (aliphatic resin) glues were designed as improvements over polyvinyl resin glues, with some very needed changes.

Heat resistance is better, making it easier to sand; but, unfortunately, set is faster than for white glues, a problem if you are assembling complex storage projects. Switch to hide glue when project assembly is going to need more than five or ten minutes.

Liquid yellow glue is an excellent general purpose glue, more suited to small projects because of fast set time. Preassemble all projects, and set up larger projects for assembly in modules to use this type of glue. It does not gum sandpaper. It resists heat and moderate dampness well. It is NOT waterproof, not even truly water resistant.

Waterproof and Water-resistant Glues

Where moisture is a real problem, there are a number of other glues you may also use. Two are plastic resin and resorcinol resin glues.

Plastic resin adhesives are highly water resistant, but the resorcinols (and epoxies) are truly waterproof.

Resorcinol resin glues are dark-red liquid resins with which a catalytic powder is mixed before use. Resorcinols have a reasonable working time, from about a quarter of an hour to two hours. Clamping pressure is high; 200 pounds per square inch. The pressure has to be uniform, which means clamps are spaced more closely.

Resorcinol resin is a difficult to use, obstinate glue, that has an ugly glue line, but that offers good working time, and a totally waterproof joint. Keep it warm during use (above 70 degrees F, preferably close to 80), and work with care, and you've got a good, strong joint. You must have a tight joint to start with, because resorcinol has poor filling qualities (use epoxy for sloppy joints that must be waterproof).

Plastic Resin Adhesives

Plastic resin adhesives are dry powders, mixed with water just before use. The resin is urea formaldehyde, a highly water-resistant adhesive, best on wood with a moisture content of no more than 12 percent. Best use and cure temperature is 70 degrees F.

The joint line is a light tan color. Gumming is not a problem as the resin resists heat well; general working is easy, and mixing from powder is quick and simple. The only reason yellow glues are used is because they are ready-mix, though the fast set is a help on many projects; plastic resin adhesives are as good or better in most areas, but less convenient.

Epoxy Adhesives

Epoxies aren't particularly handy for most of our storage projects, but new formulas have been developed that aid in using these adhesives.

Epoxy doesn't shrink, so it is a good gap filler. Some is made as putty, filling the largest gaps, though tight joint fits are still better for long project life. It has a clear joint line, good heat resistance, and is impervious to water and most chemicals; however, it is expensive, hard to use, and may present fume problems if used in large amounts.

1–56 Resorcinol glue mixes quickly: be neat, for it's costly, and ugly—you don't want smears of this stuff.

Contact Cements

Contact cements are useful for some storage project construction, especially when you work with cheaper wood composite substrates such as fiberboard. Contact cement may go over almost any wood substance, but works best over composites that are more stable dimensionally. Contact cements come in two basic types. One uses a water solvent, while the other uses another nonflammable solvent base. Avoid professional types that use flammable solvents.

Vapors are harmful even with newer solvents: make sure you work with proper ventilation. Do not use flammable contact cements.

Contact cements give a quick bond with cleanup and trim of the final project possible immediately. Use is simple. Coat both surfaces with the cement, using a brush or a roller. Let the surfaces dry (to the touch: the cement will appear clear).

A slip sheet of Kraft paper or waxed paper may be used, covering the entire adhesive surface. Leave enough to grip outside the two pieces being joined, bring the top piece down, align the two pieces, and slowly start slipping the paper out. Once the paper is out 3″, roll or tap over the cleared area to assure a bond. Pull the paper the rest of the way out, using care to not disturb the alignment. Roll or tap to make a solid bond.

Choosing Glues

The selection of the correct glue is important, but so are the application of the glue and the clamping of the parts. Also important is working with a tight-fitting joint so that there are no gap-filling problems or joints weakened by thick expanses of nothing but glue. You want your storage projects to last.

Clamps

Woodworking clamps fall into one of four categories: bar clamps; hand screws; C clamps; and band clamps. The largest number of variations probably fall in the bar clamp range, though recently, mitre and frame clamps seem to be gaining.

As with all clamps, band clamps vary. One of mine is about 1″ wide and 10′ long. Another is 2″ wide and 14′ long. Both work well. Band clamps are useful for clamping odd shapes, such as octagon frames, many storage project sizes and assemblies, and picture frames.

1–57 Contact cement ready for use.

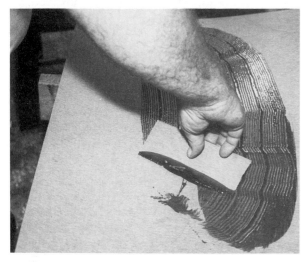

1–58 Contact cement being spread with a shop-made notched spreader.

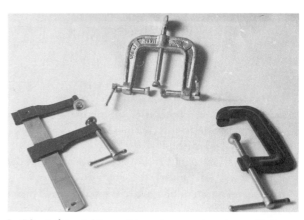

1–59 Left to right: small bar clamp; edge clamp, C clamp.

Hand screws clamp nonparallel surfaces, and don't creep as many clamps will.

Corner clamps are useful for mitred work such as picture frames and storage project carcases.

Clamping and Clamping Pressure

Clamps are used for three reasons. Wood surfaces must be in direct and close contact with the glue; the glue must become a thin, continuous film; and the joint must be held steady until the glue dries.

1–62 Jorgenson-brand aluminum bar clamps, like these 6' and 2' models, are excellent on case assemblies like this hope chest where medium pressure is sufficient.

1–60 Black & Decker's clinch clamp is a variation on band clamps, and is extremely easy to use where light clamping pressure is enough.

1–63 Short bar clamps do well when you're putting together two-by material for legs and similar parts.

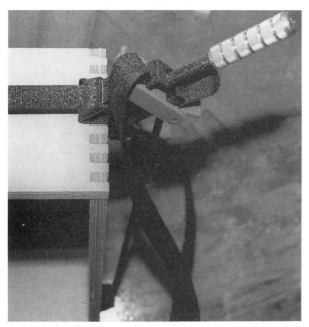

1–61 Vermont-American makes an excellent band clamp that is easy to use, and that provides a solid grip.

1–64 Medium bar clamps, like these Bessey models, are great for middle-size assemblies, and, like all bar clamps, they can be adjusted to help pull the assembly square.

Clamping pressure varies with glue type, but usually suits glue thickness: the heavier the glue, the more clamping pressure. You need a thin, smooth glue line, not a joint squeezed dry, which occurs when too much pressure is used.

Home workers may occasionally apply too much pressure using hand-tightened clamps. This happens on large surfaces with closely arrayed bar clamps, but is not a frequent problem. Most of the time getting things aligned and getting clamps tightened firmly so that there is even squeeze-out is plenty.

Resorcinol and urea resins require a lot of pressure: epoxy needs little.

Always avoid excessive pressure in favor of even pressure over the entire area. Get even glue squeeze-out over the entire joint rather than racking the project up as tight as possible.

1–65 Quick clamp versions of bar clamps work well on small assemblies such as this cherry unit.

1–67 Pinch dogs help in wide-board assembly as they pull board ends tightly together.

1–66 These bar clamps, from Leichtung, are super for assembling flat, wide boards, saving much time and sanding if used correctly.

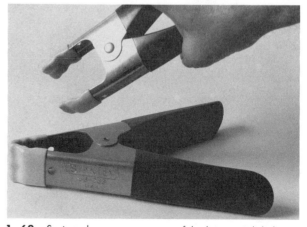

1–68 Spring clamps are very useful where quick light-to-medium pressure is needed.

◼ Finishes

Finishes for storage projects vary all over the place, from a light coat of air, to many coats of clear tung oil or similar finish. For most of these projects, a stain and clear finish is appropriate, though a few will do as well with enamel. For some people and with some woods, finishing coats begin with stain.

All finishing operations are best done "in the white." Basically, all that means is that finish is applied before exterior hardware such as handles, knobs, trim, and hinges is applied. It should all be fitted, but must be removed before the finish is applied so that finish doesn't slop over onto the hardware giving a junk look to the iob.

1–69 Tung oil is a superb finish for almost any indoor project.

If a water-based stain has been used, you will probably need to finish smoothing with a 180- or 220-grit paper, as water raises wood grain. If an oil-based stain has been used, you may not need to do any further smoothing: I like to go over most stains with 0000 steel wool to make sure there is no buildup of the stain in corners and in decorations. The steel wool is so fine it doesn't do much to reduce the coloring effects of the stain.

For final cleanup, before staining or coating with finish, always start with a wipe-down with a dry rag, and go on to vacuuming. Use a tack cloth for the final wipe-down before coating with stain or finish.

It is the selection of clear finishes that complicates the finishing procedure. Under normal circumstances, I don't bother with shellacs and lacquers, preferring to go, instead, with polyurethanes or tung oils (many tung oils today are reinforced with polyurethanes). In some cases, I'll use a Danish oil finish.

In almost every case, the finish I use will be either a satin or flat type. High gloss finishes are more difficult, usually, to lay on properly, and tend to show more of the defects in the project. Too, the glare can be blinding.

Remember, though, to always use a scrap piece of wood (or a hidden spot on a finished project) to test for color effect of any finish, or stain. Almost all finishes change the color of the underlying wood, even after it has been stained. It's up to you to decide whether or not you like a particular finish and wood combination. If you don't, check until you find one you do like.

2
Kitchen and Dining Room Projects

Large projects, especially for storage, can become overcomplicated for a variety of reasons; the shape of a cabinet is one source of complication, while excessive decoration—spurred on by an intense desire to prove oneself a fancy woodworker—is another. My aim is to provide good solid projects, with reasonably simple, or at least straightforward, construction needs.

■ Microwave Cart on Wheels

Most kitchens today have microwave ovens, and many have problems with where to stick that handy device.

Most microwaves are not really small enough to tuck up behind anything or to hang under a cabinet. Overall, they take up a good two feet of linear countertop space, often more. Probably the simplest solution is to use a cart, newly bought or built. With the addition of a drawer, a pullout shelf, and some cabinet space the cart can serve many needs. To get the quality and the flexibility for a custom fit, you shouldn't need much convincing that the best way is to make it yourself.

Begin by marking and cutting the pieces to size. When laying out on plywood, don't forget to allow for kerfs between marks—standard kerfs are about 1/8″ wide, but new narrow-kerf blades may reduce that by almost 50 percent.

2–1   Microwave cart. (*Courtesy of Georgia-Pacific Corporation*)

Assembly

Begin the assembly with the frame, using the narrower front and side pieces for the top where space is needed for the ¾″ pullout board. Cut a ¾″ x ⅜″ rabbet at both ends of each front and back frame, and fasten the side frames to the front with glue and 4d finishing nails. Keep a check on square as you go. Glue and nail the bottom panel to the bottom frame using 2d finishing nails.

Lay the frames on one of the sides, keeping the bottom frame flush with the front and bottom edges of the side panel. The top frame should be flush with the front edge, but ¾″ below the top edge of the side panel.

Tools

- table or circular saw
- mitre box
- cordless drill, screwdiver bits
- 16-oz and 13-oz claw hammer
- nail set
- square
- measuring tape or rule
- marking tool—scribe or carpenter's pencil
- paint brush
- finishing sander
- tack cloth
- 0000 steel wool
- laminate trimming bit
- laminate trimmer or router
- laminate knife

The third frame supports the drawers, and it is positioned 6″ below the top frame. Setting the frames this way allows a ¾″ slot at the rear to hold the back and a ¾″ space at the top for a pullout shelf.

Attach frames to the side panels with glue and 2d finishing nails. Keep a check on square as you go, and adjust as needed.

Glue and nail stiles to the side panels, flush with the back edges of the frames. Now, turn the assembly face down, and coat the edges of the stiles and the back frames with wood glue. Put the back in place, keeping the panel's bottom edge flush with the bottom edge of the case. Fasten the back to the stiles and frames with ¾″ brads.

Set the case on its side, and coat the back edges of the stiles with glue. Fit them into place. Toenail the stiles to the front and back frames with 2d finishing nails.

Turn the unit over and fit the stiles into place, so that the middle of each cleat is 12¾″ from each edge. Glue and toenail the middle cleats in place.

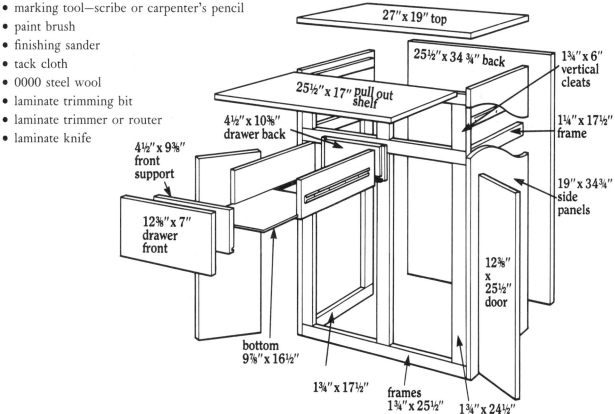

2–2 Microwave cart. (*Courtesy of Georgia-Pacific Corporation*)

Materials

(All wood, unless otherwise specified, is ³⁄₄″)

- five 1¾″ x 25½″, pine, for front and back cabinet horizontal frame pieces (rails)
- 1¼″ x 25½″ pine, top front rail
- four 1¾″ x 17½″ side rails
- two 1¼″ x 17½″ side rails
- ¼″ x 15½″ x 17½″ hardboard, bottom panel
- two 19″ x 34¾″ sides
- two 1¾″ x 26″ pine, back vertical members (stiles)
- 25½″ x 34¾″ plywood, back
- three 1¾″ x 24½″ pine, front stiles
- three 1¾″ x 6″ pine, front stiles
- 1″ x 1¼″ stile
- two ½″ x 12⅜″ x 25½″ plywood, doors
- 17″ x 25½″ plywood, pullout shelf
- 19″ x 27″ plywood, top
- 22″ x 30″ plastic laminate, for top and edges
- two 12⅜″ x 7″ plywood, drawer (false) fronts
- two ½″ x 4½″ x 9⅜″ plywood, drawer fronts
- two pair of drawer slides to fit finished drawers
- three spacers 1¾″ x 1¾″, from two-by-four pine
- four ½″ x 4½″ x 17″ plywood, drawer sides
- two ½″ x 4½″ x 10⅜″ plywood, drawer backs
- two ¼″ x 9⅞″ x 16½″ hardboard, drawer bottoms
- ¼ lb 4d finishing nails
- ¼ lb 2d finishing nails
- ½ lb 6d common nails
- twelve 1¼″ No. 6 flathead wood screws
- box ¾″ brads
- wood filler
- four 2″ white porcelain knobs
- four 2″ cabinet hinges, self-closing
- ¾″ plywood edging tape, or filler if plywood is to be painted
- one set of 2″ diameter casters
- paint or clear finish
- wood glue
- contact cement
- 100- and 150-grit sandpaper

Cut drawer parts now, if you haven't already.

Use the router to cut a ⅛″-wide groove, ¼″ deep (or use a table saw: the ⅛″ wide groove is just about the exact width of the kerf a standard 10″ saw blade cuts), and ¼″ from the bottom edges of the sides, back, and interior front backer piece.

Cut rabbets ½″ wide and ¼″ deep on each end of the drawer's back panel. Assemble the front support, sides, back and bottom using glue and 2d finishing nails.

Attach the drawer fronts with 2d finishing nails and glue. Attach drawer slides to frame cleats, and install the cleats to the box using 1¼″ No. 6 flathead screws.

Attach any remaining slide parts as directed by the manufacturer. Drill the drawer fronts and install knobs. Attach hinges to doors and frames. Check all movement of drawers, doors, and the slide-out board.

Use a nail set to sink any visible nail heads, and fill the holes with putty. Fill any edging holes with wood putty in areas to be painted.

Sand, using 100-grit, and then 120-grit, sandpaper. Paint, applying two coats of enamel over doors, sides, frame, etc.

Apply contact cement to the top, and to the trimmed laminate (cut with a laminate knife so that you've got edging pieces as well). Do the same to the pullout board's top. Allow the contact cement on laminate and boards to dry before joining.

Apply the laminate to the boards, and to the edges, making sure to apply plenty of pressure. To apply pressure, use a rubber hammer or a two-by-four that you can strike solidly with a hammer. The best way to apply enough pressure is to use a laminate roller.

Use the laminate trimmer to trim the edges of the laminate on the top, then coat the laminate edging and board edges with contact cement and apply that when the cement dries. Apply and trim in the same way. You may do the edges first if you prefer.

Install casters and reinstall hinges and knobs, and your microwave cart is ready for use.

If you wish to add the towel rack as shown, cut two half circles on a 6″ diameter, and a piece of ¾″ wood backing 6″ by 16″. Also cut a ¾″ dowel 14½″ long. Assemble the half circles to the backing board using 2d finishing nails and glue. The dowel is centered 1″ down from the top arc of the half circles, and is installed with a 1¼″ No. 6 wood screw at each end. Fill edges and nail holes, and paint to match; install the assembly on the cart end with two more 1¼″ No. 6 wood screws.

■ Bar Cart

This one's a toss-up: is the storage available most appropriate in the dining room, the living room, or the den? It will vary from household to household, and some will prefer to customize the design to their needs. It contains a very handy wine-storage area and drawers for accessories, with a roomy top and large liquor and mixer drawer. It's possible to change the emphasis of the pattern by exchanging the wine storage inserts for shelves. (Do it the easy way, and leave out all the vertical panels and half of the horizontal panels for the honeycomb. Of course, don't cut the slots in the remaining shelves, since there's nothing to fit into them.)

extra ⅛″ or so needed at the top, and the expanded size of the drawers when covered. Laminates vary in thickness; so keep a careful check where drawers slide flush and edges are to be covered.

Cut all pieces to size, except for the honeycomb internals in the wine rack.

Begin assembly with the frame at the cart bottom, butt-joining the side pieces inside the front and back. Screw together with No. 6 1½″ drive screws. Check the fit of the corner blocks, and then coat the edges with wood glue. Screw them in place, again with the 1½″ screws. The casters attach to these corner blocks.

Use the router to cut ¾″-wide by ¼″-deep dadoes in the left side panel, and the middle panel, as shown.

2–3 Bar cart. (*Courtesy of Georgia-Pacific Corporation*)

The amount of laminate indicated at the end of the Materials List is enough for the sides and ends of top. If you wish to cover the entire unit, wait until after you construct the project, and then take surface and edge measurements. Then you can get the correct amounts in the colors desired. You may also figure the amount needed from the plan drawing; make sure, if the entire unit is to be covered, that you allow for the

Space equally to accept wine rack shelves and dividers.

Cut the dadoes in the right side of the middle panel and the inside of the right side panel to hold the divider that fits between the large drawer and the top smaller drawer.

Nail the front trim piece in place on the right side of the frame. Nail the wine rack base to the frame, after checking fit and spreading glue on the frame.

Position the middle panel, and nail it to the wine rack bottom, also placing a line of glue on the joint. Use 4d finishing nails for the nailing.

Position the top, and check the fit. Remove and coat the top edges of the sides and middle panel with wood glue, and nail down through the top into those pieces, using three or four 6d finishing nails per panel.

Check the slip-fit of drawer dividers in their grooves. Remove and add glue to the sides of the dividers, and slide them back in place. Nail each divider at its outside edge with three 6d finishing nails.

Tools

- table or circular saw
- mitre box
- cordless drill, screwdriver bits
- 13-oz. claw hammer
- nail set
- square
- measuring tape or rule
- marking tool—scribe or carpenter's pencil
- paintbrush
- finishing sander
- tack cloth
- laminate trimming bit
- laminate trimmer or router
- laminate knife
- jigsaw and blades

You can now cut the wine rack dividers and go on to cut the slots that fit them together—like old-fashioned egg cartons. Cut ¾″-wide and 1″-deep notches in the front edges of the uprights, every 4″. Use the router and a ¾″ straight bit to dado each side from there back, making the dado ⅛″ deep, extending from the notch at the front of the board to the back of the board. For the wine rack shelves, cut notches ½″ wide by 1½″ deep every 4″.

When all of the grooves and notches are cut, slip them together to check the fit. If the fit is okay, disassemble, and reassemble with a few dollops of glue at each crossing. Then slip the entire unit into the space for it, and nail (4d finishing nails) into edges.

Gather the small drawer parts. Route a ¼″ by ¼″ groove on the insides of the sides and back of the drawer front and the inside of the back. Assemble the drawers with 4d nails and glue.

Attach the drawer slides and install the assemblies inside the case.

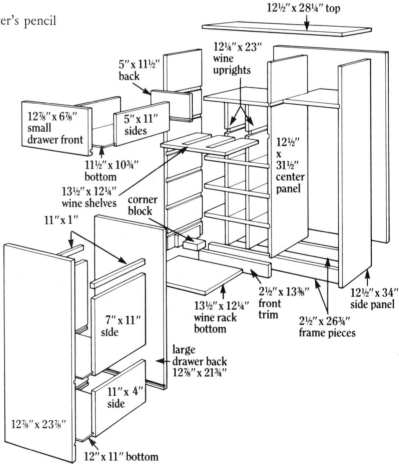

2–4 Bar cart. (*Courtesy of Georgia-Pacific Corporation*)

Materials

(All wood is ¾″ stock unless otherwise specified. All plywood to be B-C or better unless otherwise noted.)

- two 12½″ x 34″ plywood, for sides
- 12½″ x 31½″ plywood, for center divider
- 12½″ x 28¼″ plywood, for top
- two 2½″ x 26¾″ pine, side front and back frame pieces
- two 2½″ x 10¾″ pine, side frame pieces
- 2½″ x 13⅜″ pine, front trim piece
- two 12¼″ x 23″ plywood, for wine rack uprights
- four 13½″ x 12¼″ plywood, for wine shelves
- two 12⅞″ x 6⅞″ plywood, for upper drawer fronts
- 12⅞″ x 23⅞″ plywood, for large drawer front
- four ½″ x 5″ x 11″ plywood, for small drawer sides
- two ½″ x 5″ x 11½″ plywood, for small drawer backs
- two ¼″ x 11½″ x 10¾″ plywood or hardboard, for small drawer bottoms
- two 11″ x 4″ plywood, lower drawer sides for large drawer
- two 11″ x 7″ plywood, upper drawer sides for large drawer
- 12⅞″ x 21¾″ plywood, large drawer back
- two 11″ x ¾″ x 1″ pine, large drawer rails
- ¼″ x 12″ x 11½″ plywood, large drawer bottom, lower
- ½″ x 11½″ x 11½″ plywood, upper drawer bottom
- 13½″ x 12¼″ plywood, wine rack bottom
- Four 3½″ x 3½″ x 1½″ pine, corner blocks
- two 13½″ x 12¼″ plywood, dividers (upper)
- ¼″ x 28¼″ x 33¼″ luaun plywood, back
- two pair drawer slides, 10″
- two pair drawer slides, 10″ heavy duty
- three drawer pulls
- two pair 2″ casters
- twenty-four No. 6 1¼″ flathead wood screws
- twelve No. 6 1½″ flathead drive screws
- ¼ lb 6d finishing nails
- ¼ lb 4d finishing nails
- wood glue
- contact cement
- wood putty, to fill edges for painting
- edge tape, as an alternative to wood putty
- 16″ x 31″ laminate to cover top.

Next, for the parts of the bottom drawer, you need to run a ¼″ by ¼″ dado around the inside bottom and ½″ up, of the front, back, and both sides of the bottom drawer case pieces.

For the large drawer, extra support is provided by the rails above the top part of the case assembly. The two drawer cases and rails are assembled at the same time. Run the rails about 4″ above the top of the top drawer case—the same height on each side, of course.

The bottom of the top drawer case is 13″ from the top of the drawer front. This entire case is made of ¾″ material for strength. Sides sit directly on the bottom, and are attached with No. 6 1¼″ flathead wood screws and glue. If you use drive screws, it still pays to prepare a small pilot hole, though you don't have to drill for the countersink—drive screws automatically countersink themselves.

Use screws and glue to attach the back and front of the drawer, too. Remember, the back is 2⅛″ shorter, a distance taken up at the *bottom* rear of the assembly. Top edges are flush with each other.

Assemble one side inside the front and back, with grooves aligned, using No. 6 1¼″ screws and glue. Slip in the ¼″ thick bottom, and install the second side also with screws and glue.

Install drawer slides, and locate and drill holes for drawer pulls.

Remove hardware, sand with 100- and 150-grit sandpapers, and paint as desired.

The top is laminated; cut laminate to near finished size (about 13″ by 28¾″) and spread contact cement on both the back of the laminate and the top. When the cement dries, carefully align the laminate using a slip sheet of Kraft or waxed paper, and pull the slip sheet. Make sure the laminate is pounded or rolled to get good contact. Trim the laminate with the trim bit in a laminate trimmer or in the router. Repeat the cementing process with the side and end edges using the thinner pieces of laminate. Trim.

Install casters and other hardware. Load with napkins, corkscrew, and other necessities and you're ready to go.

■ Kitchen Island

Like microwave carts, kitchen islands are exceptionally handy. Portable versions may be pulled to whatever area in the kitchen needs the extra working and storage space, easing almost any food preparation job. This version is easy to make and might make a good weekend project if the parts are on hand.

the big sheets on the ground, or hanging off the end of a workbench, and the two-by-fours used will be strong enough for this sort of use at least a dozen times, and probably two or three times that many.

For the fewest splinters, place masking tape along the cut lines.

Begin assembly by drawing lines parallel to all the ends of the bottom and top, 1½" in from the ends.

2–5 Kitchen island. (*Courtesy of the American Plywood Association*)

Start by laying out the parts on the two sheets of plywood. If cutting is primarily to be done with a table saw, lay out only the straight cuts, with the good face of the wood *up* (marked side will be the good face). For later curved cuts, done with a jigsaw or bayonet saw, make cuts with the good face *down*. If main cutting is done with a circular saw, make all cuts with good face *down*. Whatever saw you use, allow ⅛" between marks for the kerf.

I've found the easiest way to work with many cuts on plywood using a circular saw is to use at least three two-by-fours to support the work on sawhorses, then to make the cuts, guided by a straightedge, with the blade set so that it clears the material being cut by ⅛". This is much easier on the back than trying to cut

The slightly curved top and bottom edges face front; so mark accordingly. Support the end pieces, and apply glue on the ends. Lay the bottom in place and align, after which drive 4d finishing nails through the bottom and into the sides. Use a nail every 6". Place the bottom on the floor, and install the top in the same manner. In both cases you may, if you choose, use 1¼" or 1½" No. 6 drive screws to replace nails, at about 8" intervals.

Install back and side cleats for the inside shelf so that the *top* of the shelf will fall 14¾" above the bottom. That gives a space of 11" on top of that shelf. Cleats for the sides are cut 1" shorter than side depth, or 22". Cut the back cleat to fit inside the side cleats, or 42". Install with glue and 1¼" drive screws.

Tools

- table or circular saw
- mitre box
- cordless drill, screwdriver bits
- 16-oz and 13-oz claw hammer
- nail set
- square
- measuring tape or rule
- marking tool—scribe or carpenter's pencil
- 48″ or longer straightedge
- paintbrush
- finishing sander
- tack cloth
- 0000 steel wool
- laminate trimmer or router, laminate trimming bit
- laminate knife

Materials

- two 4′ x 8′ x ¾″ A-B or Medium Density Overlay plywood
- four 2″ screw base casters
- sixteen 1″ No. 6 wood screws, for casters
- two drawer pulls
- two pairs of drawer slides
- two 8′ x 1″ x 2″ lumber, for drawer and bread board blocking
- wood glue
- ¼ lb each, 2d and 4d finish nails
- paint
- 30″ x 48″ laminate
- two 48″ x 1″ laminate
- two 30″ x 1″ laminate
- contact cement

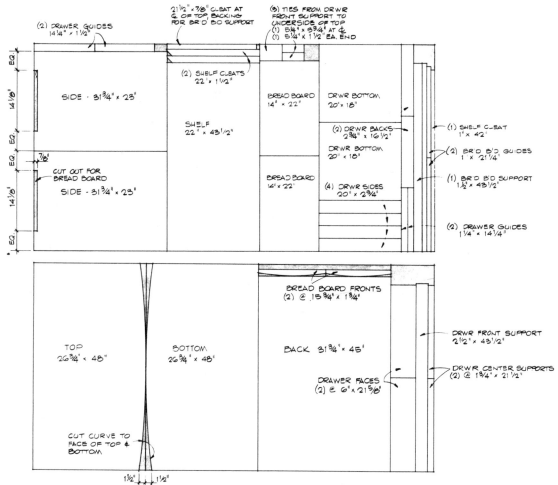

2–6 Panel layout. (*Courtesy of the American Plywood Association*)

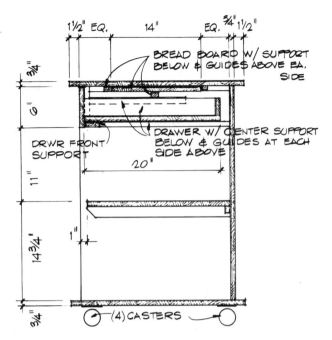

2-7 Plan section. (*Courtesy of the American Plywood Association*)

Assemble drawers as per drawings, using butt joints, glue, and 4d finishing nails. You may, here, replace the nails with No. 10 biscuits and a biscuit joiner, if you wish. Install drawer pulls and slides. Install casters.

Fill edges with wood putty. (You may also use wood tape, or iron-on plastic tape, to cover edges; if plastic tape is used, select to match or contrast with other colors, and apply *after* all painting is done. Also, if using plastic tape, avoid getting excess paint on edges.)

Remove all hardware, and sand with 120-grit paper. Vacuum and use a tack cloth to remove dust. Paint in selected colors.

Coat the back of the laminate with contact cement, and apply an even coat to the edges and ends of the top as well. Apply the laminate, and tap all the way around with a rubber mallet to get a good bond. Use the laminate trimmer to trim top and bottom of the laminate.

Coat the back of the laminate with contact cement, and apply an even coat to the top surface as well. Let dry. Provide a slip sheet of Kraft or wax paper, and set the laminate in place, aligning carefully. Pull the slip sheet about 1″ out, and tap the laminate to bond cement at that point. Pull the slip sheet all the way out, and tap to bond. If possible, use a laminate roller (or a top quality maple rolling pin) to get the needed bonding pressure for the contact cement. If not, tap a two-by-four with a hammer to provide the bonding.

Applying the laminate to the sides first gives a very slight overlap that may increase the durability of the top.

Reinstall the hardware, and it's ready for use.

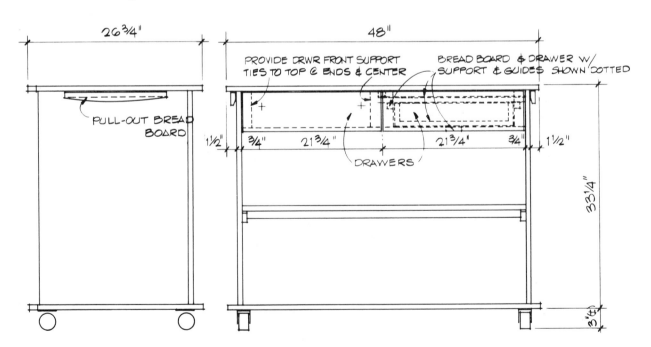

2-8 Side view and front view. (*Courtesy of the American Plywood Association*)

■ Cart/Island

Combining the advantages of the microwave cart and the kitchen island, this project may be built either way you desire, with simple changes (note different materials lists). The microwave cart is simpler to make, and forms the basis of the kitchen island.

This cart need not be used just as a microwave cart, of course (in its simpler version). It makes a very nice one-shelf work cart, with its large top. You can, if you so desire, switch over the towel holder edging from the more complex cart, and add a simple knife rack; then you'll have the equivalent of an expensive factory-made cart. The more complex cart is designed to have its own enclosed storage, plus an open shelf, but works on a similar base to the simpler cart.

General Assembly

For both the island and the microwave cart, begin by cutting the 6" material down to 3½"; this assures square edges, but also allows you to select and cut for the most attractive pieces. If you are using hardwoods for either cart, you can simply buy exactly at the sizes needed—1½" by 3½" in both cases.

Then make the frame, cutting four stretchers 18½" long from the two-by-four (1½" by 3½") and four more 25" long also from two-by-four material. The four legs are 30" long and are also of two-by-four.

Through the height of the stretchers, drill and counterbore holes for later attachment of the butcher block top. Through the width of the same stretchers, drill and counterbore holes for attaching the stretchers to the legs. If you're building the movable kitchen island, make sure there is clearance for the drawer; that means the inside holes in the frame *must* be counterbored.

Now, assemble the frame using wood glue and lag bolts with washers.

Before attaching the upper shelf cleats, drill and counterbore them for 1¼" No. 8 screws (cleats are ¾" wide by ⅞" high; the ⅞" dimension is *always* vertical).

Materials, Microwave Oven Cart

- 10' two-by-six (cut down to 1½" x 3½")
- two 8' two-by-six (cut down to 1½" x 3½")
- 4' two-by-four (cut down to 1½" x 1½")
- 8' one-by-one
- 48" x 48" x ½" AC birch or oak plywood, for top and bottom shelves only
- 1½" x 25" x 31" butcher-block top
- wood glue
- wood putty
- twenty ¼" x 2½" lag bolts with washers
- sixteen ¼" x 3" lag bolts with washers
- twelve No. 10 flathead wood screws
- twelve No. 8 flathead wood screws
- four 2" ball casters
- 1" brads

2–9 Microwave cart.

Drilling and counterboring comes in from the underside of the cleat. Install the cleats, with their top edge 13½″ from the bottom top of the base frame.

Shelves go on next. Cut and install the top and bottom shelves; the top shelf is 21¼″ by 25″, while the bottom shelf is 20⅜″ by 25″. Use No. 8 1¼″ screws through predrilled, countersunk holes to attach the top shelf. Attach the bottom shelf with 1″ brads, spaced 6″ apart; also use wood glue.

At this point in the assembly, you have to decide which version to make, if you haven't already. You may go on to make the simpler microwave cart, or you may decide to construct the more complex movable kitchen island.

Microwave Cart

If you go with the simpler cart, add the fourth top stretcher, as in the first step (lag bolts, etc.). Attach the butcher-block top for the cart, through the already drilled holes using No. 10 screws 3″ long. If you decide to go with a plywood top, use at least ¾″ A-B plywood, and cover it with plastic laminate using contact cement. This, if you truly leave a microwave on the top all the time, is a good alternative to the cost of the butcher-block top. You may prefer to laminate ¾″ plywood pieces to form a 1½″ thick top for extra strength. If you do use a ¾″ top, shorten the attaching screws to 2½″.

Install plate casters according to the manufacturer's instructions. Most use four screws into the leg bottoms.

Finish the butcher-block top with a salad-bowl finish, and use a good oil finish or polyurethane on the remainder, over stain if you wish. If you've used pine, you may prefer to paint, but light stain will also work well. I'd recommend using oak for legs and stretchers for a combination of great appearance and fine durability.

Kitchen Island

To make the kitchen island, a few more, and different, steps are needed. The island has an optional outlet strip for kitchen appliances, and a drawer for utensils; you may also add the simple knife rack. If you've got small children around the house, it might be a good idea to omit the knife rack on a piece this low.

The changes start with the top stretchers, as already mentioned. The heads of the lag bolts used must be countersunk to prevent interference with the drawer runners. The drawer as well replaces the top front stretcher.

Materials, Kitchen Island

- four 8′ two-by-six (cut to 1½″ x 3½″)
- two ¾″ x ⅞″ x 8′ pine
- ½″ x ½″ x 12′ pine
- 1″ x 36″ dowel
- 48″ x 48″ x ½″ birch or oak plywood
- 48″ x 48″ x ¼″ birch or oak plywood
- 3′ x 1″ x 4″
- 24″ pine lath
- 1½″ x 25″ x 31″ butcher-block top
- wood glue
- wood putty
- sixteen ¼″ x 2½″ lag bolts with washers
- twelve ¼″ x 3″ lag bolts with washers
- twenty-four No. 8 1¼″ flathead wood screws
- seven No. 10 3″ flathead wood screws
- twelve No. 8 1″ flathead wood screws
- ¾″ and 1″ brads
- six No. 8 1¼″ pan-head screws
- No. 8 2¼″ pan-head screw for knife rack
- 1⅙″ x 30″ continuous hinges
- one pair of magnetic cabinet catch
- four 4″ cabinet pulls
- four 2″ ball casters, plate
- multiple outlet strip (optional)
- drawer stop

Once the frames and shelf cleats are installed, cut side panels (29⅞″ by 15″) from ¼″ plywood. Attach using 1″ brads and glue. Set nails and fill with wood putty. If you're planning to stain the finished project, simply glue and clamp the sides until dry. No wood patch material—and I've used almost all of them—accepts stain exactly like the wood around it.

To get exact spacing between the drawer guides, use the glide to check. Set the bottom guide flush with bottom edges of the frame pieces, place the glide on there, and mark for the upper guide piece with it laying lightly on the glide. Guides are 17¾″ by ½″ by ½″, and are attached to stretchers with glue and 1″ brads at 4″ intervals.

Cut two pieces of 34″ by 1½″ by ¾″ stock for the handle assembly, and round one end of each. You may use a coping saw or scroll saw and sandpaper, or simply clamp and rotate the pieces together on a disc or belt sander. Keeping the pieces clamped together, drill the 1″ hole for the 1″ dowel. Cut the dowel to length, which is the width of the butcher block plus the width of the two handle pieces. Notch dowel ends ⅝" deep, vertically. Cut two wedges from scrap one-by-four, making wedges ¾" long by 1" wide by ⅛" thick. Insert the dowel in its holes, and glue in place. Tap the wedges, with a coating of glue, into the slots in the ends of the dowels. Allow the glue to dry and trim off any excess wedge material. Sand smooth.

Attach the handle assembly to the butcher block with waterproof glue, and clamp until dry. If you wish, add three (per side) round-head brass wood screws; with correctly spread glue, and firm clamping, they're not actually necessary.

Attach the butcher-block top to the frame, using predrilled and counterbored holes in the three upper frame stretchers.

The next step is to make the drawer. Choose one 19¾" piece for the drawer front. Drill and countersink six ³⁄₁₆" holes. Assemble the four cut pieces to form the box. Pay attention to squareness. Use 1" brads, and glue at each corner joint.

Attach the already cut bottom to the drawer, and nail around, after spreading glue on the bottom edges of the drawer frame. Keep the plywood edges flush with the frame edges.

Attach the front facing piece of 24¾" by 3½" by ¾" pine with six No. 8 1" screws in the predrilled and countersunk holes. Make sure the drawer frame is *centered* on the front face piece.

With glue and 1" brads, attach the 18" by ½" by ½" glides to the 18" box sides. Glides are mounted ⁹⁄₁₆" up from the bottom edge. Mount handles selected to the drawer front following the manufacturer's instructions.

Add four cleats, using glue. Cut the back panel to final size after assembly of sides, etc. is complete. The panel must fit tightly in the space between the upper shelf and bottom stretcher. Use 1" brads and glue.

Next, the drawers go on. Use a hacksaw to cut two pieces of piano hinge to 13⁷⁄₁₆" lengths. Attach one to each door, and then attach the other sides of the hinges to the frame.

Now, before adding any more hardware, strip off what you've already put on. Sand the entire assembly lightly with 120- or 150-grit sandpaper, and seal the plywood and other wood parts. Stain or paint as desired (use only a salad-bowl or other nontoxic finish).

Add magnetic door catches and plate casters as desired. Attach the outlet strip, if wanted, keeping it below the overhang of the butcher-block top.

Add the knife rack; use pine lath to separate two 10"-wide by 12"-high squares of plywood. Space the lath to allow your knife blades to fit. Drill all four corners for screws. Drill ³⁄₁₆" holes through dowel spacers (1" by 1"), and use 2½" round-head brass screws to attach the knife rack to the unit.

This unit will serve well both for storage and as a work area for many years.

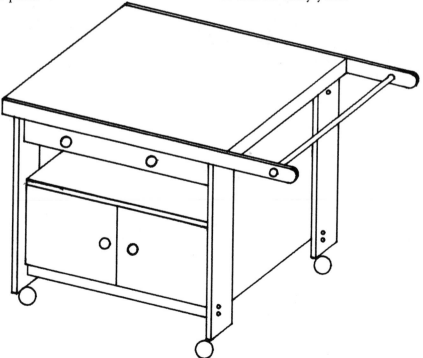

2–10 Kitchen island.

■ Pastry Center with Storage

I've presented a number of kitchen island and other mobile storage ideas already, but this center is designed for the pastry cook who needs space for rolling doughs, kneading, and generally taking care of business in the form of pies, cakes, tarts, popovers, and similar items. With the shelf extended, you'll find more than eight square feet of countertop to work on, but with the shelf rolled down, the unit is small enough to roll out of the way with ease. The drawer provides room for smaller items, while shelves allow space for mixing bowls, cookie tins, and other baking needs. The cart is sized so it will roll *under* a standard countertop. If you desire extra working height, simply add more leg and side panel length.

2-11 This pastry or baking cart looks as good as the results produced with it will taste. (*Courtesy of the Western Wood Products Association*)

Materials

(*Unless otherwise specified, all wood is pine, spruce, fir or hem-fir. You may wish to substitute hardwoods such as oak for appearance.*)

- 60′ one-by-one
- 15′ one-by-two
- 160′ one-by-four
- 5′ one-by-five
- 3′ one-by-twelve
- 10′ 1¼″ x 2½″
- 24″ x 24′ x ¼″ plywood (final size 23¼″ x 22″)
- one pair of lift-up shelf brackets
- ¾″ polished marble, 24½″ x 31½″
- drawer knob

- four 2½″ brass ball-style casters
- 1 lb 3d finishing nails
- ¼ lb 6d finishing nails
- ¼ lb 8d finishing nails
- wood glue
- adhesive for marble top
- wood filler
- stain (if desired)
- clear finish, either satin tung oil or water-based polyurethane

Cut one-by-four boards to 27¼" lengths for panels A and B, a total of sixteen boards, two of which will have to be trimmed to make the final panels come out right. Cut three-quarter-by-five stock for cleats, two to ½" by 2½" by 17½" and two to ½" by 2½" by 24½". Rip two end boards for panel A to 1¹⁵⁄₁₆" wide and 2¹¹⁄₁₆" wide, so that the resulting panel is 22⅛" wide, with cleats installed as shown. The B or back panel is 29½" wide, and end boards are both 2½" wide. All cleats are nailed (with 3d nails) and glued in place.

Edge-glue and clamp the above panels, being sure to keep the panel units *flat* during gluing up. Use only moderate clamp pressure and cupping can be kept to a minimum.

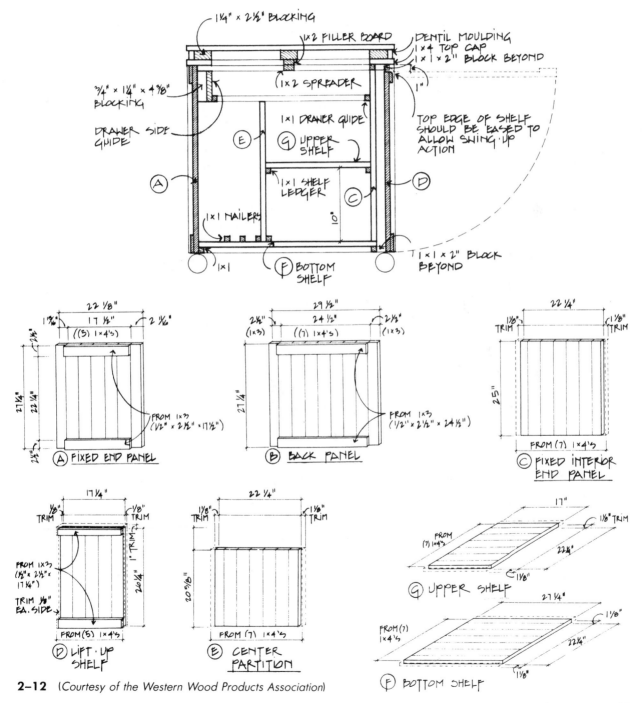

2–12 (*Courtesy of the Western Wood Products Association*)

Panel C, the interior end panel, is made up from seven 25"-long one-by-fours, and then is trimmed to a final 22¼" width by trimming 1⅛" from each edge. Again, edge-glue carefully.

Panel D, the lift-up shelf, is made similar to A and B (it has cleats), but uses only five 26¼" one-by-fours, trimmed ⅛" off each side for a resulting width of 17¼". Cleats are one-by-three stock cut to ½" by 2½" by 17¼".

Make temporary stop blocks that allow a 2" margin at the top and bottom of all end posts. Use one-by-four stock, and set the first routed groove ¾" in from the left side, and the second ¾" in from the right side. The middle groove is set ½" to the left of the right-hand groove. Rip-mitre one edge per board, and glue and nail to form corner posts. To eliminate clamping

problems with long glue ups such as this, place boards undecorated faces down, with the mitred edges touching. Every 6" to 8" along the boards' lengths, place a strip of reinforced packing tape, allowing enough extra tape to completely extend across the opening that results when the boards are properly clamped by the tape.

Turn the taped units over, and apply glue. Then draw the units into place and nail from both sides of the mitre, after which the tape is drawn across the opening and left in place overnight. (It's best to give

Tools

- table saw, radial arm saw, or circular saw
- mitre box or power mitre saw
- electric drill and drill bits, for hardware holes
- router, router bits (¼" and ½" straight bits)
- jigsaw
- four 3' bar clamps
- two large "C" clamps
- screwdriver
- chisel
- carpenter's hammer
- nail set
- tape measure
- framing square
- brush
- steel wool
- 100- and 150-grit sandpaper
- finishing sander

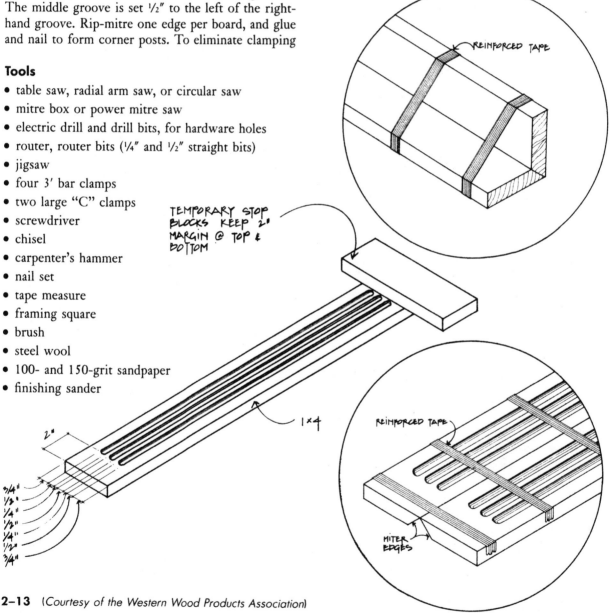

2–13 (Courtesy of the Western Wood Products Association)

such joints at least a dozen hours to set up, because the glue joint will be stressed as they're installed, and as other work is done on the pastry cart.)

When the glue has dried, apply the back panel to the insides of two of the legs, butting the legs against the end of the cleats. Install panel A to the left end of the unit in the same manner. Use glue and 3d nails—from the inside—to hold the pieces in place.

From one-by-one framing cut four 29¼" lengths, two 20¾" lengths, and four 2" blocks. Install as shown in the drawing using glue and 6d finishing nails (use 3d nails if 6d nails will penetrate fully).

The drawer guide board is ¾" by 4⅜" by 21½", and needs three blocks, ¾" by 1¼" by 4⅜", one at each end and one in the middle, as shown, glued and nailed in place. From one-by-two cut a 20¾"-long spreader. Position the spreader, nailing and gluing in place. From one-by-four cut bottom shelf boards 27¼" long. These are glued and nailed to the one-by-one frame. You'll need to measure for and rip the outside pieces (lay the shelf boards both ways from the middle); check actual measurements for the shelf boards and keep the boards flush with the left side.

2–14 (Courtesy of the Western Wood Products Association)

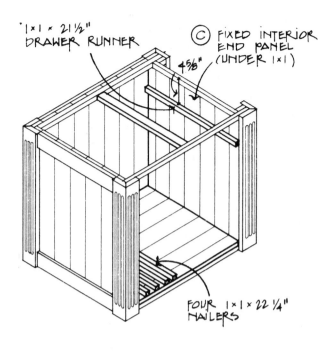

'1 × 1 × 21½"
DRAWER RUNNER

4⅜"

C FIXED INTERIOR
END PANEL
(UNDER 1×1)

FOUR 1 × 1 × 22¼"
NAILERS

Panel C now goes in at the right, under the one-by-one framing and on top of the bottom shelf. Nail and glue in place, and attach a one-by-one 21½" drawer runner 4⅜" below the top of the framing.

Next, fasten four one-by-one 22¼" separators to the bottom shelf, two spaced ¾" apart, with the left edge of the first 17" from the left edge of the right-hand leg. The third one-by-one is spaced 1½" from the second, and the fourth is spaced 1½" from that (using the left side as a measuring mark in both cases).

Fasten a one-by-one 21½" drawer runner to the left inside panel, flush with the bottom of drawer guide board. That one-by-one is set back ¾" from the front. Install a one-by-one 23" to the back panel, aligned with both drawer runners. Attach the front drawer frame to runners on either side. Use 1¼" nails and glue to attach all the preceding parts, except for the end nailing, which should be done with 6d nails (carefully, to avoid splitting the one-by-one material).

Glue and nail a one-by-one 22¼" shelf cleat to the middle partition (E), and to the right panel, both 14" above the bottom shelf. Slip partition E between the one-by-one nailers, and nail to the drawer frame at the top. Then glue and nail the upper shelf into place, and cap the whole works with one-by-four stock, set flush with the outer edges of legs, with mitred corners glued and nailed to legs using 3d and 6d nails, as appropriate. Install upper shelf (17" lengths of one-by-four) with 3d nails and glue; you'll have to rip the front piece to fit, after measuring.

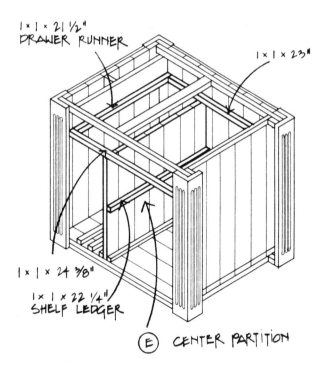

1 × 1 × 21½"
DRAWER RUNNER

1 × 1 × 23"

1 × 1 × 24 ⅜"

1 × 1 × 22¼"
SHELF LEDGER

E CENTER PARTITION

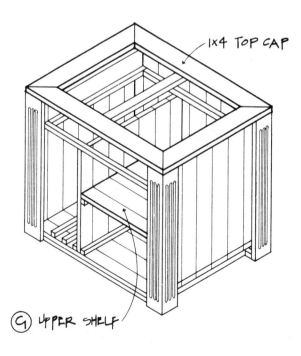

1×4 TOP CAP

G UPPER SHELF

Cut and fit 1¼″ by 2½″ by 23½″ (two) and 1¼″ by 2½″ by 24½″ (two) blocking, front and back, using 6d nails and glue. Place a one-by-two 17⅝″ filler board on top of the spreader, and nail and glue it in place. Next, cut more ½″ thick stock, with the base front trim piece at ½″ by 2½″ by 24½″, and the shelf edge trim ½″ by 1½″ by 17¾″. Use 3d nails and glue.

You may buy dentil moulding at many specialty woodworking stores, or you may make your own in a number of ways. Use an 8″-wide board at least 33″ long, and, with a ½″ router bit, cut grooves 1¼″ apart. Clamp a guide in place for the router. After clean-up sanding, rip the board into 1¼″ wide pieces.

Allowing a full block at corners, mitre the ends of the dentil moulding with outside edges of 31″ (two sides) and 24″ (two ends). Attach the dentil moulding to the face of the blocking, inset ¼″ from the top cap edge. Add a 1¼″ by 2½″ by 17⅝″ top block on top of the spreader and filler.

Install the lift-up shelf brackets so that the bottom of the lift-up shelf will be flush with the bottom of the baking cart; this spacing allows a 1″ gap at the top to allow the shelf into its raised position. Ease (bevel) the top edge of the shelf to free up the swing-up action.

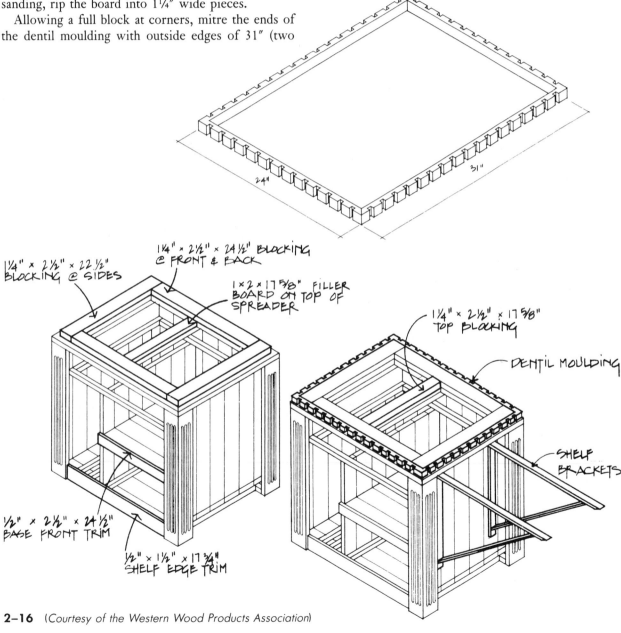

2-16 (*Courtesy of the Western Wood Products Association*)

To make the drawer, cut two ¾" by 3½" by 22" sides, and a 22¾" x 3½" back, plus a ¾" by 2⅞" by 22¾" front. You also are using a ½" by 4½" by 24¼" fascia, or drawer facing. The drawer bottom is ¼" plywood, cut to 23¼" by 22". Rout a ¼" by ¼" deep groove in both sides and the back, ⅜" up from the board bottom edges.

Assemble (using glue and nails) the back, front, and sides, and apply glue to the grooves. Slide the plywood into the grooves, and align the corners using a square. Nail the plywood to the bottom edge of the front, after squaring up the unit. Use 3d nails throughout, nailing carefully.

Put the drawer in place, and place the fascia against it. Mark the facing for final installation, remove the drawer, and glue the fascia to the drawer front. Drill a hole and install the drawer knob.

Turn the cart upside down, and install the casters.

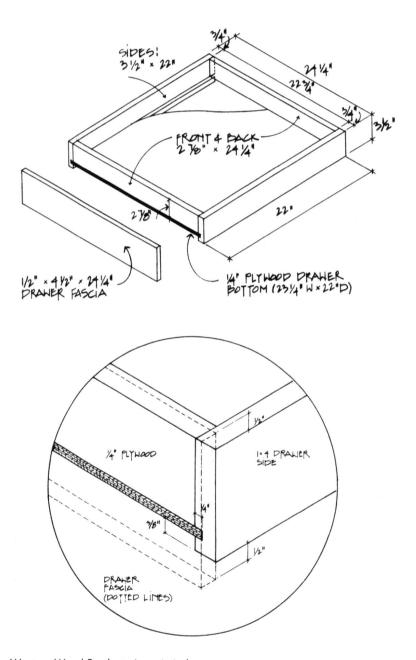

2-17 (Courtesy of the Western Wood Products Association)

After you right the cart, do whatever finishing work is needed (remove the drawer pull first)—final sanding, stain, and clear finish, or paint. Do not apply paint or finish to the areas to which the marble top will be glued.

Apply adhesive and install the marble top.

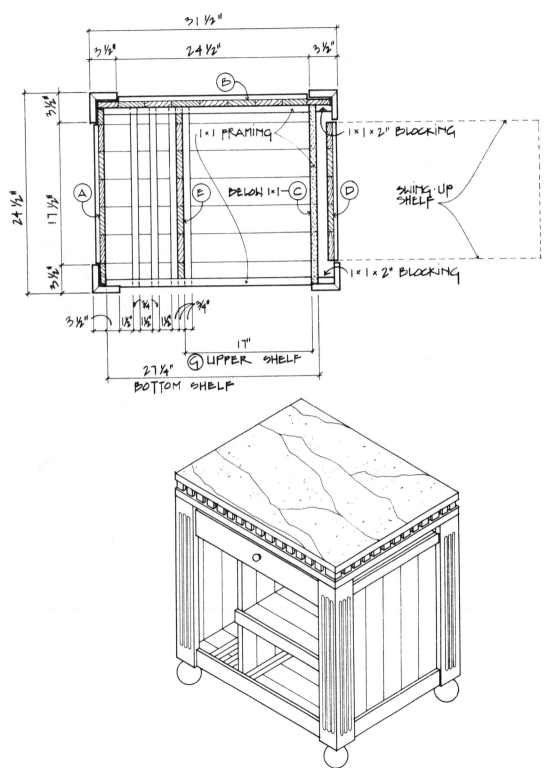

■ Double-Duty Kitchen Island

This kitchen island differs in several respects from the others in this chapter, but the most unusual feature is the rack, or series of slots, available for storing spatulas, whisks, and similar bulky, drawer-jamming items.

struction, and nail the kick plate to the base with 4d finishing nails, after applying glue to the back of the one-by-four.

With the three one-by-sixes cut to length for the bottom shelf, rip the middle board to 3⅛″ wide, and edge-glue the shelf boards; clamp with moderate pres-

2–19 The double-duty kitchen island may be made easily movable, or as here not so easily movable; this offset version must be bolted to the floor to prevent tip-over. (*Courtesy of the Western Wood Products Association*)

The wood top is similar to a butcher-block top (this is softwood, unless you want to use maple or other hardwood; a real butcher-block top has only end grain maple on its surface). This top is nearly 4″ thick.

This is a heavy project once done, but may be moved by two people around the kitchen, or other room, as needed.

With extreme care, cut all lumber to the listed sizes, keeping a careful check on accuracy as you go.

Start construction with the bottom frame, using the two-by-fours already cut to 15¾″ as the ends, short two-by-twos as blocking, and two-by-two corner posts set as shown. The one-by-four kick plate is also installed at this time, with all work being carried out with nails and glue. Use 8d nails and glue for con-

sure, keeping the resulting board as flat as possible. Cut a 1½″ notch in the back corners of the shelving (to fit around the posts), and glue and nail it to the base (allow at least six hours glue drying time before the latter operation).

To make the top frame, glue and nail two-by-threes on edge for the sides and back, and then nail the 35½″ one-by-three across the front, using 4d finishing nails and glue, between the side members. Glue and nail two-by-four blocking to the middle of the top frame, allowing ¼″ spacing for the one-by-six partition. Glue and nail the 38½″ one-by-three, with 4d finishing nails, to the front overlapping the ends. Keep edges even with the posts at front, sides, and back, and toenail in place.

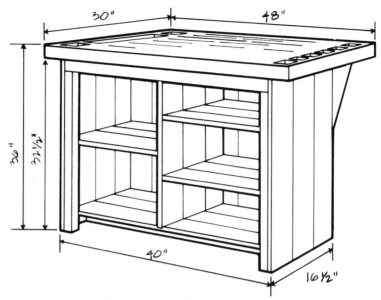

2-20 (Courtesy of the Western Wood Products Association)

Materials

(*Unless otherwise specified, all wood is pine, spruce, fir, or hem-fir. You may wish to substitute hardwoods for the butcher-block top.*)

Frame
- two two-by-four x 35½″
- two two-by-four x 12¾″
- four two-by-two x 30″ (posts)
- two two-by-two x 9″ (blocking)

Kickplate
- one-by-four x 35½″

Bottom Shelf
- three one-by-six x 38½″ (final width 14⅛″)

Top Frame
- two-by-three x 35½″
- two two-by-three x 15¾″
- one-by-three x 35½″
- one-by-three x 38½″

Upper Partition Supports
- two two-by-four x 14⅛″

Lower Partition Supports:
- two one-by-one x 14⅛″

Partition:
- three one-by-six x 25¾″ (final width 14⅛″)

Shelves (3):
- nine one-by-six x 18⅝″ (final width 14⅛″)

Outside:
- thirteen one-by-six x 32½″

Top
- twenty-eight one-by-four x 41½″
- two one-by-four x 46½″
- eight one-by-four x 44″
- two one-by-three x 48″
- two one-by-three x 30″

Top Support
- two-by-twelve x 22½″ or two purchased shelf brackets

For support with moulding instead:
- three two-by-twelves, cut 12″ high x 9⅞″ wide x 15⅝″ face, or cut to fit moulding you select
- 38½″ moulding
- two one-by-twelve x 14″ end panels

Tools and Some Further Materials

- table saw, radial-arm saw, or circular saw
- mitre box or power mitre saw
- electric drill and drill bits, for hardware holes
- router and router bits (¼″ and ½″ straight bits)
- jigsaw
- four 3′ bar clamps
- screwdriver
- chisel
- carpenter's hammer
- nail set
- tape measure
- framing square
- brush

- steel wool
- 100- and 150-grit sandpaper
- finishing sander
- wood glue
- waterproof glue
- 1 lb 4d finishing nails
- 1 lb 8d nails
- 2″, 2½″, and 3″ screws
- four 3″ lag screws
- four 5″ lag screws

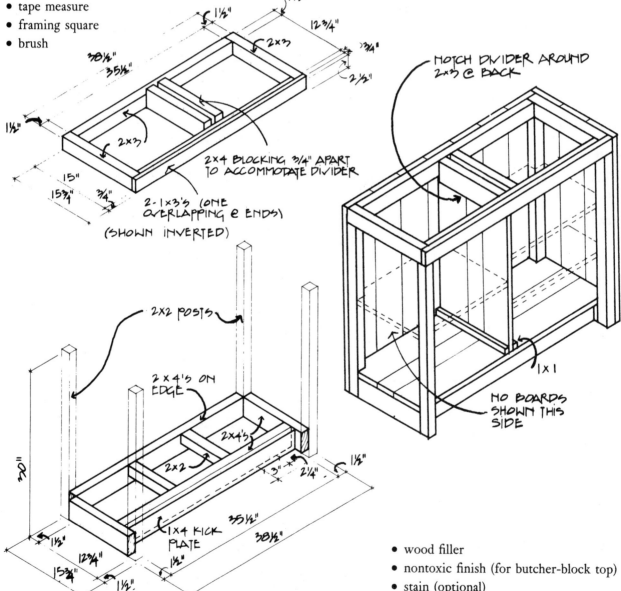

- wood filler
- nontoxic finish (for butcher-block top)
- stain (optional)
- clear finish

2–21 (Courtesy of the Western Wood Products Association)

To make the vertical partition, use three one-by-sixes and again rip the middle board to 3⅛" wide for a finished partition width of 14⅛". Edge-glue and clamp with moderate pressure, endeavoring to keep the boards as flat as possible. The finished partition is 25¾" long. Use one-by-one cleats on the bottom shelf (14⅛" long), spaced ¾" apart, and placed in the middle, just as are the two-by-fours on the top frame.

The outside is covered with one-by-six boards, sides and back, using 1½" (4d) finishing nails.

Use one-by-one shelf cleats to install shelves as illustrated. Cut 1½" notches for corner posts before installing shelves. Cleats are installed with 3d nails and glue, and the shelves are then glued and nailed, with 3d nails, to the cleats.

The butcher-block top comes next. Notch the one-by-fours that extend the furthest to fit the one-by-three trim (¾" by 2½").

You must have a level surface on which to assemble the butcher-block top; a helper will also be handy. Check the assembly pattern to see it matches the drawers, and then number the boards, from 1 through 38, to keep them in sequence as the construction goes on.

Use a framing square to set up a tack-nailed temporary framework of one-by-one material to hold boards across the back and down one side, thus forcing them to stay square as you assemble the unit. Use waterproof adhesive and 4d nails to assemble the top.

Keep on assembling until you reach the end, and clamp with moderate pressure until the glue sets. Wipe off excess glue with a damp rag. Sand when finished.

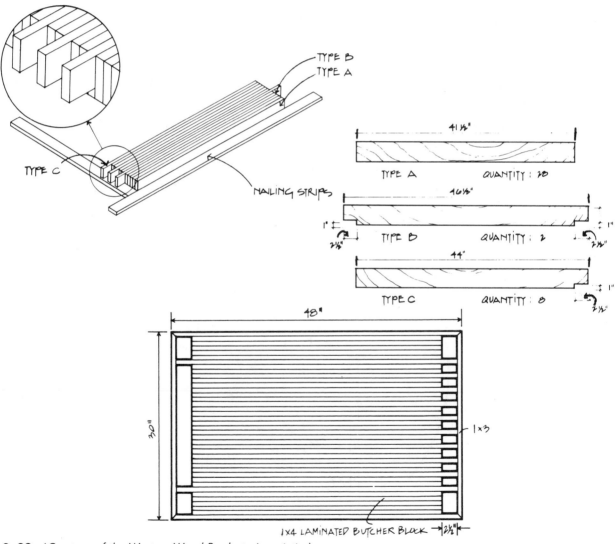

2-22 *(Courtesy of the Western Wood Products Association)*

51

Cut top supports into triangles as shown (you may use commercial shelf supports if you wish, but moulding will fit a great deal better on wood triangles). For the moulding specified, you'll get a fit with triangles 12″ high by 9⅞″ wide (top) with a 15⅜″ hypotenuse. Another moulding pattern will force you to make adjustments; so check before cutting if you've gotten any other pattern. One block is mounted in the middle, and the other two at the ends, inset ¾″ from outside edges to accommodate one-by-twelve end panels. Apply wood moulding using 3d nails and glue.

To make the end panels, clamp a one-by-twelve to the outside edge of the support and the moulding (which is flush with the support), and trace the moulding profile. Cut the moulding profile with a jigsaw or a scroll saw; glue, nail, and clamp in place until the glue sets.

You may skip the moulding step if you wish—retaining the movability and possibly reducing the work—or simply use commercial shelf supports. Cut an 11¼″ length of two-by-twelve on the diagonal to make the supports, and mount them to outside edges using 2½″ screws. Predrill and countersink the holes, and finish with wooden plugs (after doing a slight—¼″ or so—counterbore).

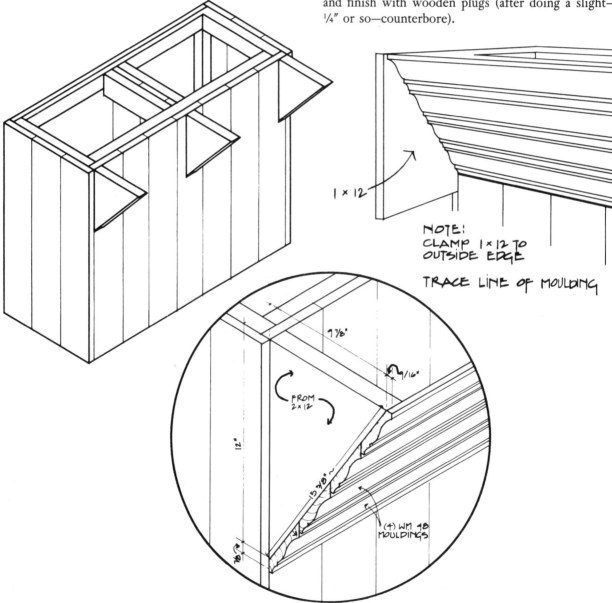

NOTE!
CLAMP 1 × 12 TO
OUTSIDE EDGE

TRACE LINE OF MOULDING

1 × 12

9⅞″

9/16″

FROM
2 × 12

12″

15⅜″

(4) WM 48
MOULDINGS

2–23 (*Courtesy of the Western Wood Products Association*)

To attach the top, get help to turn the base unit right side up. Secure the base to the top with four 3″ lag screws. Predrill the holes, and drill a counterbore that will allow you to slip in the appropriate-size socket wrench for the lag screw head. If you offset the top in the manner shown, the unit cannot be used as a movable unit, for to keep from tipping it must be secured to the floor with 5″ lag screws. To make the unit freestanding and movable, simply center the base on the top. This also eliminates any need for the shelf supports, two-by-twelves, and moulding.

To finish up the trim, mitre one-by-three boards, and cover the outside edge of the top.

Sand completely, including the top, then stain (if desired) and coat the base with clear finish. Use a non-toxic finish that will keep stains from penetrating the top.

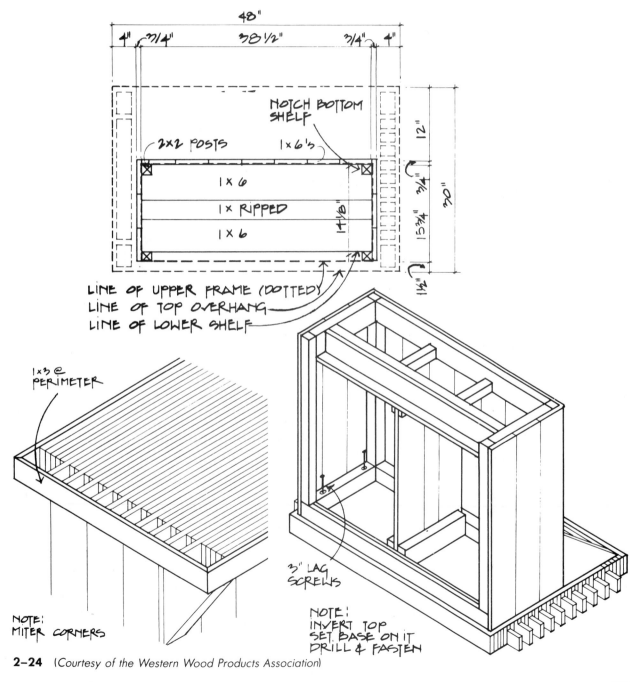

2–24 (Courtesy of the Western Wood Products Association)

◼ Expandable Bar

This rolling bar with fold-out ends may not be the life of a party, but it should make some kinds of entertaining easier—and look handsome while doing so.

Start the project with the careful layout of all parts on the two sheets of plywood, making sure to allow ⅛" spacing for kerfs.

Begin assembly with sides to the back, and then install internal shelves. Build the drawers next; position

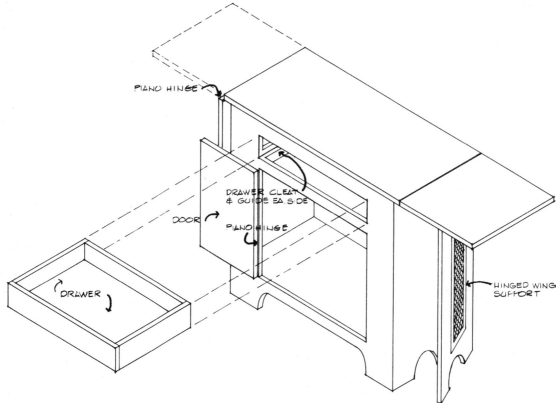

2-25 Expandable mobile bar. (*Courtesy of the American Plywood Association*)

Tools

- table saw, radial-arm saw, or circular saw
- 10- or 12-point crosscut saw
- mitre box or power mitre saw (optional)
- jigsaw or bandsaw
- laminate trimmer and bit
- electric drill and drill bits
- screwdriver
- chisel
- tape measure
- framing square
- brush
- steel wool
- 100- and 150-grit sandpaper
- finishing sander

Materials

- two ¾" x 4' x 8' MDO or A-B plywood
- three drawer pulls
- four 2" stem casters
- four ¾" x 18" continuous hinges
- eight 2½" cabinet hinges, for doors and wings
- two magnetic catches
- paper caning sufficient to fit your desired pattern (optional)
- two-by-two x 24" blocking, to fit for casters
- 28' ½" half-round moulding, to fit perimeter of caning (if caning option is desired)
- 5' x 6' laminate, for bar top
- wood glue
- contact cement

and install drawer runners as shown in the drawings. Install the front, and then install cabinet doors.

Side wings go on next. Wings and cabinet doors are attached using continuous hinges. The expanding tops are attached with the 2½″ cabinet hinges.

Build the drawer and check the fit of the glides. Wax the glides.

The laminate top goes on next and is applied with contact cement. Cut the top within 1½″ to 2″ of final size, and coat both the top of the bar and the back of

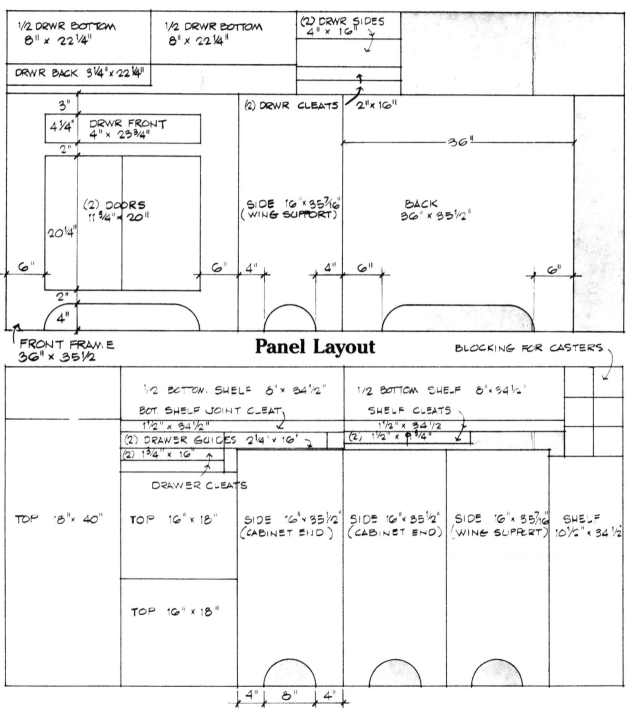

Panel Layout

2-26 (*Courtesy of the American Plywood Association*)

the laminate with a good grade of nonflammable contact cement. Allow to dry while placing about four ¾"-square by 30"-long wood spacers on the bar top. Place the laminate glue-side down on the spacers, and move into position. Remove one spacer and bring the laminate in contact with the adhesive on the bar surface. Use a rubber mallet to assure contact once you're positive it is in position. Remove the spacers and use the mallet on the laminate as you go. Finally, use a laminate or veneer roller to make certain there is total contact between the laminate and bar top.

Sand carefully; finish with your choice of paints or stains and clear coatings. Then add the cane patterns, if you want them.

The resulting movable bar will provide an attractive and durable centerpiece for many a social gathering.

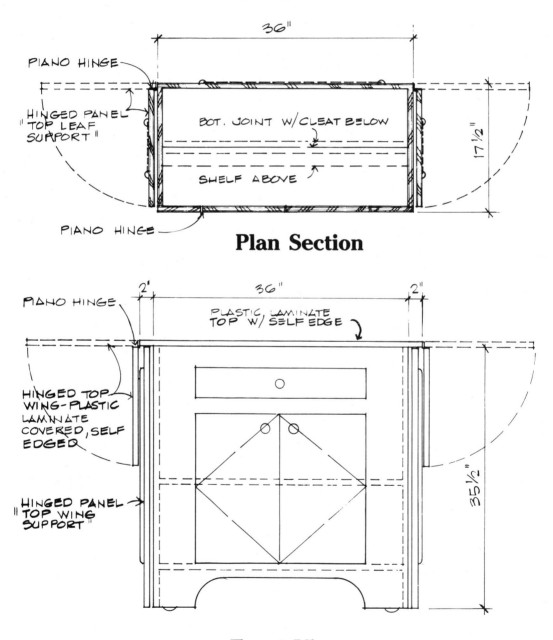

Plan Section

Front View

2–27 *(Courtesy of the American Plywood Association)*

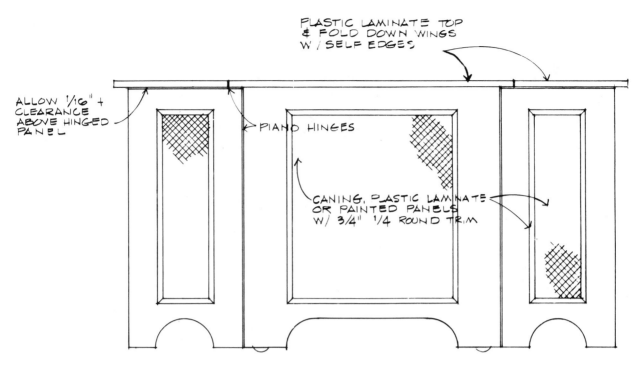

PLASTIC LAMINATE TOP
& FOLD DOWN WINGS
W/ SELF EDGES

ALLOW 1/16" +
CLEARANCE
ABOVE HINGED
PANEL

PIANO HINGES

CANING, PLASTIC LAMINATE
OR PAINTED PANELS
W/ 3/4" 1/4 ROUND TRIM

Back View

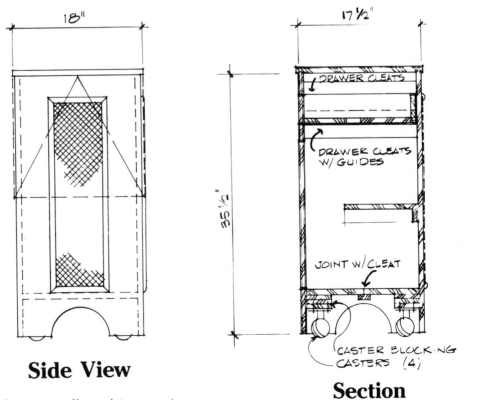

18"

17 1/2"

35 1/2"

DRAWER CLEATS

DRAWER CLEATS
W/ GUIDES

JOINT W/ CLEAT

CASTER BLOCKING
CASTERS (4)

Side View

Section

2-28 *(Courtesy of the American Plywood Association)*

3

Home Office Storage and Work Space

These projects relate to home office needs, with computer desks being the most prominent; any desk, of course, may be used to hold typewriters or anything else you wish. As well, there's no need to set up a professional office to find these projects exceptionally handy. With home computer use on the rise, and the old chores such as bill paying ever present, some form of simple home office is essential to all of us.

Projects range from simple to moderately complex, with the starting point being a place to store floppy disks—a disk holder that is adaptable to other uses, such as holding CDs.

■ Stacking Floppy Disk Files

This is a relatively simple solid-wood file, little more than a box surrounding a drawer in its single phase, that may be built in multiples and stacked, with or without the described 4″ high frame. I like the frame because my desk is always awash in papers, often 2″ to 4″ in depth; so raising the front of the file drawers a few inches off the desk makes the drawers simpler to open without shifting piles of paper.

Tools

- table or radial-arm saw
- dado head or ¼″ rabbeting router bit
- planer
- router
- drill and drill bit, ⁵⁄₃₂″ (check diameter of knob)
- square
- measuring tape
- six or eight 12″ bar clamps
- 13-oz hammer
- 150-grit sandpaper
- finishing sander
- tack cloth
- screwdriver for knob screw

As presented, the files will hold both CDs and 5¼″ floppy disks. Change a couple of dimensions—specifically, remove 1½″ from the height and width of all parts—and the unit works equally well with 3½″ floppy disks.

I recommend making two or more files at the same time. Begin by planing walnut to ½″ thickness (you may buy your walnut already planed, of course), and go on to the next step, cutting pieces to the listed sizes. For those who wish to do so, there's no real reason not to use poplar or a similar species of wood for the drawer bottom, sides, and back.

Check edges for square; then set up and cut rabbets as shown. Rabbets are all ¼″ wide (into the ½″ wood) and ½″ deep to accept wood at its full thickness.

Mark the side-to-side center on the case bottom front, and drill a countersunk hole 2″ to each side of the center for No. 6 ¾″ flathead wood screws. Predrilling in this manner allows you to readily stack a second, third, and even fourth tier of boxes without worrying about slipping. The predrilling isn't needed for the first tier, fitting onto the rack, but if done it eliminates the need for the long (3½″) counterbore in that part.

Materials

- four ½″ x 8½″ x 10″ walnut, sides, top and bottom
- ½″ x 8″ x 7½″ walnut, back
- two ½″ x 7½″ x 9½″ walnut, drawer sides
- ½″ x 7½″ x 9½″ walnut, drawer bottom
- ½″ x 7½″ x 6½″ walnut, drawer back
- ½″ x 8½″ x 8⅜″ walnut, drawer front
- ½″ x 5½″ x 7⅝″ drawer front
- 1″ porcelain knob
- wood glue
- ⅝″ brads
- satin clear finish
- walnut stain (if desired)

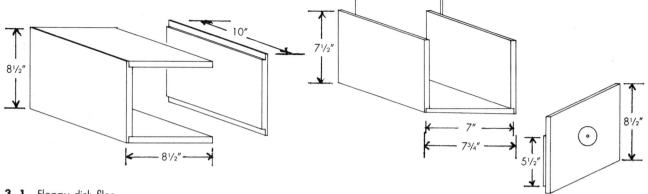

3-1 Floppy disk files.

Check the fit of all parts. Backs fit inside the parts to which they are joined with simple butt joints. Make any needed adjustments; add glue, clamp, square, and set aside for a few hours.

Assemble the drawer front by placing the 5½″ x 7⅝″ backup drawer front ½″ up from the bottom of the actual drawer front and gluing it in place. Assemble and glue up the drawer.

At this point, it's a good idea to check and see if the drawer will fit in place. If it doesn't, a small amount of sanding will correct the problem.

Sand with 150-grit sandpaper, and apply the first coat of satin clear finish. I suggest keeping hands off until a couple hours have passed. At that point, given normal drying conditions, you can lightly sand the finish in preparation for the next coat. Use at least three coats.

Rack for File Boxes

The rack that holds a stack of these file boxes is made to fit the number you expect to stack horizontally, and does nothing more than raise them off the desk and look decorative. Make it as wide as needed after measuring your versions of the file boxes: here, I give dimensions for a two-box width for 5¼″ floppy disks.

Rack Materials and Additional Tools

- two ¾″ x 18″ x 4″ walnut
- two ¾″ x 10″ x 4″ walnut
- ¾″ x 22″ x 1½″ walnut shop-made moulding
- two ¾″ x 12″ x 1½″ shop-made moulding
- eight No. 0 joinery biscuits
- wood glue
- finish, as above
- biscuit joiner
- router moulding bit

Simply designed, this is nothing more than a squared-up box designed to fit the underside of the outer floppy disk file boxes. Cut the pieces to size, and make and mitre the moulding.

Start by assembling the square frame, making sure that, front to back, it's the same size as the underside of the boxes (10″ for our example). Keep it *square*.

Once the glue has had a couple of hours to dry, you can unclamp and assemble the cut-to-fit moulding, which is glued in place.

Sand, stain, and finish as above.

To make the best assembly, drill a hole through the bottom of the ¾″ stock, counterboring until you're within about ½″ of the top of the stock (use a ½″ brad-point drill here for best results). Follow that with a ⅛″ pilot hole, and drive a ¾″ No. 6 wood screw up into the bottom of the file cabinet. That prevents excessive movement when you pull a drawer out. For the next tier, you've got to drill and sink a ¾″ or ⅝″ screw from the top—with very little room to place the drill—if you haven't already made and drilled a stack of these cabinets beforehand. Follow the above recommendations for drilling ahead of time, and that problem is solved.

You could, of course, simply stack the files and glue the boxes together, but then their mobility is severely limited. And it's kind of nice to have at least one extra, *loose* file box, so you can slip a drawer out with needed disks, and transport those disks elsewhere. I suggest making an extra case, adding a centered suitcase handle, and some kind of spinning latch to keep the drawer from sliding out. The simplest kind of latch is a screen window latch, but you can make your own from one screw and a ½″-thick walnut piece ½″ wide by 1¼″ long. Drive a No. 4 1″ round-head wood screw through the walnut spinner into the center edge of the case top.

■ Sliding-End Bookshelf

This is my version of a handy little bookshelf that you may have seen in several catalogs or stores at a reasonably low price. My major change is to enlarge the end stop to the same size as the sliding end (and the other end), while increasing the size of all the ends. I had been using a standard version to hold books—mainly computer manuals and similar stuff—on my desk for a couple of years, and I got tired of everything toppling from it almost daily. The reason everything topples is quite simple: the manuals are much larger than the 5½"-wide x 7"-tall end pieces.

nothing wider than 5". After the glue dries, sand, and cut to size.

Cut the dowels to size.

Tape the three boards together, and round the upper corners with a belt sander or a jigsaw, scroll saw, or band saw. Back the area to be drilled through with a piece of ¼" hardboard or plywood scrap.

Mark the hole centers for the dowels, and drill through all three boards. Check dowel fit. Disassemble and sand lightly.

Insert the dowels into the center plate. Use no glue there. Coat the inside of the end plate holes with wood glue and insert the dowels in one plate. Stand on top

End and Center Pieces 10" Wide × 11½"

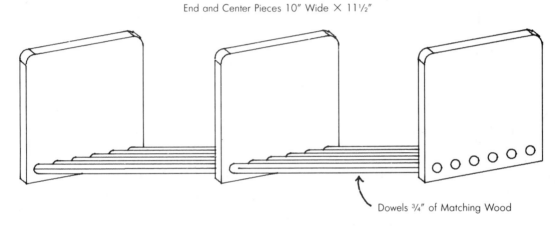

Dowels ¾" of Matching Wood

3–2 Bookshelf with sliding center.

Thus, going for an overall end piece size of 11½" high by 10" wide works well, even though it uses a bit more desk space. The extra size also means you can grab the shelf and take your manuals to another desk or work area with no problems.

Begin by gluing up narrow boards to make the wider boards for the ends and sliding center. I'd suggest using

edges and insert dowels in the glued holes for the second end plate.

Square as you go, and drive a 2d finishing nail into the bottom of each dowel, through the bottom of the ends. Use care here to keep from splitting the wood; though when nailing this way, it should be no problem *if* you nail straight. Do not nail through the sliding center piece.

Allow the glue to dry, then sand with 150-grit paper, and stain as desired. Put on at least three coats of tung oil, sanding lightly (or use 0000 steel wool) between coats, and cleaning off with a tack cloth.

When the finish dries, flip it over and load it up.

Tools

- table, radial-arm, or circular saw
- mitre box (for cutting dowels)
- drill and ¾" Forstner or brad-point drill bit
- square
- measuring tape
- 150-grit sandpaper
- tack cloth
- 13-oz claw hammer
- six to nine 12" bar clamps
- planer or belt sander, to smooth 10"-wide panels

Materials

- six ¾" walnut, cherry or other dowels
- three ¾" x 10" x 11½" walnut, cherry or oak
- wood glue
- twelve 2d finishing nails
- stain and tung oil

■ Drop-Leaf Computer Desk

The drop-leaf feature of this desk makes it suitable for small or crowded homes, and for apartments, while the adjustable shelves make it easy to adapt to almost any use—including noncomputer uses. The overall finished size, folded, is only 13″ x 46″ wide; so it really doesn't use a lot of space (and it fits through doors easily).

Begin by laying out the patterns on the plywood. The American Plywood Association layout pattern provided allows for ⅛″ kerfs for your saw cuts: you *must* do the same. Always make cuts from the roughest face of the wood. I'd suggest adding a good tight line of masking tape along cut lines. While this doesn't eliminate splintering, it does reduce it, especially with jigsaws.

3-3 Drop-leaf computer desk. (*Courtesy of the American Plywood Association*)

Tools

- circular saw
- jigsaw
- measuring tape
- square
- compass
- four two-by-fours (to support plywood while it's cut)
- screwdriver, for hinge screws
- screwdriver, for No. 6 wood screws
- cordless drill and driver bit
- drill bit to fit stem casings for casters, ³⁄₃₂″ drill bit, ¼″ drill bit for shelf holders
- nail set
- paintbrush
- 100-grit sandpaper
- finishing sander
- section of ¼″ pegboard, 10″ high by about 10″ wide

Materials

- ⅝" x 4' x 8' plywood: use either Medium Density Overlay (both sides) or A-B
- seven ⅜" butt hinges
- twelve adjustable shelf supports
- six ball casters, stem type
- ½ lb 4d or 6d finishing nails
- thirty-six No. 6 1¼" flathead wood screws (or drive screws)
- twelve No. 6 1" drive screws
- twelve adjustable shelf holders
- wood filler
- paint

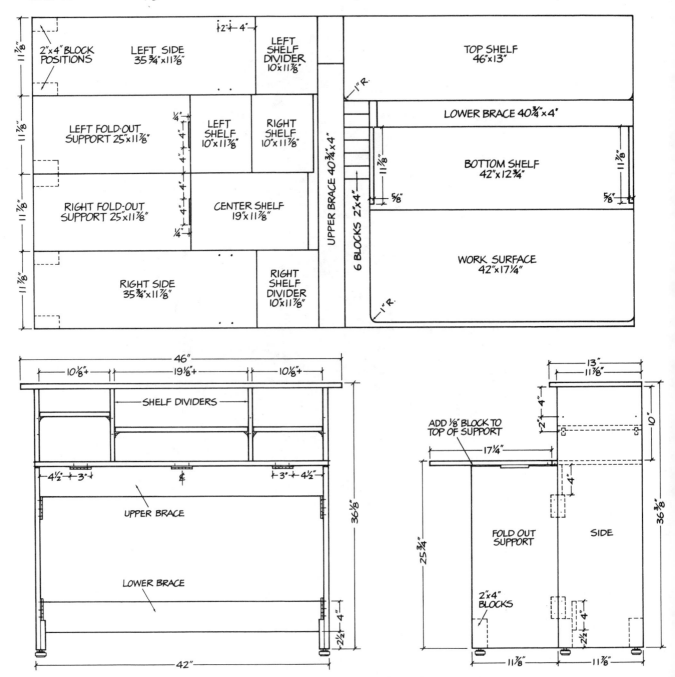

3-4 Panel layout with front and side views. (*Courtesy of the American Plywood Association*)

Carefully cut the pieces to size, and then lightly smooth the edges.

Assembly begins with the shelf unit, using the 1/4″ drill bit in conjunction with the pegboard to drill holes for the adjustable shelf holders. The pegboard makes sure the holes are in line and spot on—at equal distances up and down from each end. Simply center it on each spot, and drill a 3/8″ deep hole. For the two center shelf dividers, you may go ahead and drill right through the dividers; back the plywood with a piece of scrap material, clamped tightly in place, to prevent splintering.

With the holes drilled, notch the bottom shelf as shown in the plans, going 5/8″ deep. Attach the bottom shelf to the sides, 10″ down from the top edges (to the top of the shelf), using glue and 4d or 6d finishing nails.

The top shelf is now positioned, set in 2″ from each end, flush back, with a small front overhang. Do this with glue and 4d or 6d finishing nails, making sure the assembly stays square at this time.

Place the upper and lower braces at this time, securing those with 1¼″ drive screws and glue.

The left and right fold-out supports are now hung using the hinges. These are surface-mount hinges; so they do not need to be mortised in, which greatly simplifies the work. With the supports folded out, install the drop-leaf part of the desk.

Add blocks on the desk and the fold-out supports using 1″ drive screws and glue.

Install the shelf dividers by first coating the top and bottom edges with glue (mark the edge and a center line on the top shelf and below the bottom shelf to ease nailing and correct insertion). Insert the dividers from the back, and nail three times per unit, upper and lower.

Lay the unit on its back, and drill for the stem holders. Install, and add the casters.

Now comes the fun part. Sand with 100-grit sandpaper, and fill all edges with wood putty. Sand those when dry.

Unless you wish to paint over the hinges, all hardware, including the casters, should be removed at this point; then the unit should be painted. When the paint is applied to your satisfaction, reinstall the hardware, including the casters; pop in the adjustable shelf holders and the shelves to suit your needs, and go to work.

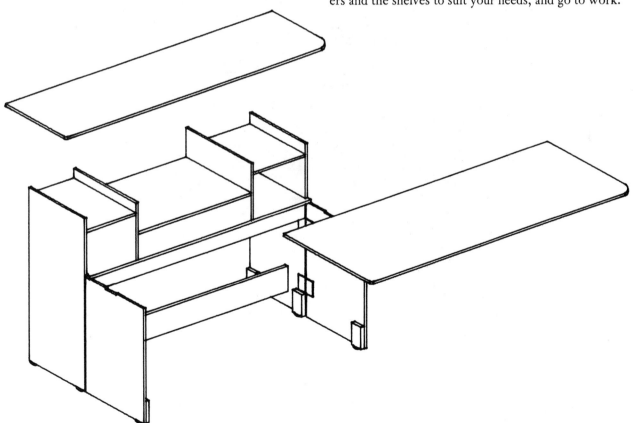

3-5 Drop-leaf computer desk. (*Courtesy of the American Plywood Association*)

■ Secretary Desk

This unit is a traditional idea gone modern—to the point where it's simply made of plywood. With adjustable shelves, a small light, and a host of other handy features that will provide easily moved, easily changed work and pleasure space, the unit may serve as a child's study area, a home desk for bills, and whatnot—or even a computer desk. Its overall size makes it useful, while construction makes it adaptable.

3-6 Secretary desk. (*Courtesy of the American Plywood Association*)

Tools

- circular saw
- jigsaw
- measuring tape
- square
- compass
- four two-by-fours (to support plywood while it's cut)
- screwdriver, for hinge screws
- screwdriver, for No. 6 wood screws
- claw hammer
- cordless drill and driver bit, ¼″ drill bit for shelf holders
- nail set
- paintbrush
- 100-grit sandpaper
- finishing sander
- section of ¼″ pegboard, 28″ high by about 10″ wide

Materials

- two ¾″ x 4′ x 8′ plywood, A-B or MDO overlaid both sides
- ⅜″ x 4′ x 8′ cut to 48″ x 79″ for unit back
- four 2″ cabinet hinges
- two door handles
- two magnetic door latches
- 24″ fluorescent light
- twelve adjustable shelf holders
- wood glue
- ½ lb 4d or 6d finishing nails
- box No. 6 1¼″ drive screws
- wood putty
- paint or other finish

Start by laying out the parts on the sheets. Of course, the back is the only part on the ⅜″ sheet; so it may be laid out at any time. I suggest that you leave it for last—and by that I mean for the last measuring, layout and cutting step, *after* the major box unit is assembled.

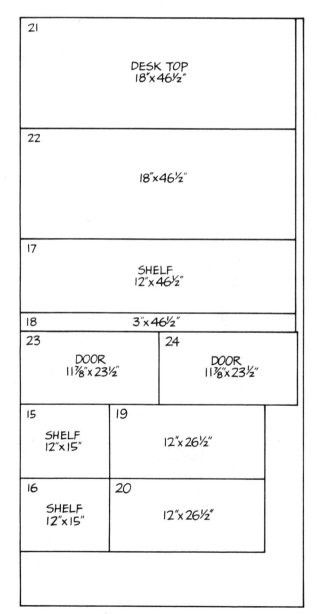

3–7 Panel layout. (*Courtesy of the American Plywood Association*)

If you've drifted off anywhere, it's a lot nicer to be able to cut the back to a larger size, instead of having to buy another sheet.

Sand edges to remove splinters.

Drill the upper inside of the sides and both sides of the shelf dividers for the shelf adjusters. Drill the holes ³/₈" deep in the side pieces. You may tape the dividers together and drill right through them—making sure to have scrap material as a backup to prevent splintering along each line of drill holes. Use the 10" by 28" pegboard to spot the drill hole centers.

Begin assembly with the outside box: use 4d finishing nails and glue to assemble the top inside ends. Keep a running check with the square on the assembly every time you add a part. Position the 12" by 46½" shelf 28" from the top of the unit to the bottom of the shelf,

and nail and glue in place. Glue and nail in the shelf brace about 4" in from the front (this brace also serves to shield one's eyes from the direct glare of the fluorescent light). Leave the assembly face down on the floor while you put together the desk top section.

As the glue dries on the desk top section, check your measurements on the overall unit. Now you can cut the back to fit. Install with 2d finishing nails and glue.

Place the entire unit on its back after the glue has had an hour or so to dry. Install the desktop, with its lower edges 24½" up from the bottom of the unit. Use six 1¼" drive screws, of brass, on each side to secure this unit. Again, keep a running check on square.

Install the shelf dividers using 4d or 6d finishing nails and glue. Draw both edge and centerlines for this installation.

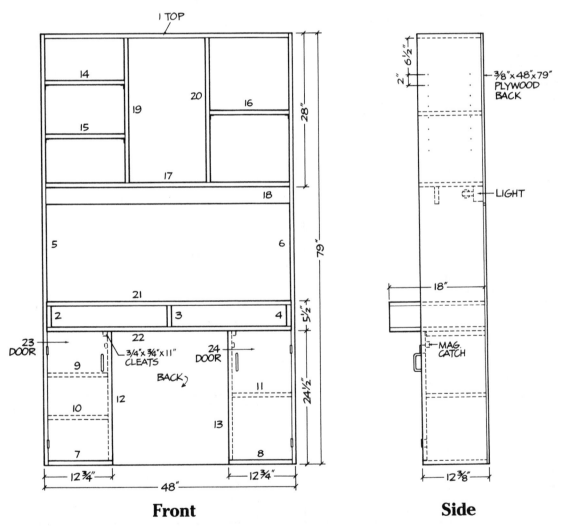

Front   **Side**

3–8 Dimension drawings. (*Courtesy of the American Plywood Association*)

Install the bottom and side of each desk base. You need a ¾″ by ¾″ cleat at the top inside of each short side for a brace; install these with 2d nails and glue. Install the shelves in the bases.

Check the fit of the doors, and install with the cabinet hinges. Install the catches and handles.

Now, remove all of the hardware, right down to taking the doors off. You may, if you wish, remove the brass wood screws used to hold the desktop module in place. They look better if there's no paint on them.

Sand with 100-grit sandpaper, and make sure all edges are fully filled with wood putty. Sand them smooth. Clean with vacuum and tack cloth, and paint to suit.

Reassemble, and you're certain to be pleased with this handy, attractive unit.

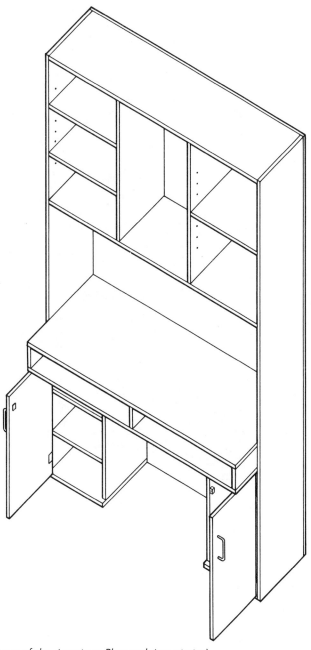

3–9 Secretary desk. (*Courtesy of the American Plywood Association*)

■ Computer Work Center

This is a more advanced unit than the drop-leaf model; it is built to hold more computer gear and is less adaptable to other modes of work. It can be adapted, however, to different computer configurations. I made two of the carts because my plotter and my laser printer each require so much space. At the same time as it supplies a great deal of space, the basic configuration here needs only two 4' by 8' plywood panels.

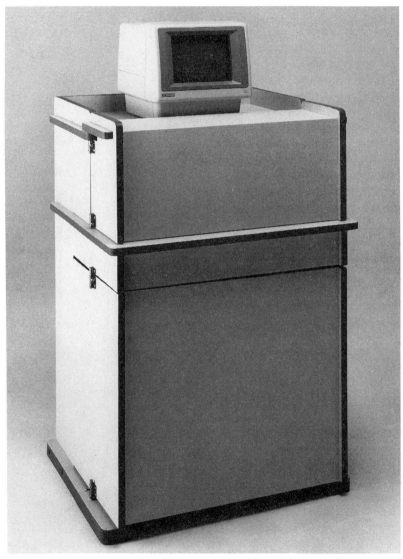

3–10 Computer work center. (*Courtesy of the American Plywood Association*)

Materials
- ¾" x 4' x 8' A-C plywood
- ⅜" x 4' x 8' A-C plywood
- two-by-four x 8' pine
- ¼ lb 4d finishing nails
- forty No. 8 1" wood screws
- four ¼" x 4" carriage bolts with nuts and washers
- eight ¼" brass barrel bolt latches
- two 2" plate casters
- wood glue
- contact cement
- wood putty
- paint

Lay out the thicker (¾") panel first, making sure to allow for the ⅛" kerf. Carefully make the cuts. Repeat the process with the ⅜" panel.

Use sandpaper to smooth the edges and to remove splinters, and begin the assembly with the software cabinet. Cut a bottom rabbet to accept the ¾" depth of the bottom (pieces laminated together using contact cement), on ⅜"-wide rabbets. Dado the back edges of the sides to accept the front; the dado is ⅜" by ⅜" set back from front edge ⅝" (1" to the inside edge of the dado). This is a stopped dado, quitting 1" from the end. Stopping a dado in this manner gives a curved edge. Use a chisel or corner chisel to cut it out square. Insert the bottom, and then insert the top into the ends. Use 2d or 4d nails, as suitable, and glue during assembly.

Mark locations for the barrel bolts on the right side, and drill holes for screws. Do not mount yet.

Computer Desk

Now, assemble the computer desk. Start with the sides, cutting a ⅜" by ⅜" rabbet in the front desk lips. This accepts the desk fascia, where a drawer might be on a standard desk. Next, cut a ¼" rabbet (again, ⅜" deep) on each side, as shown. The actual distance may vary an inch or so in either direction depending on equipment; but make sure the two rabbets are at *exactly* the same height. There is another ⅜" rabbet, stopped at 22¼", set in ⅝" from the back edge, and one at the bottom of the back edge, set in the same distance, stopped at 10".

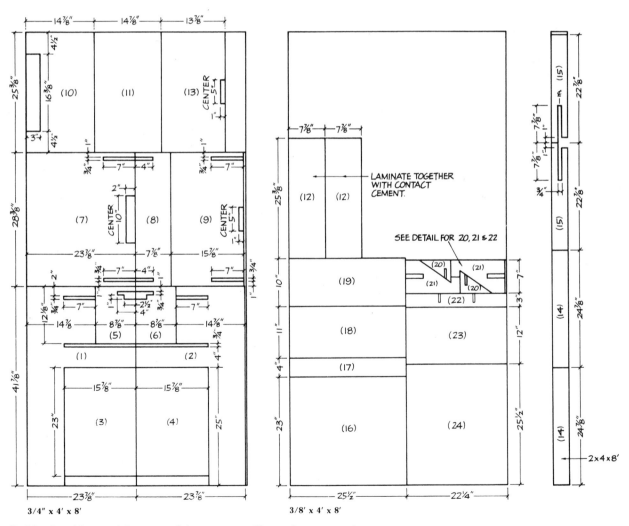

3–11 Panel layout. (*Courtesy of the American Plywood Association*)

Tools

- circular saw
- jigsaw
- router
- edge guide
- ¾″ straight bit
- ⅜″ straight bit
- corner chisel
- measuring tape
- square
- compass
- four two-by-fours (to support plywood while it's cut)
- screwdriver for No. 8 wood screws
- claw hammer
- cordless drill and driver bit
- nail set
- paintbrush
- 100-grit sandpaper
- finishing sander

With the two-by-four feet set down, mark and rabbet for the sides; the rabbet will be ¾″ wide and stopped at an 8″ mark. This rabbet may be cut with a jigsaw.

Insert sides into the feet, and drill for carriage bolts (¼″ brad-point bit). Insert carriage washers and bolts.

Place one side, with installed foot, with dadoes facing up. Place glue in the dadoes, and insert the lower brace and the back. Install the top side, and use 2d or 4d nails to hold it while the glue sets. Nail every 4″.

Insert the front fascia into its dadoes, and nail and glue.

Check square as you go.

Slip the center shelf in place with glue, and nail with 4d nails through the ends. Do the same with the top shelf and the desktop. Set aside for the glue to dry, and assemble the book rack using 2d nails and glue.

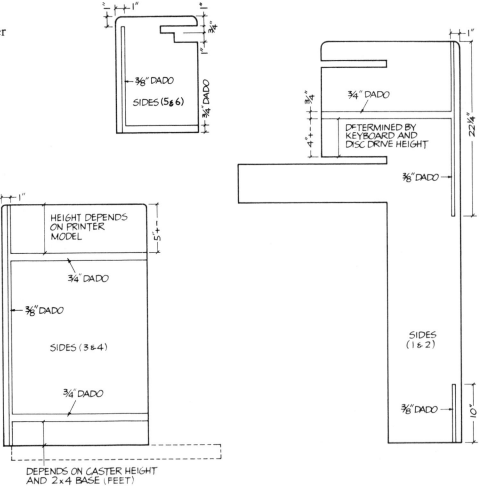

3–12 Dado details. (*Courtesy of the American Plywood Association*)

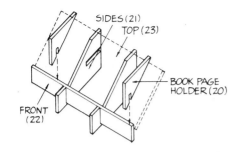

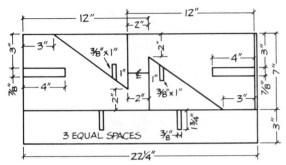

3–13 Book rack detail with exploded view. (*Courtesy of the American Plywood Association*)

Printer Cabinet

The assembly of the printer cabinet can be done while the desk is setting up. Make sure all dadoes are cut: 5″ down from the top edge, there's a ¾″ by ⅜″ dado; ⅝″ in from the back edge there's a ⅜″ by ⅜″ dado. At the bottom, there's a ¼″ dado; its height from the bottom depends on the height of the casters you're using combined with the two-by-fours used to hold the casters. Both ¾″ dadoes stop at the ⅜″ dado.

Assemble the printer stand with 4d finishing nails and glue around the bottom and top shelves and the back. Keep all components square as assembly progresses.

Assemble the two-by-four frame using 6d finishing nails and glue, from the top of the bottom shelf.

Install casters, as shown, to provide a pivoting unit that locks to the main unit for closing up at night. To use as a freestanding unit, simply install four casters, one in each corner, and leave off the barrel bolts.

Sand with 100-grit sandpaper after filling all edges with wood filler, and paint to suit. Then go ahead and install the barrel bolts, and set the unit up for use.

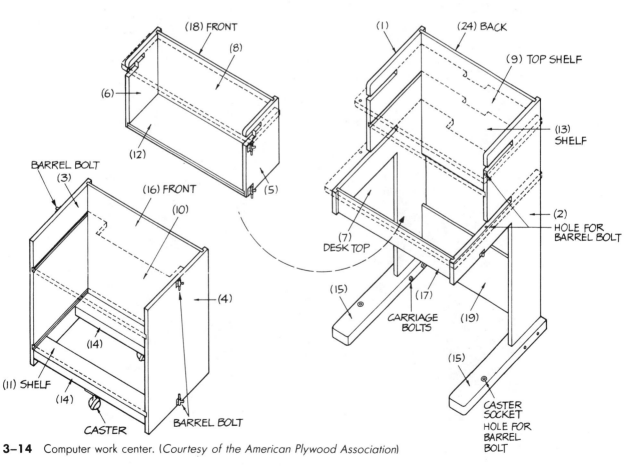

3–14 Computer work center. (*Courtesy of the American Plywood Association*)

■ Cube

Probably one of the most useful projects of all is one of the simplest—at least in its basic form: the cube. Depending on the size of the individual units, the storage possibilities range from LPs (increasingly a rare need with audio tapes and CDs), books, and use as a space for stereo components. In office use, cubes may hold files, fax machines, and similar items. Here, the materials listed form a single cube, with mitred corners, an inset back, and a door. Leave off the door for open units, and make other changes as you wish—for larger machines, the cube may be changed to a rectangle, simply by doubling the width of two sides and the back; that provides a space to hold the largest fax or answering machine unit.

3–15 Cubes. (*Courtesy of Georgia-Pacific Corporation*)

There are probably as many ways to construct cubes as there are uses for the cubes when finished. These are designed to be made with biscuit-joined mitred corners, but they may be made with simple mitred corners or with butt joints with only minor changes. For simple mitre corners, just drop the biscuits and the joiner from the list. Add 4d finishing nails to hold the corners together with glue. Set the nail heads and fill with wood putty.

For butt joints, make two sides shorter—by 1½″—to fit inside the longer sides; that is, two pieces will remain 14″ by 14″, while two will be 12½″ by 12½″. Use 6d nails and glue to assemble. In both cases, make sure the assembly is square.

Start by cutting the pieces to size. Cut slots for biscuits about 3″ in from each end on each mitre after marking. Use two biscuits per joint (eight per cube). Clamp for at least two hours.

For simple mitre joints, simply drive a 4d nail into the glue-coated assembled joint, and allow a couple of hours to dry.

Insert the back immediately, coated with glue and from the *back*. Drive 4d nails in at 4″ intervals. Set nail heads. Set the assembly aside to dry, and construct the next cube, if more are desired.

Install doors with cabinet hinges (¾″ by 2″) mortised into the edges of doors and cases.

Remove the hinges and knob, if used, and sand the entire unit with 100-grit sandpaper. Paint or stain, and coat with clear finish as desired. Reinstall the hardware.

Materials

- four ¾″ x 14″ x 14″ A-B plywood, for sides
- ½″ x 12½″ x 12½″ A-B plywood, for back
- ¾″ x 12⅜″ x 12⅜″ A-B plywood, door
  (12½″ x 12½″ reduced to allow free movement)
- eight No. 10 biscuits (optional)
- wood glue
- ¼ lb 4d finishing nails
- ½ lb 6d finishing nails
- two cabinet hinges
- magnetic latch
- wood filler
- paint or stain
- clear finish, if stain is desired

Tools

- circular saw or table saw
- sawhorses and three or four two-by-fours if circular saw is used
- claw hammer
- nail set
- screwdriver, for hinge screws
- drill, drill bit of suitable size to drill pilot holes for hinge screws, and 1¼″ drill bit for finger hole in door (you may also use a knob)
- chisel, for recessing hinges
- measuring tape
- square
- biscuit joiner (optional)
- eight 24″ bar clamps
- 100-grit sandpaper (120- or 150-grit sandpaper for hardwood plywood to be finished with stain and a clear finish)
- finishing sander
- brush

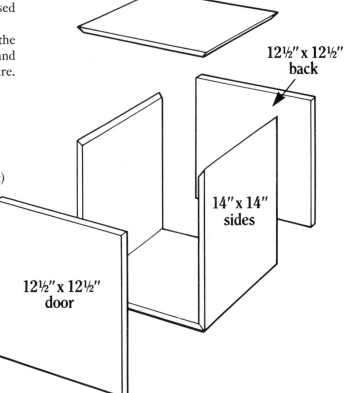

3–16 Cube. (*Courtesy of Georgia-Pacific Corporation*)

12½″ x 12½″ back

14″ x 14″ sides

12½″ x 12½″ door

■ Nesting Computer Center

There are two other computer centers in this chapter, but this one uses only a single sheet of plywood and a few bits and pieces of one-by-four (plus some hardware and such). It will also store in very little space; the completed unit is barely over 26″ wide, so that any 30″ space will do. It also rolls to any place it may be useful. Except for the table saw or circular saw plunge cuts, there's nothing here that can't be done by the careful beginner; those plunge cuts may also be made with the jigsaw, using the circular saw to finish up the cuts. Remember always to cut with the good side down when using a jigsaw or circular saw—and the circular saw works cleaner if you get one of the accessory plates that reduces the gap around the saw blade.

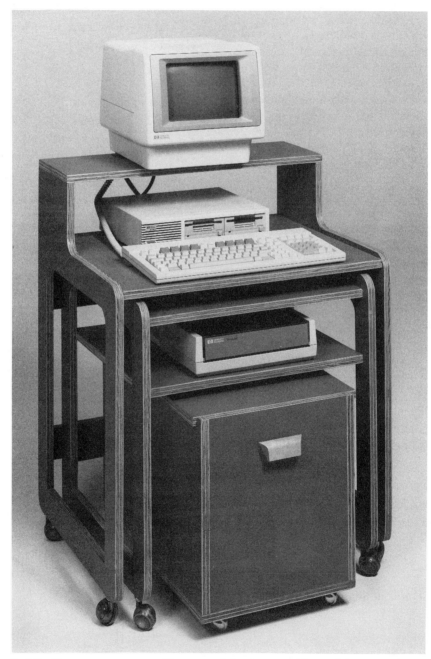

3–17   Computer cart center. (*Courtesy of the American Plywood Association*)

Tools

- circular saw or table saw
- jigsaw
- handsaw, for finishing cuts in corners
- drill and needed bits (³/₁₆″, ³/₈″, etc.)
- screwdriver, to fit heads of screws used
- measuring tape
- try or combination square
- marking tool (scribe, awl, pencil)
- four ³/₈″ dowel points
- four 24″ bar clamps
- finishing sander
- 100- , 120- or 150-grit sandpaper
- paintbrush

Mark the panels as shown in the drawing, allowing the usual ⅛″ kerf. You may make the cuts for the table and trundle table legs as plunged straight cuts (set the rip fence and feed gently and *carefully,* using a jigsaw or band saw to cut the curves afterwards; you may also make the plunge cuts using a circular saw). It is far safer to set up a guide (clamp a straightedge at a distance that allows the saw to cut on the marked line) for a jigsaw, and make the straight cuts that way. Finish up the curves freehand.

Sand rough edges, and use wood putty for edge-filling or leave the edges alone (this works best with plywoods that do not show gaps in the underlying plies).

Assemble the table and trundle table using wood screws and glue, except at the lower braces, which are placed with dowels. Drill the holes using dowel points

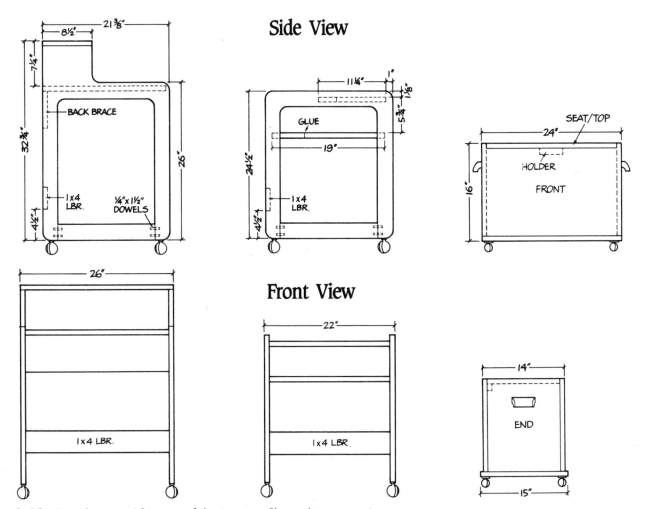

3-18 View drawings. (*Courtesy of the American Plywood Association*)

Materials

- ¾″ x 4′ x 8′ plywood, MDO, A-C or an N face
- one-by-four x 20½″ lumber
- one-by-four x 24½″ lumber
- two file drawer handles
- eight 2″ stem casters
- four 1½″ flat base casters
- forty-two No. 10 2″ wood screws
- sixteen ⅜″ x 1½″ glue dowels
- wood glue
- paint

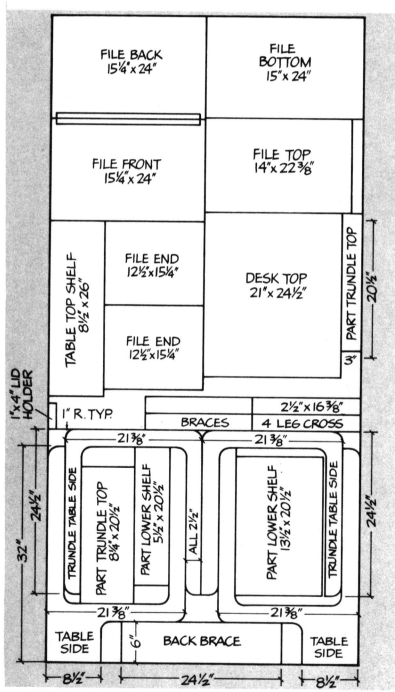

3–19 Panel layout. (*Courtesy of the American Plywood Association*)

to mark the drill settings after drilling holes in the straight bars. Check the dowel fit; take apart, and reassemble with glue and clamps. Check the square of all angles as you progress.

While the glue is drying on the above parts, assemble the file drawer. This is a simple, if sizable, box, done with butt joints that have the front and back sitting inside the sides. The bottom is spaced out an equal ½″ distance on each side. Assemble with screws and glue, keeping a careful check on square.

Sand and paint or finish as desired, then add the casters and the handle. The resulting computer work center will hold just about all you need. You can reduce the size of the top shelf on the trundle to a single narrow board, placed at the rear, if you plan to use that shelf for an extensively used printer. You can add the wider board to the bottom, and use that shelf for paper.

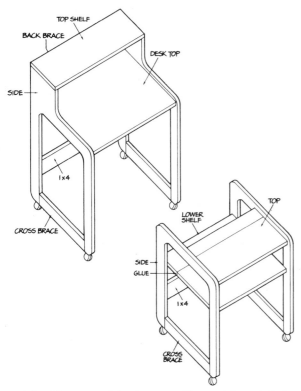

3–20 (*Courtesy of the American Plywood Association*)

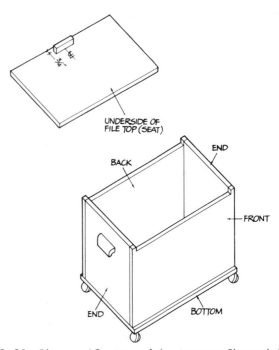

3–21 File cart. (*Courtesy of the American Plywood Association*)

4
Hobby Storage and Work Space

■ Rolling Workbench

For small areas, there's never really enough worktop space; this project not only provides a reasonable amount of extra flat space, that space is movable and may be rolled right to the job. While the 2' by 3' top isn't the largest work surface, its relatively small overall size makes this storage and work unit nearly ideal for apartments and small workshops.

Getting the fastest start here means marking the panels as the drawings show, allowing 1/8" for each kerf. To ease the work, cut the full panels down to workable size; cut the 3/4" panel long ways, 22 1/2" wide on one part. Cut the 1/2" panel short ways, 44 1/2" on one side (or make sure one side is at least 51 1/2"). This makes the panels easier to work with. Even the half panel can be cut so one side is 15 1/2" wide (the drawer backs come from this strip), easing overall handling.

4–1 Rolling workbench. (*Courtesy of the American Plywood Association*)

Next, cut all of the pieces to size, being very careful to get cuts to the final size.

Materials

- ¾" x 4' x 8' and 4' x 4' A-B plywood
- ½" x 4' x 8' A-B plywood
- two fixed and two swivel 2½" locking casters
- 16' x ¼" x ¾" screen moulding
- one pair of 2½" x ¾" offset hinges
- magnetic cabinet catch and cabinet door handle
- eighteen ¼" No. 6 screws, for drawer glides
- forty-eight 1½" No. 6 screws
- ½ lb each, 4d and 6d finishing nails
- paint, or stain and clear finish, as desired
- wood putty and wood glue

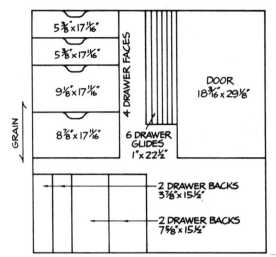

4-3 Panel layout, ¾" plywood. (*Courtesy of the American Plywood Association*)

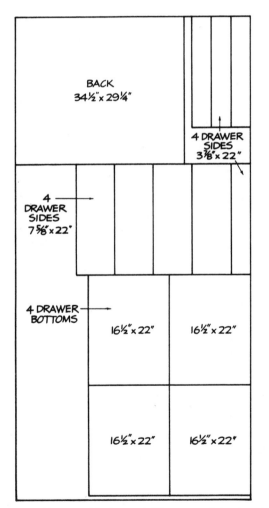

4-2 Panel layout, ½" plywood. (*Courtesy of the American Plywood Association*)

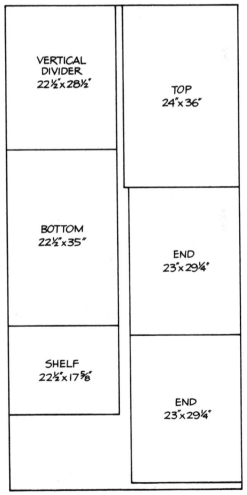

4-4 Panel layout, ¾" plywood. (*Courtesy of the American Plywood Association*)

Tools

- table saw or circular saw
- jigsaw or scroll saw
- router and edge guide, ¾" straight bit, ¼" rabbeting bit, ½" straight bit
- nail set
- cordless drill with ³⁄₃₂" bit for pilot holes and holes for handles, and driver for wood screws
- screwdriver, for hinge screws
- claw hammer
- measuring tape
- square

Mark and make a ¾" by ¼" dado cut on the inside of one side, and run a ¾"-deep by ¼"-wide rabbet on the bottom of both sides. The middle divider gets a dado matching the one on the inside of the right side in distance down from the top of both pieces. Install drawer glides in the positions shown using glue and three 1¼" nails from the glide positions into the sides, for each glide. These go on the left side of the vertical divider and on the inside of the left end.

Set the bottom inside its rabbets on the bottoms of the sides with glue, and drive 1½" or 1⅝" screws, four per end. Make sure the unit is square, and add the top with a ¼" overhang at each end using 6d nails and glue, nails spaced 3" apart. Again, check for square. Allow the glue to set up for a couple of hours, if possible.

Insert the middle divider into the marked places, and fasten with glue and screws.

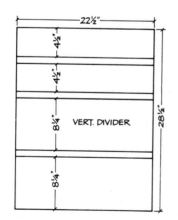

4–6 Front view. (*Courtesy of the American Plywood Association*)

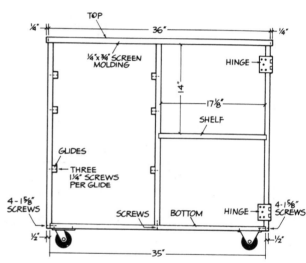

4–5 Side view. (*Courtesy of the American Plywood Association*)

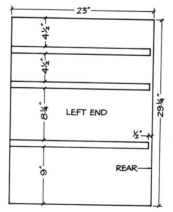

4–7 Drawer glide positions. (*Courtesy of the American Plywood Association*)

Assemble the drawers after cutting the handling arches and the ¼″ by ½″ dadoes. Use 4d nails and glue for assembly; keep a check on square, even though the assemblies are small.

Install hinges on the door and the door on the cabinet. Install the door handle and magnetic catch. Turn the unit upside down, and install the casters with ¾″ screws; you may wish to screw and glue a ¾″ by 4″ by 4″ block inset ½″ in from each corner to allow the use of 1¼″ wood screws with the casters. Otherwise, use the ¾″ screws, and inset ½″ for each side and end.

Remove the door hardware and the door. Sand the entire project with 100-grit sandpaper, and paint or stain and coat to suit. Use only a light coat or two of low-gloss finish on the top. Do not put a laminate on the top. Left plain, the top can be recovered as needed after it gets bettered by various kinds of work. To recover, you can use either ½″ or ¼″ plywood, placed with contact cement.

Reinstall the door, and go to work.

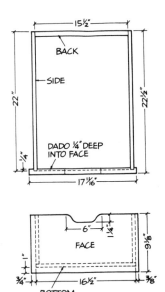

4–8 Drawing, 9⅛″ drawer. (*Courtesy of the American Plywood Association*)

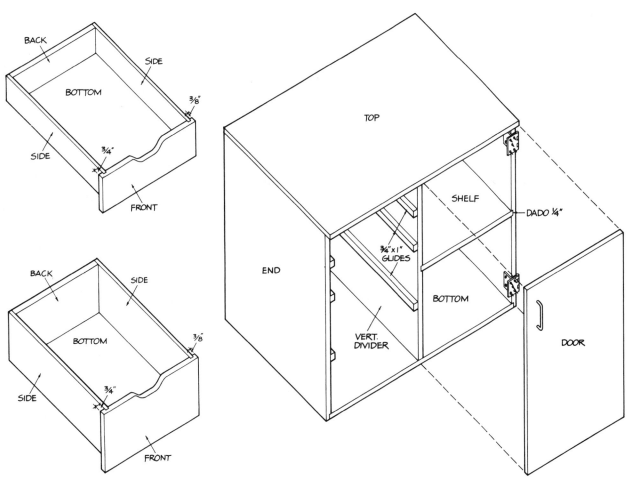

4–9 Rolling workbench. (*Courtesy of the American Plywood Association*)

◼ Equipment Box

This is a general-use box of pine. Boards are glued up and cut to width, and the dovetails, if used, are cut with a jig. All of the wide material is glued up from one one-by-eight and two one-by-six pieces and cut to exact size. Two easier-to-make variations of this equipment box are described following the instructions for the dovetail version. Follow the same basic instructions for each variant.

Tools

- router
- dovetail jig, with bits
- two C clamps
- mallet
- four 24″ bar clamps
- four 36″ bar clamps
- cabinet screwdriver
- measuring tape
- square
- table saw
- 1″ masking tape

- ⅛″ shims
- belt sander, 100-grit belt
- finishing sander, 100- and 150-grit sandpaper
- stain or paint
- clear finish (if stain is used)

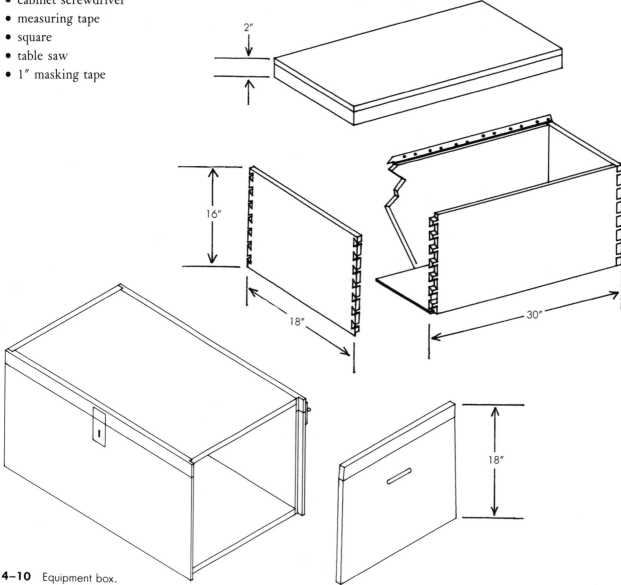

4–10 Equipment box.

Materials

- two 18″ x 18″ x 1″ pine
- three 18″ x 30″ x 1″ pine
- 18″ x 30″ x 3/8″ plywood
- 16½″ x 28½″ x ¼″ plywood
- three 2″ x 28½″ x 1″ pine
- three 2″ x 15″ x 1″ pine
- 30″ x 1½″ piano hinge
- wood glue

Start by gluing wood up as indicated, to get the above general sizes. Allow glue to dry overnight. Sand flat, after scraping off excess glue.

Lay out parts and determine top, bottom, etc. Cut 3/8″ x 3/8″ rabbet in tops of sides, back, and front. Cut same size rabbet in top, all four sides. Cut a 3/8″ x 3/8″ deep rabbet along each bottom edge (so it will face the inside). Final-cut the 3/8″ plywood to fit the bottom. Check for fit and make any needed adjustments before final-cutting the side joints.

Cut dovetails, if they're being used, and dry-assemble sides, front, and back. If fit is fine, assemble with glue and square up (check each corner with a square, or measure diagonals to see that they match). Assemble the box whole, top and all.

Cut the top loose, 2″ down from top of the box, on the table saw. Start by taping the line to be cut, with masking tape. Set the rip fence, and assemble some 1/8″ shims. Start the cut to remove the top along one long side. Shim and move to the next long side. Shim close to the next cut, and cut one end loose. Shim, turn, and cut the final end loose. Cutting the top in this manner assures a near-perfect fit.

Remove masking tape, and install tray supports with their tops 3″ below the lip of the box bottom. Assemble the tray of ¼″ plywood (set into 3/8″ x ¼″ rabbets in the bottoms of the ends and sides of the tray) so its final dimension is ¼″ less in each direction than is the inside of the constructed box.

Sand box, and stain or paint as desired. Install piano hinge and hasp.

To change this to an easier-to-make design, with fewer tool needs, the dovetails must be eliminated. That leaves two ways to go:

Finger-Jointed Equipment Box

Instead of the dovetail joint jig, use a finger joint jig to make ½″ finger joints for the box. Some dovetail jigs also work as finger joint jigs—check the instruction manual, as you may also need to rearrange the use of the templates. Otherwise, tool needs and general materials needs are similar, or the same, as outlined above. If you use finger joints, adjust the top height so that the cut line on the table saw intersects one of the joints at a point that will leave at least three-quarters of a joint on the bottom part of the box.

Rabbeted Equipment Box

The easiest way of making the basic box is to use rabbeted joints. These are 3/8″ x 3/8″ rabbets cut into opposing sides and ends to produce a fit that leaves 3/8″ of end grain. You may, if you wish, go ahead and work that rabbet depth down as much as 5/8″, exposing 1/8″ of end grain, but the joint will not be quite as strong.

This version needs no fancy jigs; you already have a 3/8″ rabbetting bit on hand for earlier uses.

As with any variant, make sure all parts fit before starting to glue up, and make sure the rabbets are all cut in properly related ways so that the rabbets result in correctly sized joints.

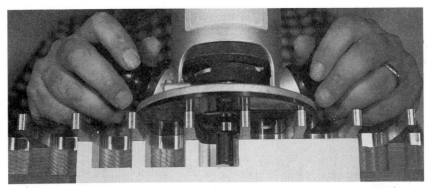

4–11 Using a dovetail jig is the fastest and easiest way to dovetail the equipment box. (*Courtesy of the Keller Company*)

■ Sewing Center I

Sewing is a popular hobby, but it is possibly made slightly less popular than it might be because it is sometimes difficult to organize all the bits and pieces around a sensible spot. Too many people feel they need an entire room to sew in; whereas a unit such as this provides all the space needed for any sewing job, and then it folds up to under 60″ tall, taking floor space of only 38½″ by 15″. It also takes only a minute or so to unfold and set up.

start by cutting ¾″-wide by ⅜″-deep dadoes to hold the long shelf and the machine cabinet divider. Cut dadoes of the same size in the right side panel to hold the short shelf and two dividers, and then dado both sides of the middle panel to match the dadoes in the sides.

Assemble top, bottom, sides, and middle panel using glue and 4d finishing nails—use 6d nails for securing the middle panel to the top and bottom assembly. Mark a midline for nailing, and nail at 4″ intervals, starting 1″ in from edges.

4–12 Sewing center. (*Courtesy of Georgia-Pacific Corporation*)

Lay out the patterns on the plywood sheets, leaving ⅛″ for the kerf, and make your cuts. Using a table saw, leave the good side up; leave the good side down for cutting with a circular saw. Cut the pieces for the box base, too. This is a simple project if you take your time; so make sure all of the parts are correctly laid out before cutting.

With the rails for the base box cut, make a ⅜″ by ¾″ wide rabbet in the ends of the outside rails. Fit the base together, and use 4d finishing nails and glue to secure parts. On the top, bottom, and sides assembly,

Make sure the shelves and dividers fit; then coat the ends with glue, and slip them into the dadoes. Drive 4d nails to secure and eliminate the need for clamping.

Route a ¼″ by ¼″ dado ¼″ up from the bottom of the sides, back, and front of the drawer parts. Assemble the drawer parts with glue (do not solidly glue the bottom in place: use about a 1″ to 2″ wide strip at each end of the bottom panel, centered on the front and back) and 2d finishing nails.

Drill a 1½″-diameter hole in the middle of each panel, 4″ in from the front edge of each panel. Use

84

the piano hinges to attach the fold-out panels to each other and to the divider shelf of the cabinet.

The legs shown are made from 2″ drapery dowel with the ends specially turned to fit ⅝″-deep by 1½″-diameter holes. You may be able to find a suitable height leg that needs no turning; if so, go ahead and get those, and, as needed, change the diameter of the hole to fit.

Use a nail set to hide all nails, covering the holes with wood filler. You may use wood veneer tape to cover the plywood edges, or go the more economical way and use wood putty. Sand with 100- or 150-grit sandpaper.

Tools

- table saw or circular saw
- sawhorse and three or four two-by-fours for supporting cuts, if circular saw is used
- router and edge guide with ¾″ straight bit, ¼″ rabbeting bit, ½″ straight bit
- nail set
- drill, ³⁄₃₂″ bit for holes for knobs, 1½″ drill bit
- screwdriver, for hinge screws
- claw hammer
- measuring tape
- square
- paintbrush
- 100- and 150-grit sandpaper
- finishing sander
- tack cloth

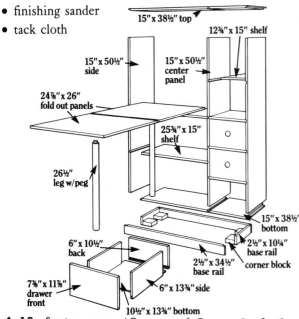

4–13 Sewing center. (*Courtesy of Georgia-Pacific Corporation*)

Remove the knobs and hinges before painting. Paint and reinstall the hardware, and you're ready to go.

Optionally, you may elect to cover the fold-out tops with laminate or to make the entire unit of a hardwood plywood; if you do the latter, use a clear finish such as tung oil, over whatever stain you select. The unit may also be set up on low—no more than 1″-diameter—plate-style casters for even greater movability.

Materials

- three ¾″ x 15″ x 50½″ plywood, A-C or better, ends and center divider
- two ¾″ x 15″ x 38½″ plywood, A-C or better, top and bottom
- ¾″ x 12¾″ x 15″ plywood, A-C or better, short shelf
- ¾″ x 15″ x 25¾″ plywood, A-C or better, long shelf
- two ¾″ x 12¾″ x 15″ plywood, A-C or better, drawer dividers
- three ¾″ x 7⅜″ x 11⅞″ plywood, A-C or better, drawer fronts
- six ½″ x 6″ x 13¾″ plywood, B-C, drawer sides
- three ½″ x 6″ x 10½″ plywood, B-C, drawer backs
- three ¼″ x 10½″ x 13¾″ plywood, B-C, drawer bottoms
- two ¾″ x 24⅞″ x 26″, plywood, A-C or better, fold out panels
- two 2″ x 26½″ legs, with dowels 1½″ x ⅝″ tall set into the top
- two ¾″ x 2½″ x 34½″ pine base rail
- two ¾″ x 2½″ x 10¼″ pine base rail ends
- four 1½″ x 3½″ x 3½″ pine corner blocks
- machine cabinet divider, ¾″ x 15″ x 25¾″ plywood, A-C or better
- three pairs of drawer slides
- two 1″ piano hinges, 24″ long
- three 1½″ wood knobs for drawers
- ½ lb 6d finishing nails
- ¼ lb 4d finishing nails
- ¼ lb 2d finishing nails
- wood glue
- wood filler
- paint

■ Sewing Center II

This sewing center is quicker to build, and a bit smaller as far as operating space goes, than the previous one but offers sufficient space for most sewing hobbies— and for some other hobbies, such as model building, that may require small parts and tool storage. Overall, it is 12″ deep, 48⅜″ tall, and 36″ wide, taking up even less wall or floor space than the preceding hobby center.

4–14 Sewing cabinet. (*Courtesy of Georgia-Pacific Corporation*)

Tools

- table saw or circular saw
- jigsaw or scroll saw
- router and edge guide, ⅜″ straight bit, ¾″ straight bit
- nail set
- cordless drill, ³⁄₃₂″ bit for holes for handles
- screwdriver, for hinge screws
- claw hammer
- measuring tape
- square
- finishing sander
- 100-grit sandpaper (120- or 150-grit sandpaper if hardwood is used)

Materials

- ¾″ x 4′ x 8′ plywood, MDO or A-C or hardwood
- ⅜″ x 4′ x 8′ plywood, MDO or A-C or hardwood
- three pairs of wraparound cabinet hinges
- one pair of invisible hinges (with stop built in)
- one pair of combination hinge-supports
- one pair of 1½″ butt hinges
- two magnetic door catches
- dowels for thread spools, knobs for doors, and similar accessories (or the appropriate accessories for your particular hobby)
- 1 lb 4d finishing nails
- wood glue and wood filler
- paint (or clear finish and veneer edging tape)

Begin by marking the panels as the drawings show, leaving the usual $\frac{1}{8}''$ kerf. Because there are so many parts in some areas, the parts cutting is extensive, and there isn't room for small parts dimensions on the drawings, so here is a list:

Tray

- SS bottom $9\frac{1}{8}''$ x $7\frac{1}{8}''$
- TT, UU front and back $9\frac{1}{8}''$ x $1''$
- WW, XX lid side $7\frac{1}{4}''$ x $1''$
- CCC, DDD, EEE, FFF, GGG dividers $3''$ x $1''$

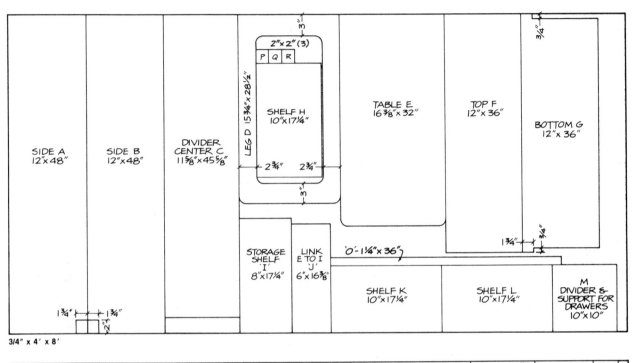

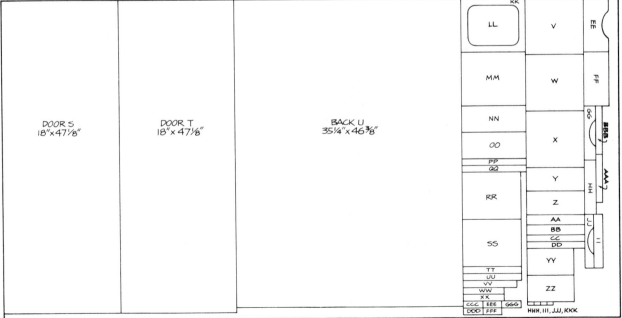

4-15 Panel layout. (*Courtesy of the American Plywood Association*)

Sewing Box

- KK top 10″ x 8″
- LL cutout for pincushion (optional) 8″ x 6″ in KK
- MM bottom 10″ x 8″
- NN, OO front and back 10″ x 4″
- PP, QQ lid front, lid back 10″ x 1″
- RR inside of lid 9⅛″ x 1⅞″
- YY, ZZ sides 7¼″ x 4″
- HHH, III, JJJ, KKK tray supports ½″ x 1″

Drawer Parts

- V, W, X drawer bottoms 9″ x 8⅛″
- Y, Z lower drawer sides 9″ x 3½″
- AA, BB middle drawer sides 9″ x 1½″
- CC, DD top drawer sides 9″ x 1″
- EE, FF lower drawer front and back 3⅞″ x 8⅛″
- GG, HH middle drawer front and back 1⅞″ x 8⅛″
- II, JJ top drawer front and back 1⅜″ x 8⅛″

The case assembly uses mostly butt joints, with the sides placed inside the bottom and top. Rabbet the ends of the top to accept the sides; ¼″ by ⅜″ rabbets. Dado for shelves as shown on the plan drawings. Assemble with 4d finishing nails and glue, keeping a tight check on square.

On the middle piece (C), and on one side of M, make ⅜″ dadoes to accept the edge guides of the drawers, as shown.

Set the middle divider in place, 17¼″ from the right side of the top and bottom (it will also be 17¼″ from the left side). Top and bottom are coated with wood glue. Mark a midline on the divider, top and bottom, and drive nails, starting 1″ in from the edges, about every 4″ using the 4d finishing nails.

Set the right side shelves at heights suitable to you, or as shown in the plan drawing. These fit into dadoes ¼″ deep, cut earlier. Coat the shelf ends with glue, and secure with 4d finishing nails.

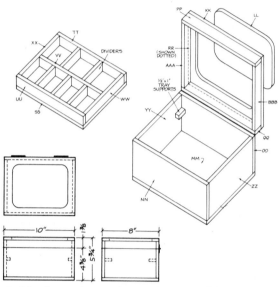

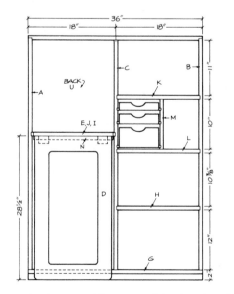

4-16 Sewing box and tray. (*Courtesy of the American Plywood Association*)

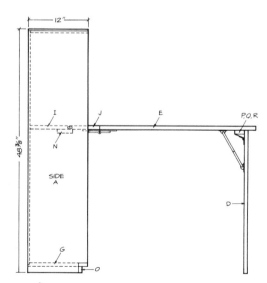

4-17 Front and side views. (*Courtesy of the American Plywood Association*)

Position O parts for toe guards.

Place J shelf link and I shelf, and then place the table. Attach leg to table using assembled, as per drawing, P, Q, R blocks.

Attach needed hardware as assembly progresses. When assembly is complete, set all nails and fill with wood putty. Fill all edges with wood putty, or cover with veneer tape. Allow the assembly to dry at least two hours, and remove all of the hardware. Then sand with 100-grit sandpaper.

Paint, or stain and coat with clear polyurethane or tung oil. Reinstall the hardware when the finish is dry.

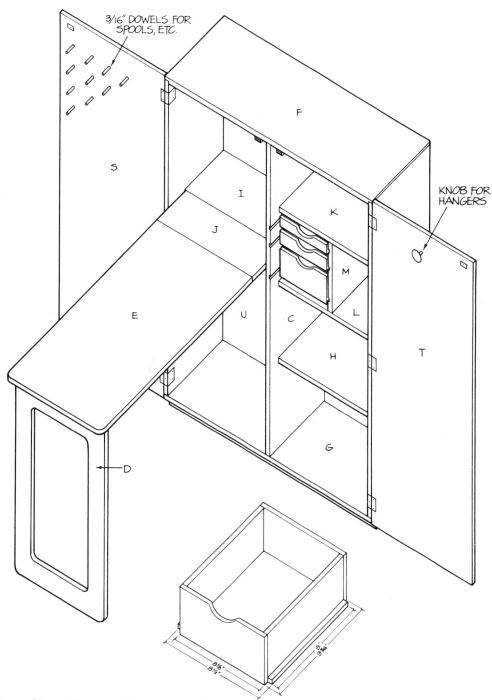

4-18 Sewing cabinet. (*Courtesy of the American Plywood Association*)

■ Changing-Top Tool Bench

This project of MDO (Medium Density Overlay) plywood (both sides) provides storage and use facilities for a series of three bench top power tools that will fit inside a space 17½" wide by 23½" long and 17" high. The tool "carrier" rotates to any of three positions and locks in place; so a single bench can store three tools, each bolted to its workbench and ready to be rotated into working position. The assembly can be easily rolled just about anywhere, and it is of only moderate difficulty to build.

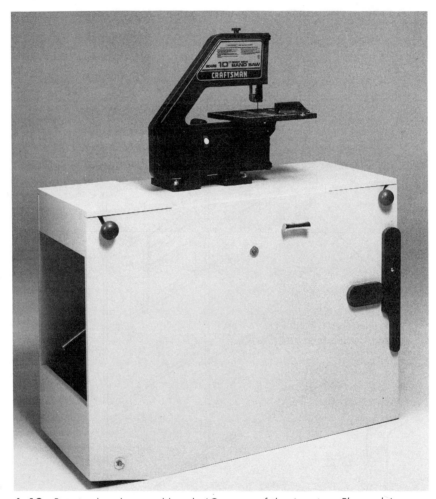

4-19 Rotating benchtop tool bench. (*Courtesy of the American Plywood Association*)

Materials

- ¾" x 4' x 8' MDO plywood
- ¾" x 2' x 8' MDO plywood
- three ½" x 24" unthreaded steel rods
- two ½" x 24" threaded steel rods
- three ½" (inside diameter), 16½"-long PVC pipe (rod guides)
- two ½" lock nuts to fit ½" threaded rods
- thirteen ½" washers
- seven 1/16" hitch pin clips
- handle with ½" hole, or 3/16" x 2" ring
- two threaded knobs, or ½" shaft hole
- two 6" tires with ½" shaft hole
- ten 1¼" No. 8 wood screws
- two 2" x ¼" machine bolts
- nuts, washers, lock washers, and 2" wood screws
- enamel or other finish

Start by carefully laying out the parts, as described, making sure to leave ⅛" for kerfs. Parts key as follows:

- A sides
- B tool mounting triangle faces
- C lower end—handle end of project
- D lower end—wheel end of project
- E work table ends
- F equilateral triangles
- G work table braces
- H handle stops
- I handles—use jigsaw to make cut to fit hands
- J bottom bracket—wheel end of project

- K bottom bracket—handle end of project
- L bottom bracket—middle
- M work tables
- R ½" rod; pivot point for triangle, includes two ½" washers, one ⅛" drilled hole ¼" from each end and 2 snap pins
- S ½" rod; stop rod to hold triangle in position, includes one ½" washer, 1 snap pin in ⅛" hole drilled ¼" from one end with a handle fastened to the other end
- T ½" threaded rods, four ½" washers, two ½" nuts and 2 threaded knobs
- U tire assembly

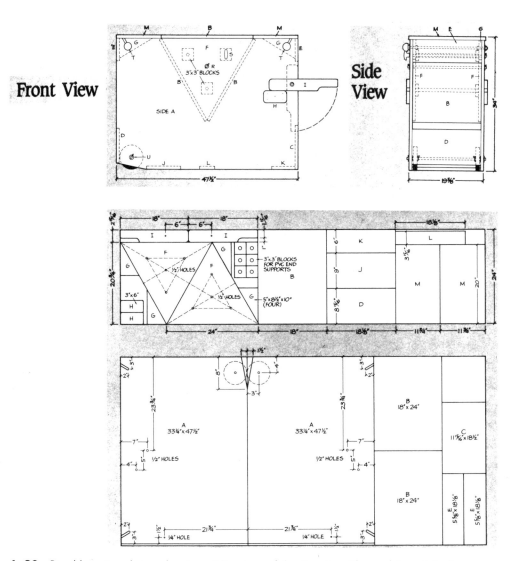

4–20 Panel layout and view drawings. (*Courtesy of the American Plywood Association*)

Tools

- circular saw or table saw
- jigsaw
- handsaw, for finishing cuts in corners
- drill and needed bits ($\frac{1}{2}''$, $\frac{1}{4}''$, screwdriver, etc.)
- screwdriver, to fit heads of screws used
- measuring tape
- try or combination square
- marking tool (scribe, awl, pencil)
- adjustable wrench
- finishing sander
- 100- , 120- or 150-grit sandpaper
- paintbrush

Assemble as indicated in the drawings; when assembling the triangular base, drill the middle hole in the two triangles (R), then drill two holes for the handles and axle. Assemble the triangle, but leave one face removable. To guide the supporting rod into place after rotating to a new tool, install $\frac{1}{2}''$ PVC pipe in the base, as shown. Drill three guide holes for the rod.

When assembly is done, remove the hardware; sand with 100- to 150-grit sandpaper, and paint. When all is dry, reinstall the hardware, and bolt your tools in place. The result is not only portable storage, but a usable tool bench space as well.

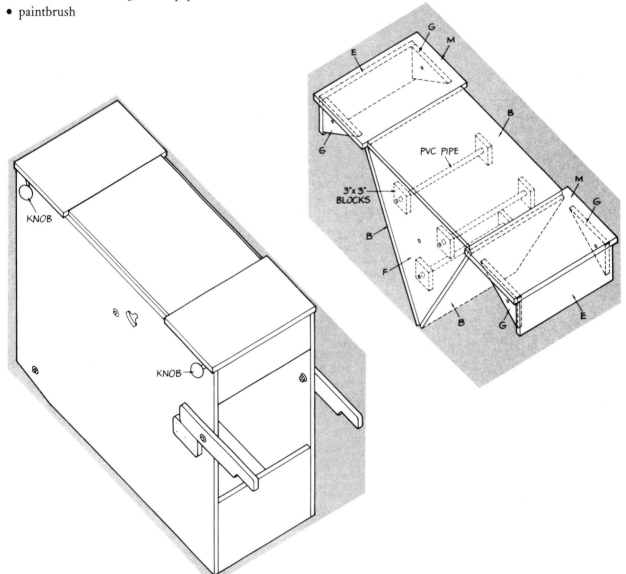

4–21 (*Courtesy of the American Plywood Association*)

■ Artist's Taboret

This design is intended for all kinds of artists; I think anyone who works on crafts of most any kind, from sewing to woodworking, will find the design handy for holding supplies and small tools. It is another project that requires some modest skill to build, though backing off and substituting thought for exceptional skill will help. This art supply organizer will brighten your work area.

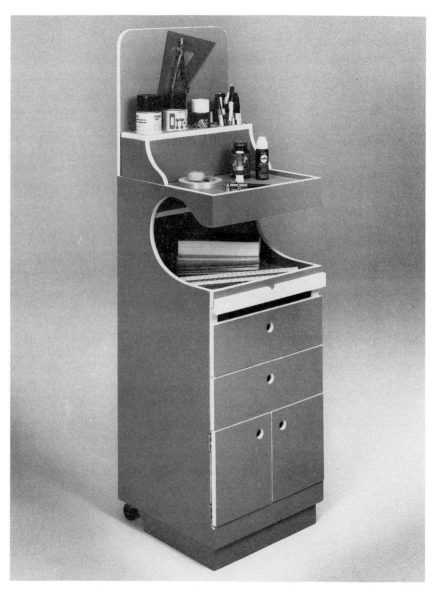

4-22 Artist's taboret. (*Courtesy of the American Plywood Association*)

Materials

- ½" x 4' x 8' MDO plywood (if you want a clear finish, use A-B, or an N face)
- two 2½" flat plate casters
- four 1½" butt hinges
- two magnetic catches
- ½ lb No. 6 finish nails
- six to eight ¾" brad nails
- wood filler
- wood glue
- paint or clear finish, as desired

Tools

- circular saw or table saw
- jigsaw
- handsaw, for finishing cuts in corners
- drill and needed bits ($\frac{1}{4}$″, $\frac{3}{16}$″, etc.)
- screwdriver, to fit heads of screws used
- 16-oz claw hammer
- nail set
- measuring tape
- try or combination square
- marking tool (scribe, awl, pencil)
- finishing sander
- 100- , 120- or 150-grit sandpaper
- paintbrush

Lay out the panel as shown in the drawing, making sure to leave the usual $\frac{1}{8}$″ allowance for the kerf.

Start the assembly with the carcass, back down on the floor, after sanding the edges and corners clean. Install the sides 2$\frac{1}{4}$ up from the bottom using glue and the finish nails, and setting the nails as you go. Keep a running check, on sides' squareness to the back, keeping it as close as possible. Nail the bottom inside the sides; position the appropriate shelves and other parts and nail them in place. Once this nailing is done, using a thread of glue along joints, make sure the carcass is square, and let it sit for at least two hours.

Assemble the drawers while you're waiting for the above glue to set solid (six to eight hours is an even

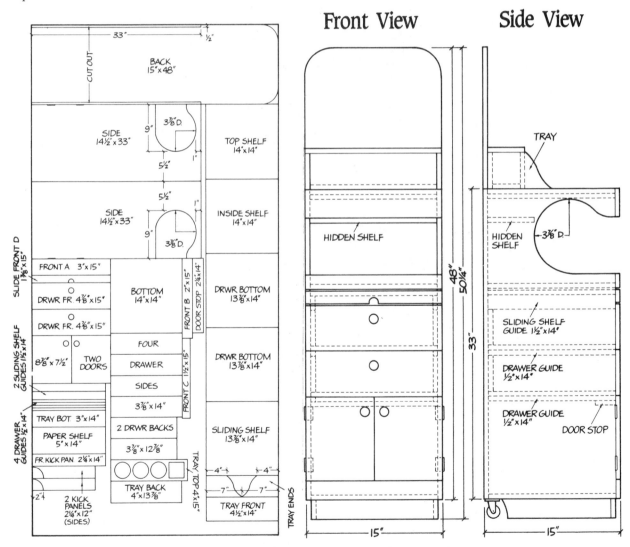

4-23 Panel layout and view drawings. (*Courtesy of the American Plywood Association*)

better setting time). Drawers are simple butt-joint construction, with the bottoms nailed and glued under the assembled sides. That assembly is nailed and glued to the fronts.

If you have time left, make the sliding shelf and assemble the tray. If you're working with something other than drawing or painting supplies, you may decide to design your own tray, or even eliminate it.

Now, install shelf and drawer guides and the hidden shelf; use ¾" brad nails and glue for the shelf sides, and No. 6 nails and glue for the back.

Sand carefully and paint, or apply other finish. Add the hardware, and install the doors. Add the two casters, and you're ready to go.

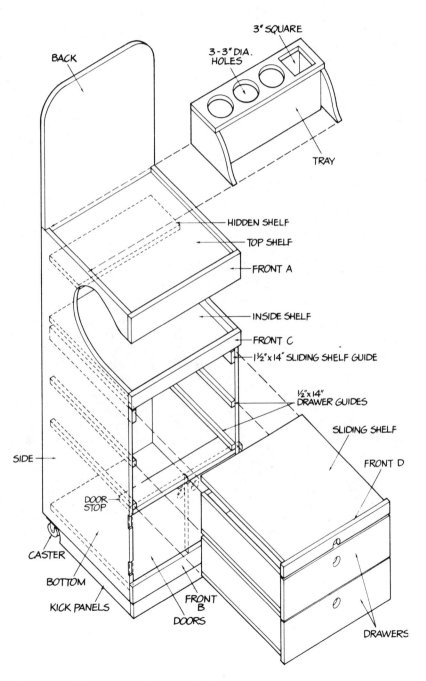

4-24 Exploded view. (*Courtesy of the American Plywood Association*)

■ Car-Care Cart

Even with today's high-tech computer-controlled automobiles, much maintenance can still be performed with a modest investment in wrenches, screwdrivers and similar items. This leaves the need for a low-cost way to store such tools where they'll be handy for use when needed. The cart provides the answer, using just 1½″ sheets of ½″ plywood. And it gets out of the way and stores in a tiny space, when work is done and it is closed up (storage needs are down to about 26″ by 14″, from a working size of 24″ by 48″).

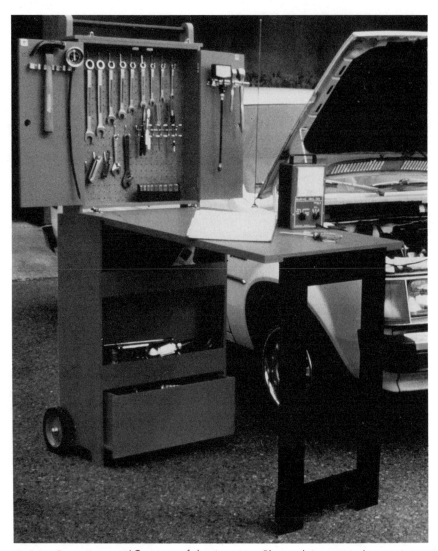

4-25 Car care cart. (*Courtesy of the American Plywood Association*)

Tools

- circular saw or table saw
- jigsaw
- handsaw, for finishing cuts in corners
- drill and needed bits (1″, ¼″, ³⁄₁₆″, etc.)
- screwdriver, to fit heads of screws used
- 16-oz claw hammer

- nail set
- measuring tape
- try or combination square
- marking tool (scribe, awl, pencil)
- finishing sander
- 100- , 120- , or 150-grit sandpaper

Do the layout of the pieces as shown in the drawings, leaving the standard 1/8″ kerf. Drill holes as required, or wait until later for drilling. Carefully cut all straight-sided pieces, and make straight cuts. Make the curved cuts with the jigsaw. Sand edges.

Begin the assembly with the box back, with sides added flush to the top using No. 6 finishing nails and glue. Keep the sides square to the back; then add shelves, back of shelves, and shelf fronts, making sure all is square. Set the assembly aside for the glue to set (at least 45 minutes with most glues; longer, even overnight, is better). Assemble the bottom drawer, sides outside the back, and side and back assembly centered on the 23″-wide front. Add the 23″-wide bottom, making sure the drawer is square. The overhang on the bottom will fit the drawer guides to provide a smooth-moving drawer.

Assemble the upper section tool box, with the perforated hardboard using glue and nails. Make sure the assembly is square, and check the door fit. Once this glue has set, install the doors to check fit once more.

Materials

- 1/2″ x 4′ x 8′ MDO plywood (if you want a clear finish, use A-B, or an N face)
- 1/2″ x 4′ x 4′ MDO, as above
- 24″ x 21⅞″ perforated hardboard (stock 24″ x 24″)
- 1″ x 23″ wood dowel
- two 6″ x 1″ (up to 8″ is fine) wheels, with axle, four nuts, and six washers; axle holes to accept the size axle to fit your wheels
- four 1″ x 1½″ butt hinges
- two magnetic catches
- two 1¹⁄₁₆″ x 18″ continuous hinges and screws, for toolbox doors
- 1/2 lb No. 6 finish nails
- wood filler
- wood glue
- paint or clear finish as desired

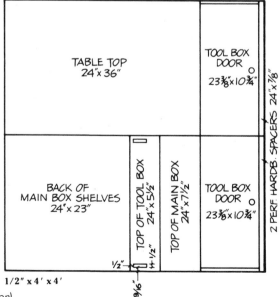

4-26 Panel layout. (*Courtesy of the American Plywood Association*)

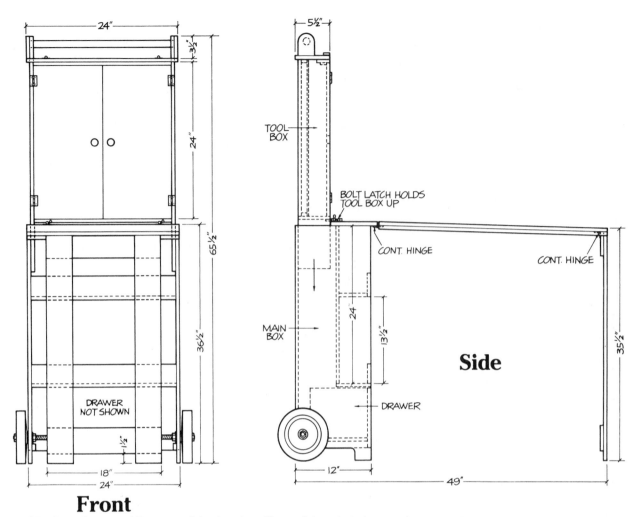

Front

4–27 View drawings. (*Courtesy of the American Plywood Association*)

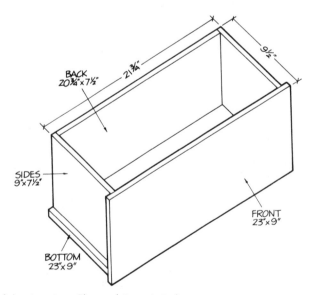

4–28 Drawer. (*Courtesy of the American Plywood Association*)

Now, go ahead and put the table assembly together, with the continuous hinge on the underside to be installed after finishing. You may install the hinge now, getting it sited, all screwholes drilled and ready, and so on, but the hinge needs to be removed for finishing, unless you intend it to be the same color as the box.

Finish assembling the unit with such parts as the toolbox dowel handle. Sand and paint according to your own color preferences.

Reassemble with all of the hardware, and check the fit and lift of the toolbox in the back area of the base. If all is well, that will fit perfectly (much depends on making both units square), lift out and drop back easily, while locking readily into place with the barrel bolts when it is lifted.

The car care cart is adaptable to other tool types, too, since it is a good size for small project tools such as drills, handsaws, etc.

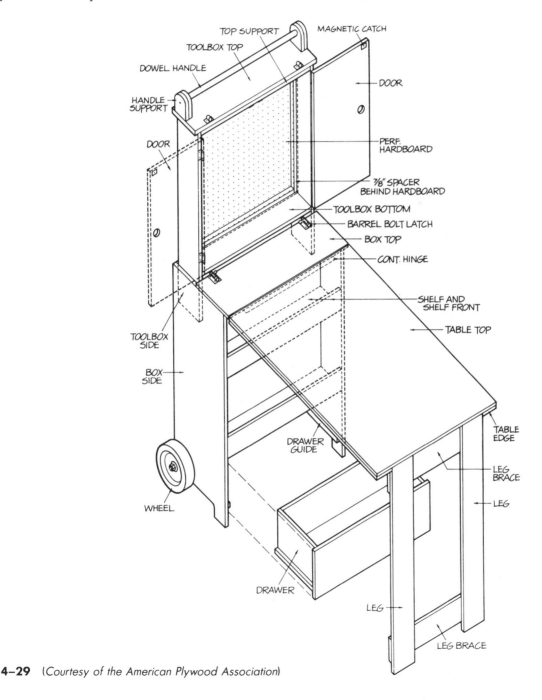

4-29 (*Courtesy of the American Plywood Association*)

■ Mobile Workbench

Workshop storage is as essential as workbench space. If storage and workbench space are combined, and made mobile, even the largest, most complete shop benefits. For smaller shops where everything must do double duty, the benefit is correspondingly greater. The project has four large drawers and two open shelves for storage. The design offers great stability as well as storage, work space, and mobility. The top is a generous 26″ by 54″ of solid one-by-four lumber, ample for most woodworking needs.

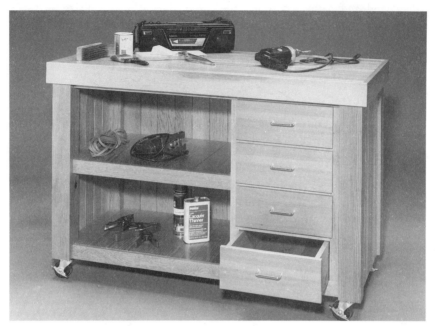

4–30 A mobile workbench with plenty of tool storage makes all sorts of jobs easier. (*Courtesy of the Western Wood Products Association*)

Materials

(*Unless otherwise specified, all wood is pine, spruce, fir or hem-fir*)
- 22′ one-by-one
- 40′ one-by-two
- 95′ one-by-four
- 15′ one-by-six
- 30′ one-by-eight
- 30′ two-by-two
- 10′ two-by-four
- 11′ four-by-four
- ½ lb 3d finish nails, 1¼″
- 1 lb 4d finish nails, 1½″
- 1 lb 6d finish nails, 2″
- 1 lb 10d finish nails, 3″
- four drawer pulls with 1¾″ or longer screws
- four locking swivel casters, stem type, at least 3″
- wood glue
- clear finish

Tools

- table saw, radial-arm saw or circular saw
- router and edge guide, ¼″ straight and ¼″ x ⅜″ rabbeting router bits
- mitre box or power mitre saw
- electric drill, drill bits to fit drawer pull screws, bit for caster stems
- screwdriver
- chisel
- tape measure
- framing square
- brush
- steel wool
- 100-grit sandpaper
- finishing sander

Frame Assembly

Begin by cutting wood to lengths shown (four-by-fours to 31½"—cut four; two-by-fours to 48½"—cut two; two-by-twos to 48½"—cut three). Assemble the two side frame sections using the two-by-twos at the base, and the two-by-fours at the top. Spreaders overlap the four-by-four posts by 1½". Fasten with glue and 10d nails, or 2½" screws.

Cut one-by-fours and one-by-twos to 17½", and assemble the frame as shown, with the extra 48½" two-by-two spreader centered between the two on the outside. Use 6d nails and glue.

At this point, after the glue has had a few minutes (at least 30) to set, invert the frame; mark and drill caster holes.

Cut two two-by-fours and two two-by-twos to 45½", and cut two two-by-fours to 14½" lengths. Insert the short two-by-fours (blocks) inside the top two two-by-fours, placing one, to the first edge each time, 13¼" from the inside left leg and 16" from the inside right leg. Use 10d nails (and glue) right through the two-by-four side rails.

Nail and glue the outside rails in place, both two-by-four and two-by-two, in the places shown. Use 6d nails and glue at the middle, and toenail with 10d nails to the posts.

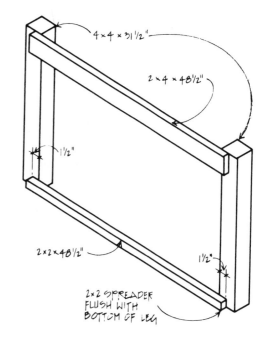

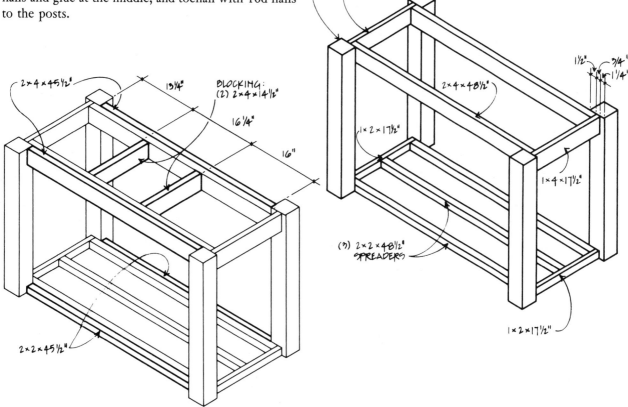

4–31 (*Courtesy of the Western Wood Products Association*)

Drawer Frame

To install the drawer frame, cut four one-by-twos to 26½", and one one-by-two to 17½". Also cut a one-by-one to 17½". Install right-side long one-by-twos to the four-by-four legs, front and back, flush with the inside edges of the legs. Use nails and glue. Toenail and glue vertical one-by-twos (again, long ones) between the top and bottom frames, flush with inside face of two-by-four blocking at the top. The one-by-twos are flush with the outside edges of the top and bottom frames; the inside measurement is 15¼". At the base of the divider, glue and nail one 17½" one-by-two between vertical one-by-twos toenailing it in place. At the top of the divider, glue and nail a 17½" one-by-one nailer between the one-by-two verticals. Use 4d nails and glue to attach.

Beginning at the frame front, nail six one-by-fours to fill the vertical space to the back side of the divider. The last one-by-four needs to be ripped to 3" wide to fit (check actual measurement before cutting).

Drawer Guides

To install the right-side drawer guides, cut four one-by-twos to 20½" long. Install one across the bottom and flush with the outside edges of the vertical one-by-twos using glue and 3d nails. You'll find it easiest to get even spacing on these guides if you cut two vertical spacing blocks 5⅛" long. Set the blocks on

the bottom one-by-two; position the next one-by-two, and glue and nail it in place. Repeat until all four are done.

For the left-side drawer guides, cut three one-by-twos to 17½" lengths. Glue and nail between the vertical one-by-twos using the same 5⅛" spacers. Next, cut eight 20½" one-by-one drawer runners. Glue and nail one flush to the bottom of each side rail using 3d nails.

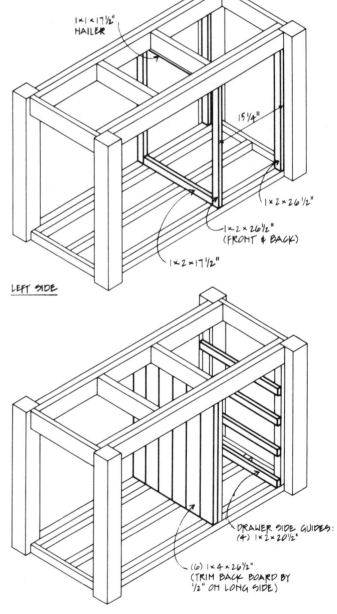

RIGHT SIDE

1×1×17½"
NAILER

15¼"

1×2×26½"

1×2×26½"
(FRONT & BACK)

1×2×17½"

LEFT SIDE

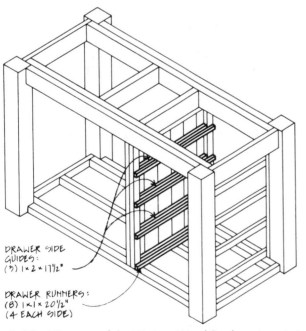

DRAWER SIDE
GUIDES:
(3) 1×2×17½"

DRAWER RUNNERS:
(8) 1×1×20½"
(4 EACH SIDE)

DRAWER SIDE GUIDES:
(4) 1×2×20½"

(6) 1×4×26½"
(TRIM BACK BOARD BY
½" ON LONG SIDE)

4–32 (Courtesy of the Western Wood Products Association)

To close up the storage space, cut 13 one-by-fours to 31½" lengths, and glue and nail them to the back of the workbench using 6d nails. Start the enclosing at both ends; work to the middle, so that any adjustment of width is in the middle board. Cut nine one-by-fours to 17½" length, and start at the left side of the drawer unit enclosure, gluing and nailing the boards in place. The last board is ripped to fit; if all works out, the rip will be 2¼" wide, but measure before cutting.

Cut two one-by-two drawer guides to 14½", and position the left-side guide with its bottom flush with the bottom of the two-by-four frame and blocking (check detail A). Glue and toenail in place. On the right side, cut two one-by-two blocks, each 3¾" long. Glue and nail the blocks to the end of the drawer guide (see detail B). Glue and nail the block to the frame, front and back, so that the bottom of the guide is flush with the bottom of the two-by-four side frame and the back of the block butts on the one-by-four end frame. The blocking puts the guide in line with the drawer runners.

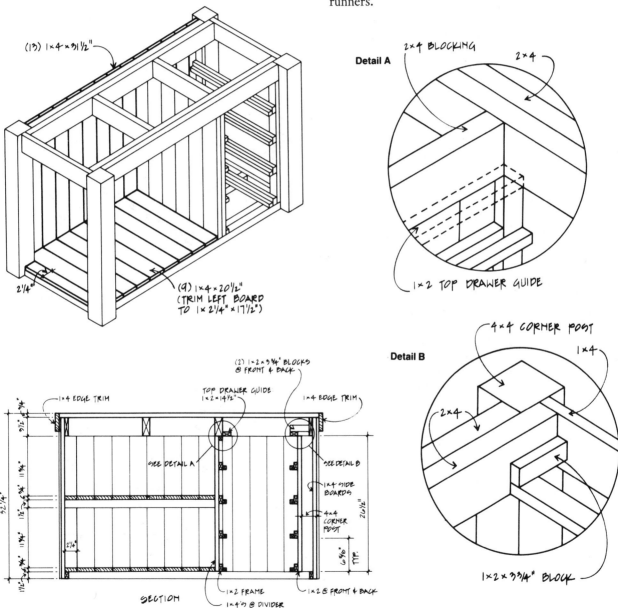

4–33 (Courtesy of the Western Wood Products Association)

Cut, glue and nail five one-by-fours to each end of the workbench, getting each one-by-four 31½" long and using 3d nails.

Cut two two-by-twos to 28" long, and glue and nail one to the back of the workbench, between the four-by-four leg and partition. It goes 11¾" above the bottom shelf. Use 6d nails. Installation is easier if you cut two spacing blocks, each 11¾" long and use those to set the ledger.

Cut two one-by-twos to 30¼" long. Nail and glue one to the installed ledger, overlapping the four-by-four leg. Use 6d nails.

Using the spacing blocks, toenail and glue the second 28" ledger across the front opening, between the leg and the partition. The front of the two-by-two is flush with the front of the partition, while the back is flush with the four-by-four leg. Glue and nail the second 30¼" ledger to the back side of the front ledger, overlapping the four-by-four leg.

Cut nine one-by-fours to 20½" long; start next to the partition, gluing and nailing the boards in place on the shelf ledgers. Use 6d nails, and rip and notch (for legs) the last board to fit.

The Top

For the top, cut seven one-by-fours to 52½" long, and glue and nail them in place using 6d nails. Attach top face trim, in the form of a one-by-four cut to 45½" long, at the top; attach shelf trim of one-by-three ripped to 12¼" and cut to a 28" length. Use a one-by-

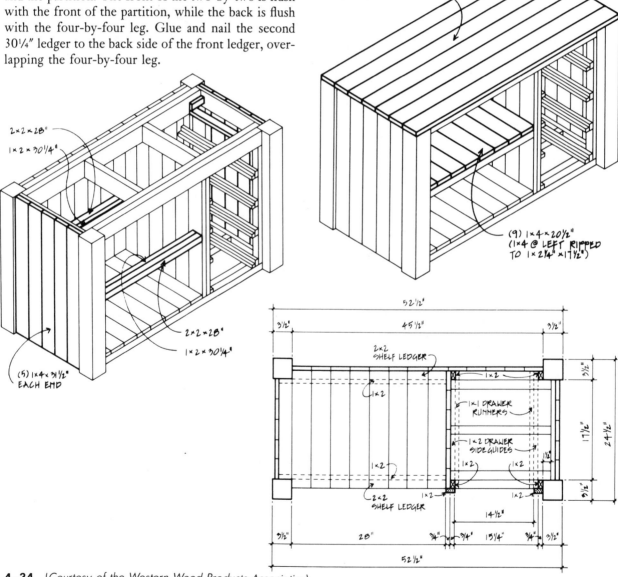

4–34 *(Courtesy of the Western Wood Products Association)*

three cut to 45½″ long and ripped to 2¼″ wide for lower face trim. Vertical trim consists of two one-by-twos cut to 25¾″. For drawer separator horizontal trim, cut three one-by-ones to 14½″ lengths. Glue and nail with 3d nails to locations as shown in the drawings.

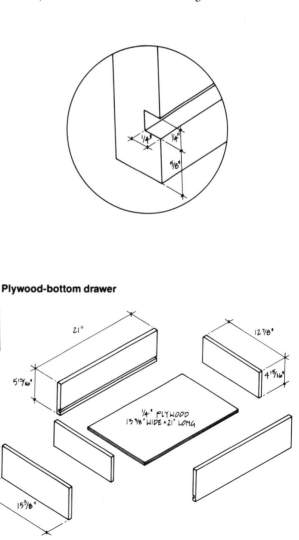

VERTICAL TRIM
1×2×25¾″

UPPER FACE TRIM
1×4×45½″

HORIZONTAL TRIM
(3) 1×1×14½″

VERTICAL TRIM
1×2×25¾″

* SHELF FACE TRIM
FROM 1×3×28″
(RIP TO 2¼″ WIDE)

LOWER FACE TRIM
FROM 1×3×45½″
(RIP TO 2¼″ WIDE)

Drawers

What now remains is drawer construction. Simple drawers are used, with the most complex work being the edge-guided routing of the ¼″ by ¼″ slots around the bottoms of both sides. Set the grooves ⅝″ up from the bottom edges, after cutting all of the sides to 21″ lengths from ¾″ by 5¹³⁄₁₆″ (actual measurement) stock. Cut the fronts and backs 4¹⁵⁄₁₆″ high and 12⅞″ long from ¾″ (actual) stock, and cut a facing 6⅛″ by 15⅜″. The plywood bottom is from ¼″ stock, 13⅜″ by 21″. Cut enough parts to assemble all three drawers (six sides, six fronts and backs, three facings, three bottoms). Use 4d nails and glue to assemble the ends inside the sides, after gluing the bottom into the side slots.

Drill holes for the drawer pulls in the facing. Apply glue to drawer facing, and line up so there is a ½″ overhang on each side, and ⁵⁄₁₆″ at the top. Nail, with 3d nails, the drawer front to the facing from the inside.

¼″   ¼″

⅝″

Plywood-bottom drawer

21″

12⅞″

5¹³⁄₁₆″

4¹⁵⁄₁₆″

¼″ PLYWOOD
13⅜″ WIDE × 21″ LONG

6⅛″

15⅜″

4–35 (Courtesy of the Western Wood Products Association)

To make drawers with solid-wood bottoms, a couple of extra steps work best. Cut all of the parts to size, as above, except for the drawer fronts and backs, and bottoms. Cut drawer fronts and backs 12⅞″ long by 5¹³/₁₆″ high. Groove as in the preceding drawer pattern, but groove front and back as well.

Assemble the solid-wood bottom from two one-by-sixes cut 20″ long, plus a one-by-three ripped to 2⅜″ wide and cut 20″ long.

Carefully edge-glue and clamp the bottom. When glue is dried (at least 12 hours is needed before the joints are stressed), rabbet the bottom edge all around so that a ¼″ lip is produced; do this in two passes, and remember to rabbet end grain first so that cuts with the grain will clean up any splintering.

Apply glue only to the front and back grooves. Do NOT glue the solid-wood drawer bottom into the side grooves, or wood movement under changing conditions of heat and humidity will rapidly split the bottom.

Solid Wood Drawer

4–36 (*Courtesy of the Western Wood Products Association*)

Keep a check on squareness as the drawers are put together. Assemble the drawers with 4d nails and glue. Drill the drawer facings for the drawer pulls, and finish drilling after assembly. Assemble as earlier, using 3d nails and glue, with nailing done from inside the drawer.

Last Steps

For the final edge trim, mitre the ends of the four-by-fours cut to measured lengths for the top, and nail and glue flush to the top at front, sides, and back.

If finish is desired, wipe on a good quality tung oil, or brush on a good polyurethane, water or oil base. I recommend sticking with satin or flat finishes.

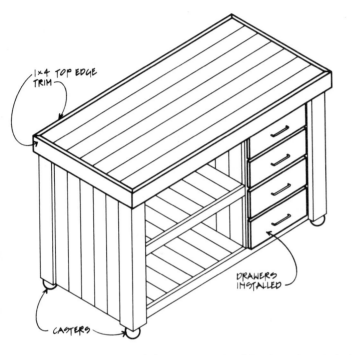

4-37 (*Courtesy of the Western Wood Products Association*)

5
General Storage

■ Arched-Top Chest

This chest is useful as a small storage trunk, or as a decorative item in almost any room, depending on the wood used. I decided on walnut, unstained, coated with the soft luster of an antique oil finish.

Begin this project by matching wood as closely as possible and preparing to glue up narrower pieces into the needed 18"-wide boards. I suggest you cut close to length, but no less than 1" extra. Joint board edges.

Lay boards out as you intend to glue them up. Mark with a swooping "V" or "W" so you can, after dis-

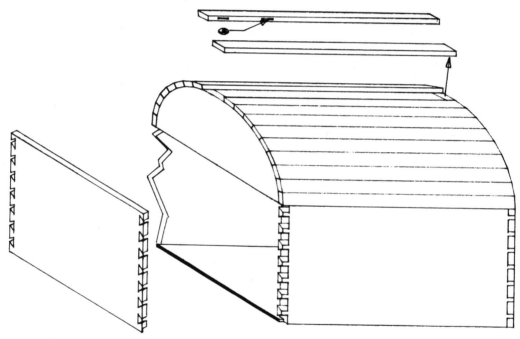

5–1 Arched-top chest.

Tools

- table saw or radial arm saw
- dado head or ⅜" rabbeting bit
- jointer
- biscuit joiner
- 1 hp or up router and dovetail jig
- soft-faced mallet
- screwdriver
- drill, ³⁄₃₂" drill bit for hinge pilot holes
- four to twelve 4' bar or pipe clamps
- square
- measuring tape

Materials

- eighteen ¾" x 2" x 36" walnut, for top slats
- ¾" x 3" x 36" walnut, for top slats
- two ¾" x 18" x 36" walnut, for sides
- two ¾" x 18" x 24" walnut, for ends
- ½" x 24" x 36" birch plywood, for bottom
- two brass hinges
- one top restraint
- No. 10 joinery biscuits
- eighteen No. 6 1¼" flathead wood screws
- wood glue
- one chest lock (optional; I omitted this)

5–2 Boards marked for joining, using a swooping V.

5–3 Cutting biscuit slots.

assembly, tell which part goes where. Mark boards for biscuit-joining at 8″ intervals. Cut the slots for the biscuits.

Set clamps within one to two inches of final size. Set biscuits near slots, and apply glue, one board at a time, assembling and clamping each wide board as glue and biscuits are applied. Make sure glue is on sides of biscuit slots as well as on bottoms and on board edges. Wipe off glue; squeeze out and set assembly aside to dry. Repeat until both sides and both ends are done. Next, rip the slats for the top. Set the table saw to cut a 15-degree angle, giving an 85-degree final angle on the board. Rip both sides of all 19 boards; you can set the angle and rip the boards at the appropriate angle as you go, but if you mess up, a great deal of resetting may be needed.

The top is most easily assembled with biscuits and a helper. It is on a radius of 7½″, but with its start well below the bottom edge of the arc, and with several side points that don't meet. Thus, drawing a pattern after you've cut the slats is the most accurate method of assembly, though it's difficult to carry out. The slats try to tumble, even with a helper; try using strips of 2″ masking tape from slat to slat to help prevent tumbling.

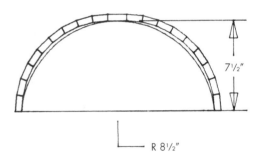

5–5 Arched-top chest, top dimensions.

5–4 Clamp and then clean up excess glue. Set aside until glue is dry.

Begin by having the helper hold half the slats, plus the middle slat, end up on a smooth piece of cardboard. Kneel down and check the fit. If all is well, draw the arc on the cardboard. Fold the cardboard over and make the arc a half circle. Cut out the template and make three plywood patterns on which you can rest the slats as they are assembled. Nail the templates the proper distances apart (36″ to the outside edges, with the third one centered) on one-by-two slats placed on the flat undersides. Let one underside slat extend out ½″ on each edge.

Start the slat assembly slowly, going up one side, placing two slats, marking for biscuits, bringing them down and cutting with the biscuit joiner, and returning to position, with glue (check biscuit fit *first*). Glue up no more than four slats on the first side, and clamp.

You may find it necessary to use C clamps to hold the first, or bottom, slat of each side in place while gluing. If so, leave it clamped so the building unit is stabilized.

Repeat the process up the other side. After two hours, come back to the first side and go up another four slats. Do the same to the opposite side.

After two or three more hours, fit the last two 2″ slats, and check the fit of the 3″ slat. Make any needed adjustments at this time; then slot, add biscuits and glue, and wait a few more hours. The top slat should be a tight enough fit that clamps are no longer needed, but you may wish to add enough weight to the top to be sure of a bond. A few volumes of an old encyclopedia per foot of length is enough.

Leave the top assembly to dry, and check the sides and ends for flatness. Sand lightly if needed. Cut to final lengths.

Cut a ½″ by ⅜″ rabbet in the bottom of all four boards; the ½″ is depth, while the ⅜″ is width, half the width of the board. This fits the birch plywood bottom when the chest is in its finishing stages.

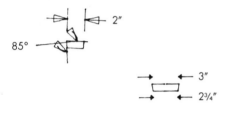

85°   2″

3″
2¾″

Ends and Sides are Rabbeted ⅜″ Wide × ⅝″ Deep Along Bottom Edges

Bottom of ⅝″ Plywood

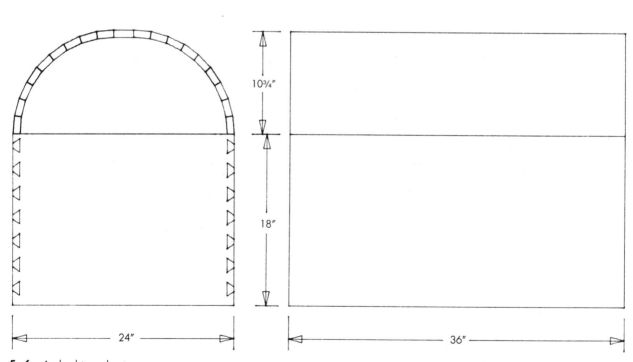

10¾″

18″

24″

36″

5–6 Arched-top chest.

110

Set up your dovetail jig system. Mount the templates to a backing board. Mounting holes (already drilled) are slightly oblong, and adjust until a test joint fits perfectly. Use a pine backing board; hardwood looks good, but because of size, weight is a problem when changing from one template to another.

Clamp the workpiece upright in a bench vise.

Set the tail template on the top of the board, and position it to get your tails where you want them. Clamp the backing board to the workpiece, and rout carefully, moving from left to right. Once the tails are cut, use them to mark the pin board. Set the pin template on the marks. Clamp and rout.

Rout carefully when using any soft-metal template. These jigs don't wear out, unless you hit the template with the router bit, which chews right through the aluminum. Make sure you are engaging the template with the template guide at the start, and the bit is no longer rotating at the end and you'll have no problems.

Cut and test-fit each set of dovetail joints, matching as you go. Good joints will be a very tight fit; so the soft-faced mallet or hammer is essential, as is a gentle technique for tapping joints apart after assembly—you will probably also have to gently drive them together.

After test assembly, gather wood glue and clamps. Set clamps to the approximate size of the box to be made. Place a square nearby. Coat one pair of joints with glue, and assemble. Coat a second pair with glue, and assemble. Coat the final two pairs with glue, and assemble. Check square. Clamp and recheck square. Allow the box to dry.

Get a final measurement of the bottom insert size, and cut the bottom to fit minus $\frac{1}{16}''$ in each dimension. Because the bottom is not the same material as the sides, it is best to spot fasten it with screws at 6″ or 8″ intervals, and glue only at the ends. No clamps are needed for this job.

Check the top fit after the chest base assembly is unclamped, and make any needed adjustments. Space and set the hinges, but do not mount. Sand the entire box with 100-grit paper, and come back with 120-grit paper.

Apply the first coat of the finish and let stand for about 10 minutes. Buff and apply a second coat. After 10 to 15 more minutes, buff again. Come back 24 hours later and apply a third coat.

Now you can install hinges and add the top restraint and a lock, if desired.

5–7 Using a dovetail jig eases the work of producing good-looking dovetails.

■ Storage Coffee Table

An easily portable storage piece, this coffee table will also serve well as a blanket chest, and in any other situation where large drawers are useful.

Lay out as shown, making sure to allow ⅛″ for kerfs.

Cut parts as indicated in drawings. Rabbet drawer fronts and backs, and cut spaces for pulls according to actual sizes needed; measure and cut after getting the hardware. You may need to cut all the way through (work with the jigsaw) or rout out the areas (or you can use a chisel to cut the areas out).

5–8 Storage coffee table. (*Courtesy of the American Plywood Association*)

Tools

- table saw or circular saw
- square
- measuring tape
- claw hammer
- nail set
- screwdriver
- drill, drill bit for pilot holes (if drive screws are substituted for nails, use ⅛″ drill bit for pilot holes, and add Phillips or square head driver bit)
- router, ⅜″ x ⅜″ rabbeting bit (may substitute dado blade and insert for table saw for bit)
- straight bit for cutting depressions for hardware, if needed
- jigsaw and blades, if needed

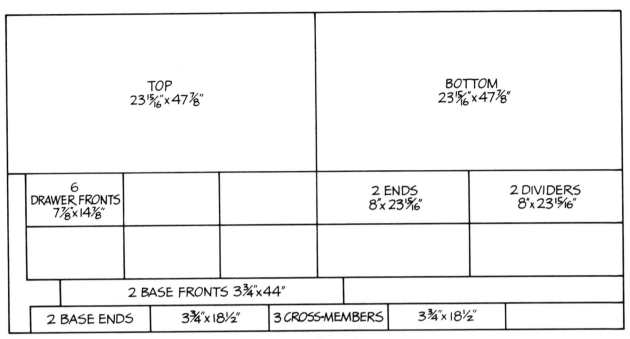

5-9 Panel layout, ¾" plywood. (*Courtesy of the American Plywood Association*)

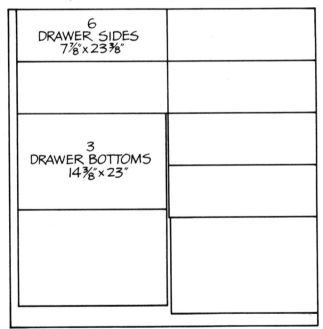

5-10 Panel layout, ½" plywood. (*Courtesy of the American Plywood Association*)

5-11 Table base. (*Courtesy of the American Plywood Association*)

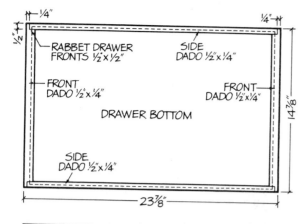

5–12 Drawer. (*Courtesy of the American Plywood Association*)

Assemble the carcass first, using all butt joints as shown in the drawing, and using nails or screws and glue. Keep a running check on square and sizing. Once carcass assembly is done, check sizes; finish-cut drawer pieces, if any changes are needed. Assemble the drawers.

Cut and assemble the base, placing one cross member at each end and one in the middle.

Sand carefully; if a natural finish is desired, you'll want to hide the cut ends of the plywood, using iron-on wood veneer tape. If paint is to be used, filling ends with wood filler works well.

Finish, add hardware, and place for use.

Materials

- ³⁄₄″ x 4′ x 8′ MDO (both sides), A-B, or natural finish plywood
- ½″ x 4′ x 4′ to match above
- six campaign style drawer pulls
- wood glue
- ¼ lb. No. 4 finishing nails (or No. 6 1¼″ drive screws)
- wood filler (to match, if clear finish used)
- 1 qt enamel, tung oil or other finish

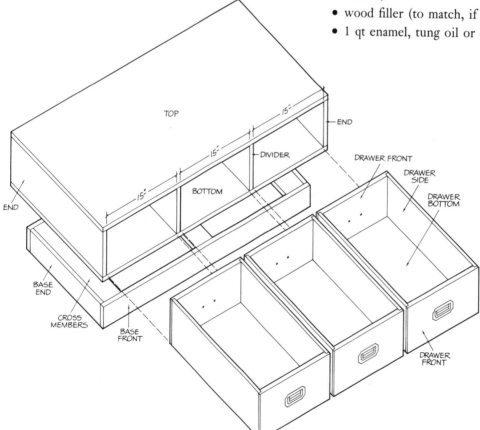

5–13 Storage coffee table. (*Courtesy of the American Plywood Association*)

■ Apple Crate

A good friend suggested that I burn in the name of a local orchard after I finished the first side of this project.

As presented, the project is 24″ long and offers 15″ of inside clearance; you may, quite easily, change the length. I suggest variations running from an inside length of 15″ (overall outside slats are 16½″) to form a square on to 30″-long slats to provide an inside dimension of 28½″. Units may be stacked.

Start by ripping all material to width, and then cut the appropriate number of pieces for each length, in each width.

Assembly is most easily done using glue on four corners. Mark all side (24″) slats ¾″ in from both ends; use a cut-off piece of stock to get an accurate measurement. Set the top slat at the top of the first two braces and mark at the bottom. Mark down 1″ (you may cut 1″ spacers if you wish; they speed marking considerably). Set on the next slat and mark at its bottom, and add ¼″ and mark. Repeat one more time.

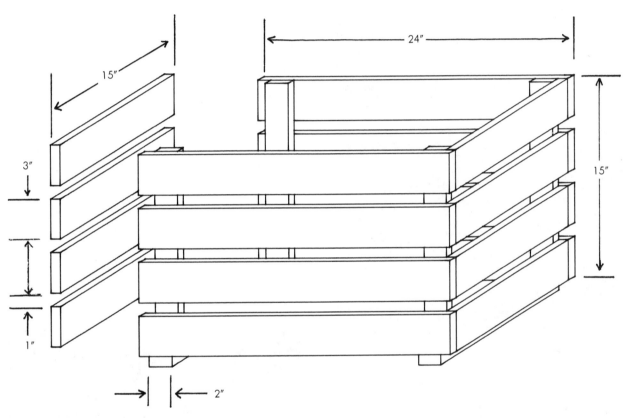

5–14 Apple crate.

Tools

- table saw
- radial-arm saw or power mitre saw
- measuring tape
- 6″ try square and 8″ flat square
- ³/₃₂″ drill bit, for pilot holes
- block finishing sander
- drill, screwdriver bit to fit screws
- eight 3″ C clamps or 6″ bar clamps

Materials

- eight ¾″ x 3″ x 24″ walnut slats, for sides
- eight ¾″ x 3″ x 15″ walnut slats, for ends
- five ¾″ x 2¼″ x 22½″ slats, for bottoms
- four ¾″ x 2¼″ x 14¼″ slats, for inside braces
- two ¾″ x 2¼″ x 16½″ slats, for bottom braces
- 1¼″ No. 6 brass-plated drive screws
- wood glue
- tung oil

This leaves a ¾" space at the bottom of the slat when it is glued and screwed to the brace, which allows the bottom to be set in.

Spread wood glue on the top slat under the brace area, and clamp the slat to the brace, making sure it is square. Repeat with the slat at the bottom of the brace, leaving the ¾" space. Repeat the process at the other end of the slats. Do the same with the second side.

After an hour or so, you may remove the clamps, and screw on the slats; drill pilot holes and then power-drive, at low speed and torque, the screws, two per slat end per brace. Repeat the gluing process on the intermediate slats if you wish, making sure of your 1" spacing. You may, instead, choose to simply drill and screw the intermediate slats in place.

Using glue and screws, assemble the end slats into the sides of the side slat braces at the same intervals as the side slats. Drill pilot holes first, making sure the holes do not line up with the already present screws in the sides; put on a small dab of glue, and drive the screws.

Keep a check on the square as you do the above assembly; square is most easily held if you install top and bottom slats on one end, with the sides standing, supported by anything that's handy. Do the same on the other end, checking square. Then install the intermediate slats.

Assemble the two outside bottom slats with 1½" spaces on the outside of the braces, and check for fit—do not use glue at this stage of assembly. The bottom braces needed to be even with the ends of the slats; you may need to make adjustments. Space the remaining three braces equally, after checking square and fit.

Place the bottom inside the crate and drive one 1¼" screw up into the bottom of each side brace, after placing a dollop of glue.

Sand lightly, clean with a tack cloth, and apply at least three coats of satin tung oil or two of satin polyurethane.

5–15 Gluing slats in place.

5–16 Slats glued, squared, and clamped in place on one side.

5–17 Fully assembled apple crate.

■ Modular Wall System

Sometimes called room dividers, this type of storage system is handy, and also serves as a home desk suitable for bill-paying and similar chores. If you'd prefer, the space can be used to hold a stereo system, records, tapes and CDs. A small television set can be placed in the drop-front desk area, instead of having it for desk use; it's not exceptionally difficult to increase the size of that space as needed. An overall height increase from (internal size) 14½″ to 16½″ doesn't require any change in materials; just place the cuts 2″ further down.

5–18 Modular wall system. (*Courtesy of the American Plywood Association*)

Tools

- table saw or circular saw
- router, ⅜″ rabbeting bit
- drill, ¼″ drill bit, ⅜″ drill bit, ⅛″ drill bit for pilot holes
- ¼″ x 14″ x 5″ pegboard (use as a template for drilling adjustable shelf-holder holes)
- six ⅜″ dowel centers
- six 24″ bar clamps

- driver, for wood screws
- screwdriver, for hinge screws
- claw hammer
- nail set
- measuring tape
- square
- paintbrush or spray outfit
- jigsaw or scroll saw

Materials

- two ¾" x 4' x 8' plywood, or MDO
- lid support for desk front
- four magnetic catches
- three pairs of cabinet hinges
- sixteen adjustable shelf supports
- eight No. 10 1¼" flathead wood screws, for fastening storage compartments to legs
- twelve ⅜" x 2" dowel pins, for joining cross pieces to legs
- wood putty and wood glue
- ¼ lb 4d finishing nails
- paint

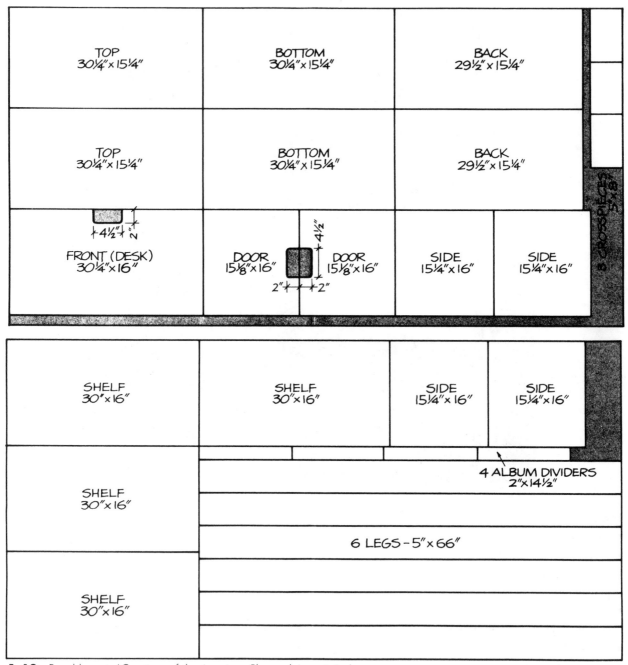

5–19 Panel layout. (*Courtesy of the American Plywood Association*)

To get an increase of 4″, you must increase sizes on both panels; instead of working with two 15¼″ by 16″ parts on one panel, use two on separate panels (there's a total of four for different uses) to get an overall *inside* height of 18½″. Anything larger will require some major redesign, and another 2′ by 4′ panel of plywood.

Modular wall systems are easily moved from place to place and readily adapted to different uses, making them nearly ideal for movable storage.

This unit is designed for permanence, in which case screws and glue are both used to assemble end pieces to sides; or it may be assembled for easy breakdown and movement, in which case only screws are used. If extra support appears desirable with a heavy television set in the desk area, simply gather three 1½″ strips of wood, and glue and nail them to the bottom, with one centered, and one 6″ towards the front and one 6″ towards the rear of the middle support.

Mark all parts on the plywood, leaving the standard ⅛″ for kerfs. Cut pieces free, and assemble the up-

rights, using dowels and glue. Clamp with moderate pressure, and let the glue set for at least two hours. Overnight is always preferable with glue.

Use the jigsaw to cut radiuses on the inside and outside upper corners of all three uprights.

Drill holes for the adjustable shelf holders.

Rabbet the back of the pieces for the cabinet units, making a ⅜″ by ¾″ rabbet. Do NOT mitre the corners first. Rabbet the top, sides, and bottom in the same size.

Now mitre the corners as shown in the drawings. Mitring the corners first might allow the router-bit pilot bearing to follow the mitre, which creates a messy rabbet.

Assemble the back, sides, top, and bottom of both cabinets, using 4d finishing nails and glue. Drive nails starting ½″ in from edges and spacing them every 4″.

Place spacers as shown, or in your own pattern, in the storage cabinet; the album dividers are 2″ x 14½″, placed as needed, using 4d finishing nails and glue.

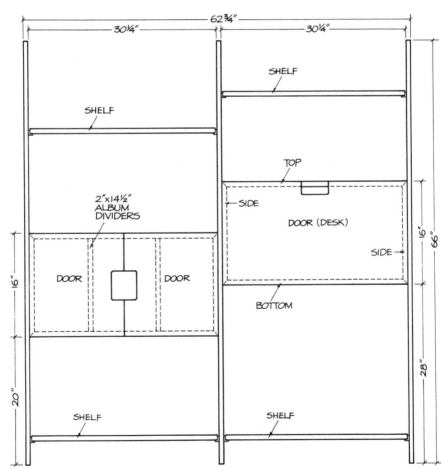

5–20 Front view. (*Courtesy of the American Plywood Association*)

Mark and drill pilot holes for wood screws into the sides of the cabinets; the storage cabinet's top is 32″ from the bottom of the end piece and the middle divider, while the top of the desk module is 44″ from the bottom of both middle divider and right-side leg. You may, of course, alter these distances as long as any pair remains equal.

Even if the desk module is enlarged and used to hold a television set, it's best to leave the top at about 48″.

Sand with 100-grit sandpaper, and place hinges and drop-front supports. Drill and mount the hardware. Remove the hardware and paint.

When the paint is dry, reinstall the hardware, and start storing whatever you desire in the system.

5–21 Side view. (*Courtesy of the American Plywood Association*)

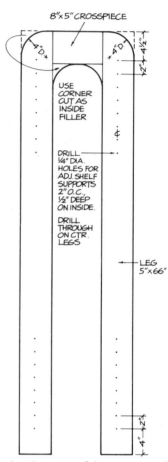

5–22 Leg details. (*Courtesy of the American Plywood Association*)

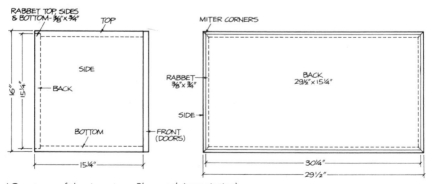

5–23 Box details. (*Courtesy of the American Plywood Association*)

■ Shaker Secretary Desk

This type of desk doesn't roll on wheels, but it does provide a great deal of adaptable storage in a unit small enough to be readily moved. It may also be made with the top section loose, so that it's even more ready to be broken down and moved from place to place.

It makes, as the original design was intended to do, an exceptionally comfortable and handy writing desk, too. The design is clean and simple. As shown here, all materials used are pine and pine plywood; there's nothing that says you can't make it from hardwood. If you do, avoid oak or ash; Shaker designs were more often done in maple, cherry and walnut.

5–24 Shaker desk. (*Courtesy of Georgia-Pacific Corporation*)

Table

- four 2¼″ x 2¼″ x 24¼″ legs
- two 2½″ x ¾″ x 32″ stretchers
- 22″ x 35″ x ¾″ top
- 33½″ x 1½″ x ¾″ facing
- 33½″ x 2¼″ x ¾″ facing
- two 19¾″ x 2¼″ x ¾″ sides

- two 12¾″ x 35″ x ¾″ short top
- 2½″ x 33½″ x ¾″ and ¾″ x 15⅞″ x 33½″ plywood lid, includes two facings as first part
- 12¾″ x 35″ x ¾″
- 1½″ x 33½″ brass piano hinge
- four 1½″ L brackets

This is not an easy project; you must be able to taper-cut the legs, for example, and there are mortises for the side stretchers that must be at least partly hand-cut. The hutch part is held together with dado joints, many of them stopped, so there's some hand-work there, too.

This construction depends less heavily than most others on nails, screws, and similar items. The back is eventually held in place with ⅜" No. 3 flathead wood screws; there is a piano hinge, and four knobs, but, otherwise, only L brackets are used to screw the top into place on the desk table.

Start the table by cutting the legs to length and thickness. Measure 2½" from the top of each leg, and cut a taper so they're 1½" at the bottoms; taper is cut on two adjacent sides that then face to the inside and back for the front legs, and inside and front for the back legs.

Measure in ¼" from the outside edge of each leg and mark the mortises for each stretcher. Mortises are ¾" wide, 2½" long, and ¾" deep. Cut mortises after drilling out the center with a ¾" brad-point or Forstner drill bit—drilling out saves a great deal of chisel work and a lot of time, and results in a neater mortise. Drilling must be done with great precision to make a tight-fitting mortise. Use a smaller drill bit if you're worried about drilling precision, and do a bit more chisel work.

Repeat the mortising for the front and rear stretchers, again cutting mortises ¾" wide by ¾" deep and 2½" long; in both cases, stretcher ends fit right into the mortise, so that no tenon cutting is needed.

Dry-fit the parts and check for squareness as well as joint tightness. Disassemble, glue, reassemble, and clamp; again check squareness.

Make triangular corner blocks from 2" scrap stock, notching the points of the triangles so the blocks fit into the corners of the desk. Glue and nail in place.

Use a ¼" round-over bit to radius the edges of the top. Place the top on the desk, making it flush at the back edge, and overlapping ¾" at all other edges. Use the L brackets to screw the top in place, which makes it removable from underneath any time the unit must be moved.

Taper the two sides, starting with a 6" measurement along the top edge of each side. Mark; then measure up 1½" on the front edge, and mark that. Draw the line, and cut off the waste to form the taper.

Sides are attached to the top with dowels. Attach a 1½" facing across the front. The back gets a 2¼" facing, both attached with dowels.

The short top, already attached, extends over the front facing ¾", leaving a 1" gap between the short

Hutch
- two 21" x 12" x ¾" sides
- 35" x 13¼" x ¾" top
- two 16½" x 11¼" x ¾" middle dividers
- two 13½" x 11¼" x ¾" supports
- two 3⅞" x 11¼" x ¾" supports
- 32¼" x 11¼" x ¾" support
- six 4" x 11¼" x ¾" dividers
- 34½" x 21½" x ¼" plywood back
- eight ⅜" x 2" dowels
- sixteen No. 3 ⅜" flathead wood screws

Drawers
- two 8½" x 3⅝" x ¾" facings
- 13⅛" x 3⅝" x ¾" facing
- 9⅜" x 3⅝" x ¾" facing
- eight 10⅛" x 3½" x ¾" sides
- 9⅜" x 9⅜" x ⅛" bottom
- 13⅛" x 9⅜" x ⅛" bottom
- two 8½" x 9⅜" x ⅛" bottom
- four Shaker-style knobs

Tools
- table saw
- router and edge guide, ¼" rabbeting bit, ⅜" rabbeting bit, ¾" straight bit, ¼" round-over bit
- drill, ¼" drill bit, ⅜" brad-point bit for dowel holes, ¾" Forstner or brad-point bit, ⅜" drill bit, ⅛" drill bit for pilot holes
- ¼" x 14" x 5" pegboard (use as a template for drilling adjustable shelf-holder holes)
- ¾" chisel, for mortises (or any mortise technique)
- six 12" bar clamps
- eight 18" bar clamps
- four 36" bar clamps
- driver, for wood screws
- screwdriver, for hinge screws
- claw hammer
- nail set
- measuring tape
- square
- paintbrush or spray outfit

top and the base of the hutch. When the time comes, the bottom of the hutch is rabbeted 1/4″ by 1/4″ along the top of its back edge to hold the back, which fits flush with the back edge, but extends 3/4″ on each side.

Attach the piano hinge to the front lip of the hutch bottom and to the edge of the lid.

Dado joints provide the holding power for the hutch. Rout the bottom of the hutch with two stop dadoes, 3/4″ by 1/4″ deep, to hold the middle supports; stop the dadoes 3/4″ from the front edge so the lid can close.

The middle supports are cut with dadoes 3/4″ by 1/8″, on each side, 3 7/8″ from the top. A second set of 3/4″ by 1/8″ dadoes is cut on the inside surfaces of the middle supports, 8 5/8″ from the top.

The board that provides a bottom for the pigeonhole units has two 3/4″ by 3/8″ dadoes on its bottom to hold the middle supports. Along the top edge, 3/4″ by 1/8″ dadoes are cut to hold the sides of the pigeonholes. Allow three inches between each of the three dadoes needed. The bottom surface of the hutch top is also dadoed, with 3/4″ by 1/4″ stopped dadoes (stop 3/4″ from the front edge) to match the lower support dadoes.

Stopped dadoes 3/4″ by 1/4″ are also cut into the inside edge of the side panels, 3 3/4″ from the top, and 8 1/4″ from the top. Again, stop the dadoes 3/4″ from the front edges.

The 1/4″ by 1/4″ rabbet is cut along the inside back edges of both sides and the bottom edge of the top to accommodate the back of the hutch unit.

Construct the case after cutting and checking the fit of all of the parts; use clamps and wood glue, and the back goes on with No. 3 3/8″ wood screws. Keep joints square during assembly. It's simpler and neater to assemble the outer case with the two middle supports and two horizontal members, with the pigeonhole and drawer dividers added last.

All drawers are 10 7/8″ deep, overall. All sides are 3 1/2″. Cut 3/4″ by 3/8″ rabbets on the back edge of each facing, and on the front of each drawer back. On the bottom edges of the backs and faces, cut a 1/8″ by 1/8″ rabbet. Glue up the backs, sides, and facings with frequent checks for squareness.

When the glue on the main drawer frame has dried, turn it over and glue in the drawer bottoms. Check the entire unit for fit, and sand carefully with 100-grit sandpaper.

Remove the hardware, and paint. Reinstall hardware and you're ready to go.

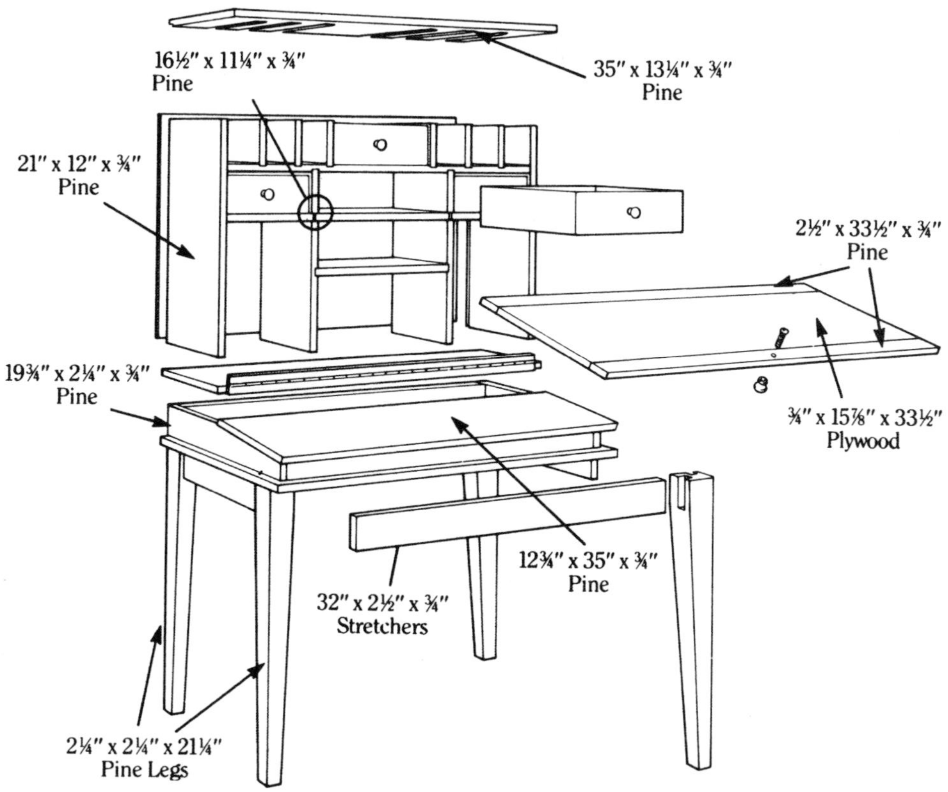

5–25 Shaker desk. (*Courtesy of Georgia-Pacific Corporation*)

■ Stacking Bookcases

This is a simple project that may be sized in almost any manner you like, provided that each stack is held to no more than six or seven individual units—if you wish to stack them higher, I'd suggest fastening the units together in some manner.

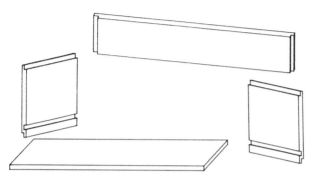

5–26 Stacking bookcase, single-assembly drawing.

Begin by cutting pieces to length; make sure the grain runs the long way in end pieces (if it's run the short way, you have to buy extra-wide wood, at higher cost, and you also weaken the joints badly). The width of the shelves given is just about the maximum for pine, but you may go out to a full 36″ shelf with oak.

Set up the router or table saw to cut the dadoes (¾″ by ⅜″) on the insides of each end piece. Make the cut so the dado is 1¼″ from the bottom edge.

Set up the router or table saw to make ¾″ rabbets and rabbet ends of end pieces, with the upper rabbet on the same side as the dado and the lower rabbet on the opposite side.

Rabbet the ends of the backing board.

Tools

- table saw, circular saw, or power mitre saw with 11½″ capacity
- dado blade
- router (instead of dado blade) and edge guide, ¾″ straight bit
- two 36″ bar clamps
- four 18″ bar clamps
- drill
- ¼″ drill bit
- measuring tape
- square

Assemble to check the joint fits and mark for dowels. Each shelf end gets four ¼″ dowels. Use through-dowelling; space 1″ in from each end and then 3″ from there on each side.

Assemble with glue, and clamp the bottom. Position the backing board, and drill that for the remaining dowels. Glue and clamp with 18″ clamps.

Sand with 120-grit paper; stain, and finish as desired.

To make a base, simply cut 1½″-wide by ⅜″ rabbets in the upper ends of one-by-six stock that you've rounded over for use as moulding; ends will be 13″ wide, while the front and back will each be 33¼″ long. Do not rabbet front and back. Assemble at corners with dowels and glue; stain and finish to match the above. Now, assemblies will fit down on the stand, and, if you wish, you may run ⅝″ wood screws into the overlapping rabbets, three per shelf end. This prevents quick movability, but also helps prevent tip-over.

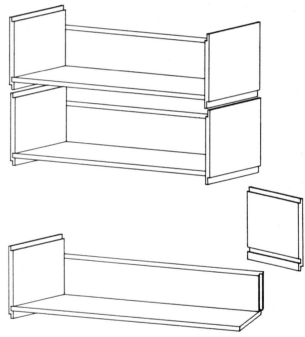

5–27 Stacking bookcase, multiple-assembly exploded drawings.

Materials

- two 11½″ x 14″ x ¾″ pine, ends
- 33¼″ x 5½″ x ¾″ pine, backing board
- 32½″ x 11½″ x ¾″ pine, shelf
- wood glue
- paint or stain, and clear finish
- fourteen ¼″ x 2″ dowels

■ Book or Curio Cabinet

This small shelf set is exceptionally handy, in large part because of its size. It's readily built from a single sheet of ¾″ or ⅝″ plywood (you must adjust plan sizes to suit the ⅝″-thick wood); or it can be built from a number of pieces of ¾″ pine or other solid wood, and a ⅜″ plywood back. It is easily moved, and the shelves rest on adjustable holders to allow the placement of many different items, or sizes of books.

This is another simple plan that provides exceptional looks, in plywood or solid wood. If you're using plywood, start by laying out the pieces on the panel, making sure there's ⅛″ between all parts to allow for the kerfs. Cut the end off the panel at the mark for the bottom pieces. Then cut up the kerf line between one side and the back. This eases further cutting operations. Remember that the circular saw is always used with the good face of the wood *down*, while the table saw cuts with the good face *up*.

5–28 Curio cabinet. (*Courtesy of the American Plywood Association*)

If you're using solid wood, cut to size, doing all ripping operations first and then moving to crosscut work unless you've gotten hold of some exceptionally long wood.

Materials

- ¾″ or ⅝″ plywood, A-B or hardwood or pine, oak, etc.
- two ¾″ x 11″ x 72″ sides
- four ¾″ x 8″ x 17″ shelves
- two ¾″ x 5⅜″ x 18″ front aprons
- ¾″ x 11⅜″ x 20″ top
- ¾″ x 9⅜″ x 18″ bottom
- two ¾″ x 1½″ x 9⅜″ bottom cleats (may be any wood, as they're hidden from view)
- ¾″ x 1½″ x 17⅞″ bottom cleat
- 10′ shelf edge moulding (picture moulding)
- sixteen ¼″-shank adjustable-shelf holders
- ¼″ lb 4d finishing nails
- box 1″ brads
- wood glue
- paint or stain and clear finish
- wood veneer edging, if you use hardwood plywood
- wood filler

Cut all curves.

Lay out the sides, and place the 11″ by 61″ pegboard flush with the top. Using a piece of masking tape, or a standard drill stop, mark the drill bit to a depth of ¼″ to ⅜″; measure the depth on the particular brand of shelf holder you're using, since they vary a bit (don't

Tools

- circular saw or table saw (if you're using hardwoods, the table saw is much easier to work with)
- four two-by-fours
- two sawhorses (if you're working with a circular saw)
- mitre box
- drill, ¼″ drill bit
- jigsaw or scroll saw
- 11″ x 61″ x ¼″ pegboard (serves as template for laying out holes for adjustable-shelf supports)
- 16-oz claw hammer
- nail set
- measuring tape
- square
- paintbrush
- sandpaper
- finishing sander

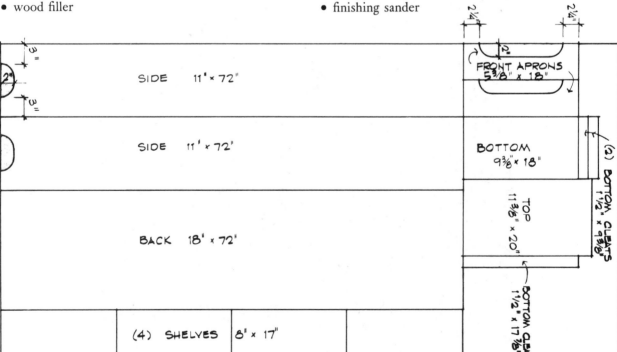

5-29   Panel layout. (*Courtesy of the American Plywood Association*)

forget, it has to also have the thickness of the pegboard added; that may be 1/8" or 1/4"). Use a bit of white or yellow marker to determine the holes you wish to use, and lay those out. You want to be about 1" in from the front and 1 1/2" from the back edges (2" from the back edge if you use 3/4" plywood as a back). Space holes at least 2" apart.

Assemble the bottom cleats to the lower bottoms, as shown (5 3/8" up from the bottom edge) using glue and nails. Assemble the back and sides, keeping a check on square. Use glue and nails, nailing every 4".

Place the front and bottom aprons and the bottom shelf, using glue and nails.

Position the top over the structure in the middle with the back edge flush.

Use picture moulding to edge the shelves and top. Mitre the corners on the top, and secure with glue and 1" brads.

Set all nails and fill holes with nail putty. Fill the edges of shelf sides, or use more picture moulding.

Sand with 100- or 120-grit paper; paint or stain and coat with clear finish.

Install the shelves and load it up.

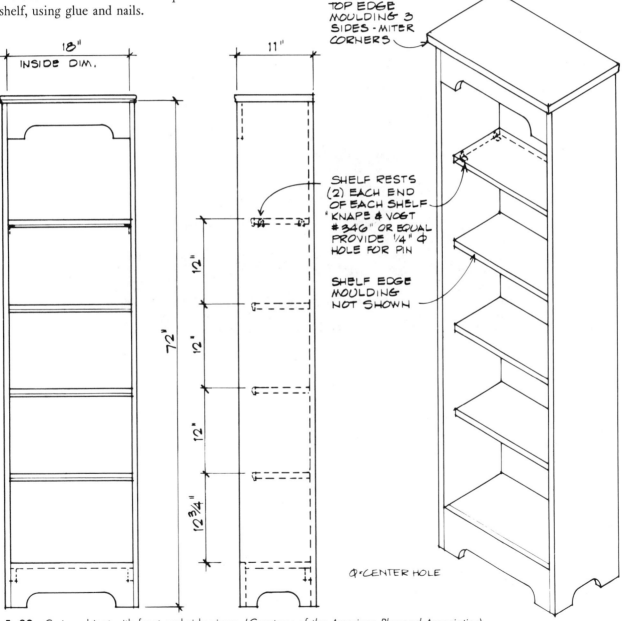

TOP EDGE MOULDING 3 SIDES - MITER CORNERS

18" INSIDE DIM.

11"

72"

12"

12"

12"

12 3/4"

SHELF RESTS (2) EACH END OF EACH SHELF "KNAPE & VOGT #346" OR EQUAL PROVIDE 1/4" ∅ HOLE FOR PIN

SHELF EDGE MOULDING NOT SHOWN

∅ CENTER HOLE

5-30 Curio cabinet with front and side views. (*Courtesy of the American Plywood Association*)

■ Barbecue Cart with Storage

Most people today use gas barbecues, with some work shelf space built in. That still leaves a considerable shortage of work space and a lack of storage space for those items you don't wish to run back and forth with each time the barbecue is used. This project solves both problems quickly. There's even a heat-resistant top area for standing those super-hot dishes that will destroy even plastic laminate tops.

Begin by assembling wood and cutting parts to the listed sizes. Then start the top frame, drilling pilot holes for the No. 8 2″ wood screws. The bottom frame is made in the same way. Next, attach the legs to the top frame in the corners and 1¼″ down from the top of the frame—longest side of the legs to the longest sides of the frame—using No. 8 1¼″ wood screws in their pilot holes.

Fit the bottom frame *inside* the legs, and drill pilot holes for No. 8 1¼″ wood screws. Assemble.

5–31   Barbecue cart. (*Courtesy of Georgia-Pacific Corporation*)

Materials

- ¾″ x 16″ x 48″, plywood, A-C, top
- two ¾″ x 14½″ x 48″, plywood, A-C, shelves
- four ¾″ x 2½″ x 49½″ pine, frame rails
- two ¾″ x 2½″ x 16″ top frame rails
- two ¾″ x 2½″ x 14½″ bottom frame rails
- two ⅜″ x 22½″ x 34¾″ A-B plywood, side panels
- two ⅜″ x 1″ x 22½″ plywood, spacers
- ¾″ x 2½″ x 18″ pine, tool rack
- four ⅜″ dowel, 2″ long, for tool holders on rack
- 1½″ x 5½″ x 14½″ pine, rest
- four ¾″ x 2½″ x 32¾″ pine, legs
- two 1½″ x 3½″ x 4½″ pine, axle supports
- two 4″ diameter wheels, 1½″ thick

- ¾″ birch dowel axle, 19″ long
- two ¾″ x 1½″ x 8″ pine, handles
- ¾″ x 14½″ birch dowel, handle rod
- six 8″ x 8″ ceramic tiles
- tile adhesive (thin set)
- sixteen No. 8 2″ flathead wood screws
- thirty-two No. 8 1¼″ flathead wood screws
- thirty-two No. 6 1″ flathead wood screws
- box 1″ brads
- ½ lb 6d finishing nails
- two ⅜″ x 2″ lag bolt
- wood glue
- stain and clear finish

128

Cut axle supports if you've not already done so, and drill the 1¼″-diameter hole with its edge ½″ from the bottom edge of the supports (set at 1⅛″ top to bottom and centered—2¼″—end to end on the supports). Fit the axle supports in place just behind the front legs, and attach them to the frame with No. 8 2″ wood screws after drilling pilot holes.

The rest is now attached to the handle side of the frame four inches from the rear edge of the frame with No. 8 1¼″ wood screws.

Spacers now go to the bottom left edges of the top rail, and are placed with glue and 1″ brads. Attach the side panels to the spacers using No. 6 1″ wood screws in pilot holes. Set the top of the side panels 1¼″ down from the top of the frame. Attach the bottom of the side panel to the frame with the same size screw.

Fit the bottom shelf in place over the bottom frame, and attach with glue and 1″ brads.

Turn the cart on its side, and fit the second shelf between the legs, 8″ below the top frame. Nail and glue with 6d finishing nails.

Drill holes in the two handles to take the handle rod. Glue the rod in place and let dry. Attach the handles to the back leg, as shown, using ⅜″ lag bolts 2″ long.

Fit the top in place, coating the top of the frame with glue and driving 6d finishing nails down through to hold it securely.

Cover a 16″ by 24″ area of the top with tile adhesive. Fit the tiles in place and wipe up any excess adhesive.

Grout when the adhesive has had time to set.

Make sure each wheel has a ¾″-diameter hole in its middle, and slip the axle rod into the axle supports. Coat the ends of the axle with glue and fit the wheels on each end.

Drill four ⅜″-diameter holes in the tool rack, and coat the ends of the ⅜″ by 3″ dowel rods with glue. Insert and let dry.

When the glue is dry, attach the tool rack to the left side panel with No. 6 wood screws.

Go over the cart and set all nails, covering the heads with wood putty. Sand with 100-grit sandpaper after all is dry; stain and coat with clear finish—for best protection, use at least three coats.

Tools

- table saw or circular saw (if circular saw, saw-horses and three or four two-by-fours for work surface)
- drill, ¾″ bit, ⅜″ bit
- claw hammer
- nail set
- screwdriver, for flathead screws
- tile cement spreader
- finishing sander
- 150-grit sandpaper
- paintbrush or stain brush

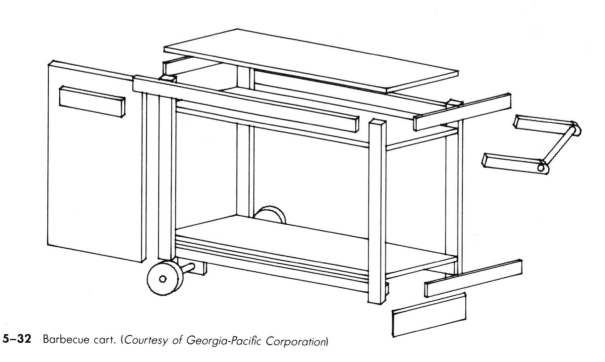

5-32 Barbecue cart. (*Courtesy of Georgia-Pacific Corporation*)

■ Build-and-Stack Modular Storage Units

Looking around my own home, I wonder why the stuff we accumulate fits so badly in the storage spaces we have, or those that were built into the house years ago.

Certainly, a quickly made, readily moved, and easily accessible series of wood box and shelving shapes to fit different spaces and to-be-stored items would be exceptionally handy. This series fits that bill, consisting mostly of simple squares and rectangles built in different sizes to suit differing storage needs. Units are easily combined for lots of space or set up singly for smaller storage requirements.

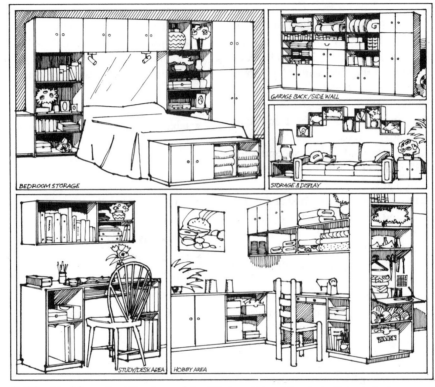

5–33   Modular units. (*Courtesy of the Western Wood Products Association*)

Materials

(Unless otherwise specified, all wood is pine, spruce, fir or hem-fir)

Basic Unit
- one (A) top 29⅜″ one-by-eight
- two (B) sides 29″ one-by-eight
- one (C) bottom 29⅜″ one-by-eight
- four (D) back 30⅞″ one-by-eight
- wood glue
- wood filler
- stain
- clear finish
- ¼ lb 1½″ finishing nails

Tools
- table saw, radial arm saw, or circular saw
- mitre box or power mitre saw
- electric drill, drill bits for hardware holes and shelf support holes (¼″ for the latter)
- section of pegboard at least 12″ long and 8″ wide, to serve as a template for drilling shelf support holes
- screwdriver and chisel
- carpenter's hammer and nail set
- tape measure and framing square
- brush and steel wool
- 100- and 150-grit sandpaper
- finishing sander

Basic Unit

Start the basic unit by cutting the parts as listed above. Use the 1½″ finishing nails and glue at each joint, using two nails per corner butt joint. Check for squareness, and then nail the back boards in place, keeping a running check on square until the first two boards are secured. Use two nails at each board end and a line of wood glue.

Allow the glue to dry at least an hour, and then use the pegboard template to drill holes for the shelves. As shown, the unit will accept one, two, or three shelves, which may be cut to 29⅛″ lengths from one-by-eight stock.

Sand carefully and coat with stain and a clear finish, or a clear finish alone.

Deep Module

The deep module is similar to the basic unit, but uses two one-by-eights to provide an actual interior depth of 14½″. Use one-by-two braces 13¾″ long to brace the corners as shown, drilling and countersinking two 1¼″ flathead screws for each brace in addition to applying glue on both contact sides of the cleat.

You may make the unit as long as you wish, but if the length is more than doubled over the base module, install a cleat as a brace at the halfway point (up to about 60″; over 60″ install two cleats).

Add shelves and finish in the same manner as the basic unit.

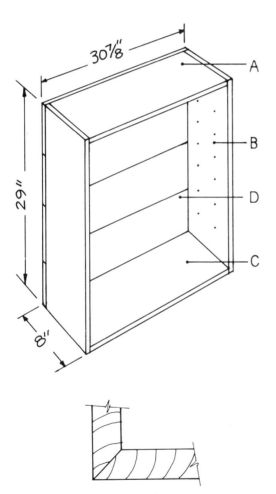

For a more finished appearance, corner joints may be mitered, then assembled as above.

5–34 Basic unit. (*Courtesy of the Western Wood Products Association*)

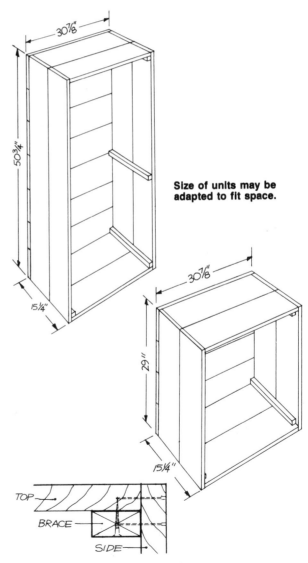

Size of units may be adapted to fit space.

5–35 Deep module. (*Courtesy of the Western Wood Products Association*)

Shelves

Shelves are added as needed, and may be installed at 29⅜″ lengths with cleats or ¼″ shorter with shelf supports. Shelf cleats are best made of either one-by-one or one-by-two lumber, glued and nailed with 1¼″ nails to the sides of the units. Make sure to set the cleats square with the sides.

Doors

Door construction for these modules is simple; it is a basic cleated construction door using two one-by-eights cut to the appropriate length for the door, with a one-by-two cleat set 2″ down from the top and another 2″ up from the bottom on each door. The cleats are screwed and glued to the doors. The door adapts well to the basic unit or the deep module in basic size, allowing for hinge installation as shown.

The door, though, sets back 1½″ inside (counting cleat depth) the unit; the shelf width must be reduced to suit the size. It's possible to use, on both units, a smaller shelf width (one-by-six by itself on the basic unit; one-by-eight and one-by-six on the deep module) to allow proper clearance. Doors themselves must be built or trimmed to provide a minimum clearance of ⅛″ all round (maximum clearance is 3/16″), which adds up to ⅜″ side to side (two sides plus the middle junction).

If a door is used on a unit higher than 36″, use three cleats per door. If the door is more than 48″ tall, use three hinges. Select your choice of door pulls and latches, and install. If you wish to make a unit with a door and of a width other than that listed above—these modules have great adaptability—simply decide on the total door width and add 1⅞″ (that is 1½″ for the wood in the unit sides plus ⅜″ for the clearance gaps). To determine height, add 1¾″ to the total height of the doors. This method allows you to build modules from stock lumber sizes, so that you can avoid having to rip boards to different widths.

Desk Module

For a handy desk, a change in door style may be used (it may be used for any other unit, too, but requires a slight bit more precision and time to build). Start with the two panels of one-by-eights (for each door side), both 25¾″ long, and add two one-by-two cleats 14½″. This door size will fit in the basic unit. Take the two cleats and counterbore 1″ down into the narrow sides, two places per board to be used. Using 1¼″ wood screws and wood glue, screw the cleats to the tops and

bottoms of the main door boards, and plug the counterbore holes with glued-in dowels. Doors built in this manner can be used for any of the modules, and add a bit more of a finished cabinetry look to the project.

To make a desk module, simply construct a basic unit, and make the door the full width (four one-by-eight boards, and two 29″ one-by-two cleats) of the unit face. Keep the door square and pull the boards together as tightly as possible. Assemble as above; then hinge in place from the bottom, so that the full width door can drop down. Use drop-desk supports to hold the door in place as a desk, or use lengths of brass or other chain.

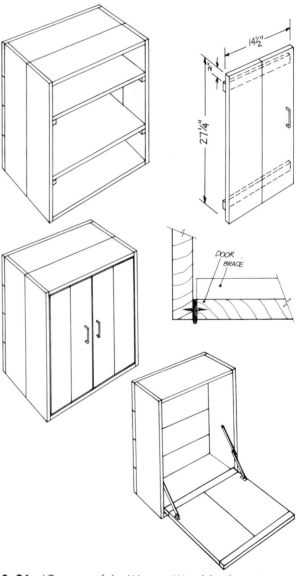

5–36 (Courtesy of the Western Wood Products Association)

■ The Organizer

I know of quite a few people who could use this unit in their basements or garages. It is simple to build and allows rearrangement at almost any time. The total dimensions of the exterior units are hard to define, because they depend on the space you intend to fill with storage organization; but the various units or modules are standardized to make changes easy. Where wide expanses of one-by-fours and one-by-sixes are listed, you may wish to substitute ¾″ plywood, cut to the same sizes (shelves, drawer bottoms, bin sides).

5–37 (*Courtesy of the Western Wood Products Association*)

Tools

- table saw, radial-arm saw, or circular saw
- mitre box or power mitre saw
- electric drill, drill bits for hardware holes
- screwdriver
- chisel
- carpenter's hammer
- nail set

- tape measure
- framing square
- level (2′ or longer)
- brush
- steel wool
- 100- and 150-grit sandpaper
- finishing sander

Material needs are going to vary widely, depending on the number of modules you want to add. I specify the wood for one module plus materials for one bin and one drawer and a wide storage area for clothing and similar items. Unless otherwise specified, all wood for the modules is pine, spruce, fir, or hem-fir. If you choose to substitute plywood in certain areas, I suggest pine or fir, B-B or B-C.

Measure the height of your installation from floor to ceiling, and cut two-by-fours (A) to length. Trim ¼″ off the upright length to ease installation. Cut one-by-six cleats (B) to 22″ lengths.

Lay the two-by-fours on the floor with the outside edges spaced 22″ apart, and glue and nail the first one-by-six cleat to the uprights, making sure it remains square to the two-by-fours. Position this cleat 1¾″ from the bottom. Fasten with three 4d nails at each end. Glue and nail the remaining cleats along the upright, allowing 1″ between cleats. To ease the setting distance, cut a spacer 24″ long and 1″ by ¾″ from one-by-two stock. Make sure the cleats remain square to the two-by-fours. Position the top cleat so it is at least 1″ down from the top of the two-by-four uprights.

Turn the unit over and add cleats on that side.

Make a second unit like the first.

Nail two one-by-four retainers to the ceiling joists (use drywall anchors if the ceiling is drywall). Space retainers 1½″ apart and make sure they're parallel. Install a second set of retainers on the ceiling, 25½″ on center. Continue to add retainers for each of the modules you've built.

Slip the two-by-four uprights of one module into the first set of retainers. Use the level to plumb the module, and then install a second set of retainers on the floor. If the floor is wood, you can use 8d nails to fasten them. If the floor is concrete, you can use masonry nails or concrete anchors.

Repeat the above process with additional modules until they're all installed.

You may now cut lumber for shelving (one-by-sixes cut to 23¾″ wide will slip right in, as will plywood cut to 21″ or 22″ by 23¾″).

Materials

Module (material for one shelving unit, 27¾″ wide):

Uprights

• four 93″ two-by-fours

Cleats

• fifty-six 22″ one-by-sixes

Retainers

• eight 22″ one-by-fours

Shelves

• one to four per shelf, 23¾″ one-by-sixes or appropriately sized 23¾″ x ¾″ plywood (up to 22″ in the other dimension, down to about 10″)

Front Brace

• one-by-four, cut to total width of modules

• ½ lb 4d finishing nails
• 1 lb 6d finishing nails
• 1 lb 8d common nails
• wood glue
• paint or clear finish, as desired
• wood filler

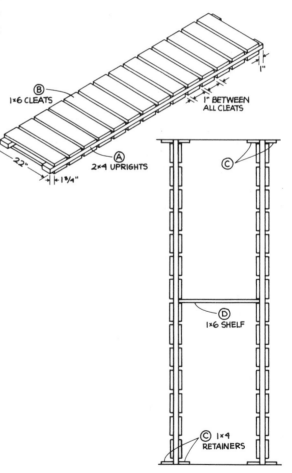

5-38 (*Courtesy of the Western Wood Products Association*)

Materials

Drawers

- Four (A) bottom 23¾″ one-by-six (or 22″ x 23¾″ x ¾″ B-B pine or fir plywood)
- two (B) sides 22″ one-by-six
- two (C) ends 20½″ one-by-six
- ½ lb 6d finish nails
- wood glue

Cut the sides and ends to length. Glue and nail the corners using 6d nails to form a square. And check the square at two adjacent corners. Center four 23¾″-long shelf boards on the drawer assembly—this gives a ⁷⁄₈″ overhang on each side. Glue and nail in place with 6d nails.

Cut the handhold, or install a drawer pull. If you wish to have drawer dividers, cut one-by-six lumber to fit, and glue and nail your dividers in place.

Drawers may be made deeper, using one-by-eight, one-by-ten, or even one-by-twelve lumber for their sides instead of the one-by-sixes. I suggest that any drawers made deeper than 8″ have sides and ends made from ¾″ plywood to help prevent warping and, thus, jamming.

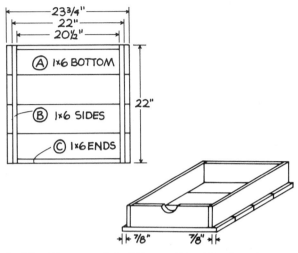

5–40 (*Courtesy of the Western Wood Products Association*)

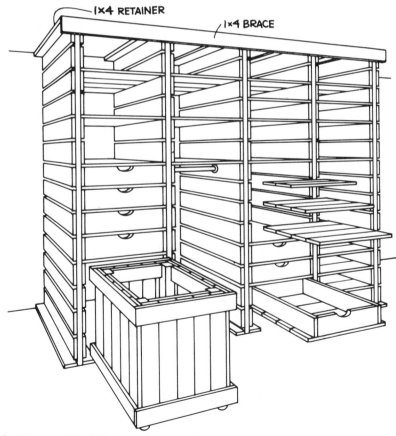

5–39 (*Courtesy of the Western Wood Products Association*)

The bin is next up, and provides good storage for heavy items, bulky items, toys, and so on.

Materials

Frame

- two 17½″ two-by-two front and back
- two 13″ two-by-two sides

Floor

- five 16″ one-by-four (or a 17½″ x 16″ piece of ¾″ pine or fir B-C or B-B plywood)

Posts

- four 19¾″ two-by-two

Side Panels

- twenty 22″ one-by-four (or ¾″ x 16″ x 17½″ plywood, but retaining posts and cleats)

Front/back panel trim

- four 20½″ one-by-four

Side panel trim

- four 17½″ one-by-four

Inside trim

- two 14½″ one-by-four front and back
- two 13″ one-by-four sides

- ¼ lb 3d finishing nails
- ¼ lb 4d finishing nails
- ¼ lb 6d finishing nails
- ½ lb 8d nails
- four 2″ casters
- wood filler
- paint or clear finish

Glue and nail up a two-by-two frame, using two 8d nails per corner. Cut flooring to length; glue and nail it to the frame using two 4d nails at each end. Hold off putting on the outside flooring pieces until you assemble the post to the base, next.

Assemble posts to the base, keeping sides square with the base. Glue and toenail with 6d finish nails, or glue and nail through the bottom of the outside flooring *before* applying the flooring to the frame.

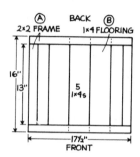

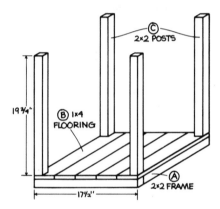

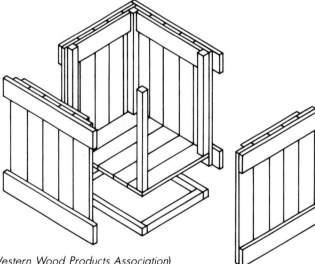

5–41 (Courtesy of the Western Wood Products Association)

To make the bin sides, use the twenty pieces of one-by-four (E) cut to length, and assemble the four side panels. Glue and nail the one-by-four trim to the top and bottom of each panel, flush, using 3d (1¼″) nails.

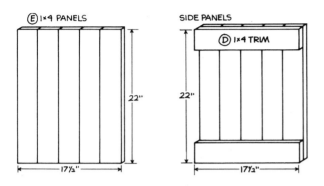

The front and back panels are made in the same manner, but the trim (F) is glued flush with the bottom edges and extends 1½″ on either side of the panel. Attach with 3d nails.

Set the front and back panels on the frame so that the base of each panel is flush with the top of the frame and the top is even with the posts. The outside edges of the vertical one-by-four panels are flush with the posts. Turn the bin on its side, and glue and nail posts to the panel using 8d nails. Glue and nail the base to the frame.

Position side panels so that the base is flush with the frame, and the outside edges are covered by the front and back panels. Glue and nail to the posts and the base: Nail the corners where front and back panels overlap the sides.

Before cutting inside trim boards, check the actual measurements between posts. Glue and nail trim to the inside, flush with top using 6d nails.

Install purchased casters after sanding and finishing the module as desired. For clothespole and wide storage areas, you might wish to omit shelving and install a clothespole about 40″ above the floor for shirts, 64″ for coveralls and longer items. Cut the pole to length, install the ends and insert the pole.

For wider shelving, cut down one module to the desired height. Install four 49½″ one-by-six shelves (or one 22″ x 49½″ piece of ¾″ plywood).

Fasten the short module to the shelves by nailing down through shelves into the cleats using 8d nails. Make sure the short module is plumb before nailing.

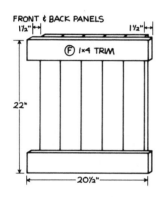

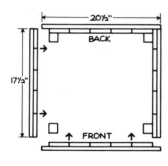

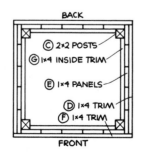

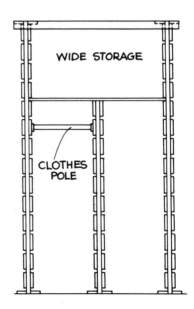

5–42 (Courtesy of the Western Wood Products Association)

■ Bookcase and Room Divider

The finished project here looks more complex than it really is. There are no complicated joints and no fancy patterns. The horizontal trim does require mitre joints, but everything else is assembled using simple butt joints. You may, if you wish, mitre the vertical joints.

The four vertical members must be ripped to size, but everything else uses standard-width lumber. Using softwood lumber, you may change dimensions to suit, but do NOT extend shelf widths beyond 2'8" or you will have problems with sag.

5–43 (*Courtesy of the Western Wood Products Association*)

Tools

- table saw, radial-arm saw, or circular saw
- cuts may be made with handsaws
- 10- or 12-point crosscut saw
- 5-point rip saw
- mitre box or power mitre saw (optional)
- electric drill, drill bits to fit screws as pilot bits
- countersink
- screwdriver
- chisel
- tape measure
- framing square
- brush
- steel wool
- finishing sander and 150-grit sandpaper

Materials

(Unless otherwise specified, all wood is pine, spruce, fir, or hem-fir.)

Frame

- two 70½" two-by-four
- three 3¾" two-by-four

Uprights

- two 55¾" two-by-four
- two 55¾" two-by-two

(If you plan to mitre uprights, use one-by-six material at each corner, and rip to 4½" wide. Omit the two-by-two middle upright.)

Base trim

- two 72" one-by-four (mitre ends)
- two 11¼" one-by-four

Shelves

- ten 26¾" one-by-twelve

Shelf supports

- sixteen 11¼" one-by-twelve

Ends

- two 48¾" one-by-twelve

Top trim

- two 72" one-by-four (mitre ends)
- two 11¾" one-by-four

Vertical trim

- four 48¾" one-by-four
- eight 48¾" one-by-three

Top

- 72" two-by-twelve
- two 1½" half-round x 11¼"

Horizontal trim

- ¾" half-round x 74" (mitre ends)

- ½ lb 4d finishing nails
- 1 lb 6d finishing nails
- 1 lb 8d finishing nails
- 2" No. 8 flathead screws
- 2½" No. 8 flathead screws
- eight pressed-wood medallions (optional) or wood blocks, 1½" square
- wood glue
- clear or other finish

Begin assembly by cutting the pieces for the frame and assembling with glue and 8d finishing nails or 2" screws. Next, rip four two-by-eights to 6" wide for the end uprights; this is the hardest work in the project if you elect to use handsaws. Glue and fasten to the outside of the frame at each corner using 8d nails. Keep the uprights flush with the base and end of the frame. Locate the middle point of the base frame, and glue and nail two-by-four and two-by-two uprights to the frame. The outside edges of the two uprights must extend 2½" on each side of the midline.

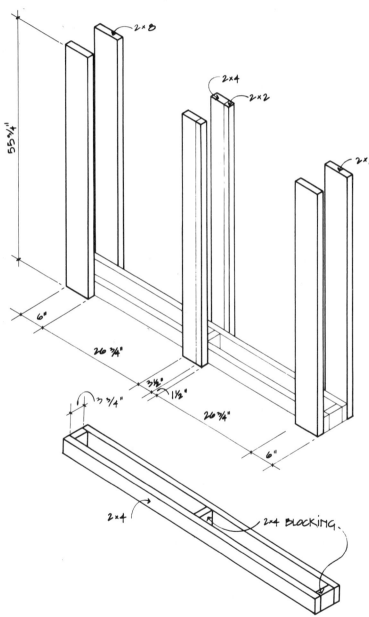

5-44 *(Courtesy of the Western Wood Products Association)*

139

For the base trim, mitre the ends, and glue and nail one-by-four trim to the bottom of the unit on the front and sides using 4d finishing nails. Then glue and nail the bottom shelves to the two-by-four frame, keeping the edges flush with the base trim. Use 4d nails again.

Shelf supports are glued and nailed to the uprights as shown, with the first tier preparing the unit for the second pair of shelves. Glue and nail in place using 4d nails. Keep the board grain vertical.

The next pair of shelves is glued and nailed to the supports, and the preceding step is repeated until all of the shelves are done.

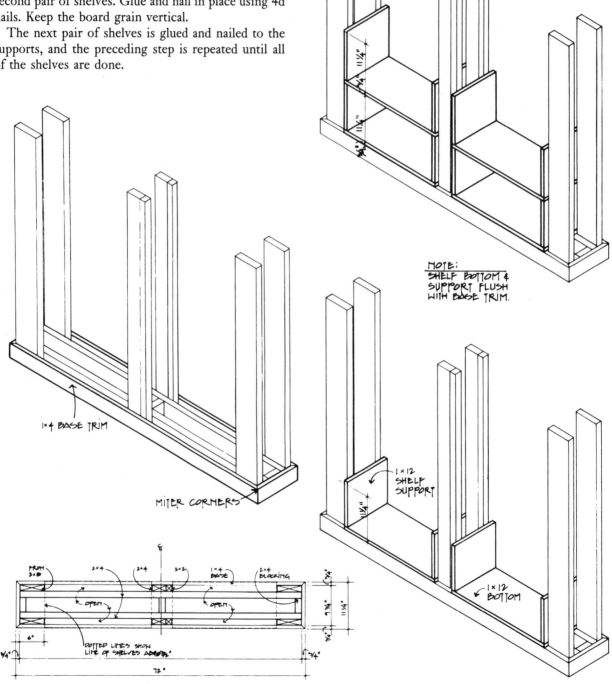

5-45 (Courtesy of the Western Wood Products Association)

The top trim goes on with mitred ends, and the one-by-fours are glued and nailed in place using 4d nails.

The two-by-twelve top cap is glued and nailed in place using 8d finishing nails. Make sure the edges are flush with the uprights and trim. Glue and nail the one-by-twelve ends in place with 4d nails. Make sure the nails are positioned in line with the shelves so that they can't penetrate intermediate spaces (or use shorter 3d nails).

Vertical trim is now applied with 3d or 4d nails and glue, as shown.

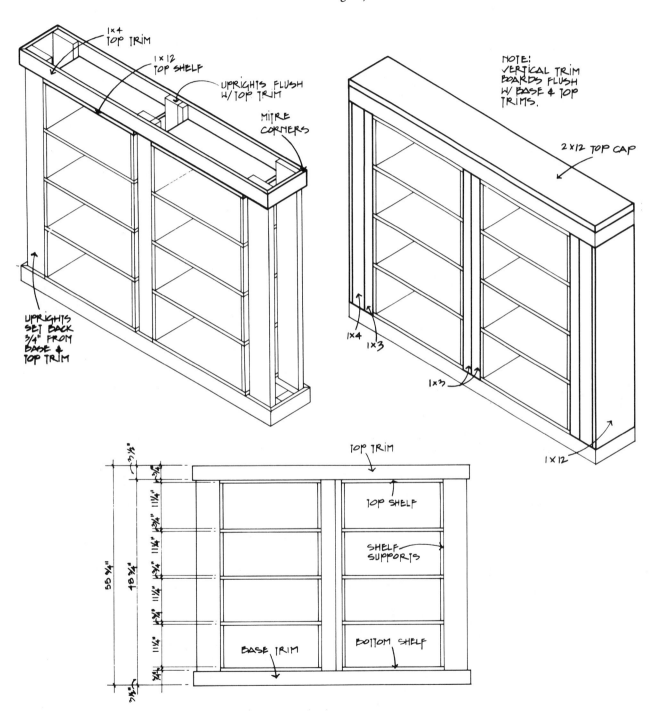

5-46 (Courtesy of the Western Wood Products Association)

141

If you wish to make this a solid-backed unit, you may use diagonal wood strips or plywood for a backing. I suggest considering luaun plywood for the back. It is inexpensive and looks good.

Top cap trim consists of 1½" half-rounds glued and nailed to the ends of the two-by-twelves. Next, cut ten lengths of ¾" half-round, each about 74" long. Mitre the ends and apply to the edges of shelves, front and back, and at the intersection of vertical trim and top trim, covering the joints. Cut ten lengths about 13" long; mitre both ends and finish off the half-round trim.

Decorative medallions or wood blocks are optional, but do much to add visual interest.

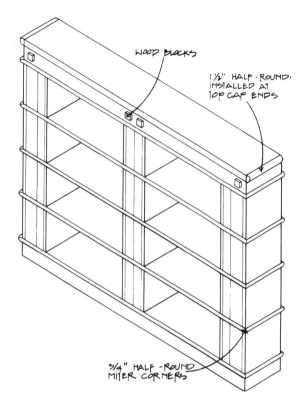

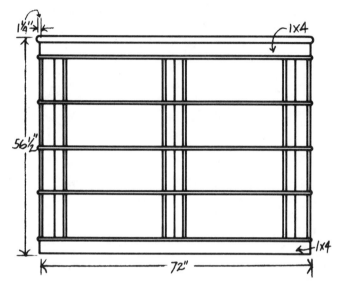

5–47 Bookcase/divider wall. (*Courtesy of the Western Wood Products Association*)

■ Versatile, Movable Under-Stair Storage

In the past, the most frequently wasted storage space in many homes was under the basement stairs—and, sometimes, under the upstairs staircase. This project provides usefully mobile storage units to fit in that space, and is readily adaptable to your specific dimensions. The rolling shelves and the rolling bin may prove handy as mobile storage units even if you have no basement or second floor, and thus have no staircase.

The tools listed will make the job easier, but you can build this project with nothing more than a hammer, crosscut saw, square, mitre box, plumb bob and a tape measure.

I don't list the materials needed for framing up and walling under the stairs. Those will vary considerably from job to job, so simply measure and estimate yourself, figuring two-by-two set with a 24″ *inside* measurement.

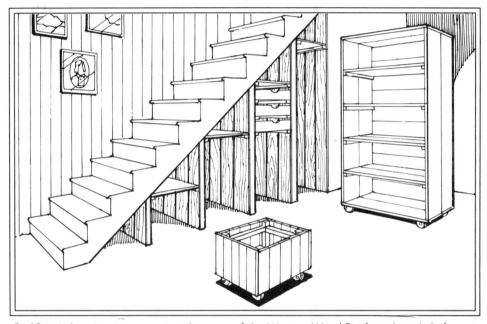

5–48 Under-stair storage units. (*Courtesy of the Western Wood Products Association*)

Materials

(Unless otherwise specified, all wood is pine, spruce, fir or hem-fir).

Pull-Out Storage Bin

- two 16½″ two-by-two bottom frame A
- two 17½″ two-by-two bottom frame
- four 12¾″ two-by-two corner posts B
- five 19½″ one-by-four bottom boards C
- two 16½″ two-by-two top frame D
- two 14½″ two-by-two top frame
- twenty-two 15″ sides E
- four 2″ casters F
- 8d and 4d finishing nails
- wood glue
- clear or other finish

Tools

- table saw, radial-arm saw, or circular saw
- 12- or 10-point crosscut saw
- mitre box or power mitre saw (optional)
- bayonet saw
- electric drill, drill bits to fit nails as pilot bits
- screwdriver
- tape measure
- framing or try square
- 2′ or 9″ torpedo level
- brush
- steel wool
- 150-grit sandpaper
- finishing sander

If your basement floor is of concrete, use concrete nails or anchors for the bottom members of the framing (sills). Screw or nail uprights to the stair stringers as shown. You may also use construction adhesive to aid security.

To check the staircase angle, simply place a sheet of shirt cardboard with one end square on the floor, and the top end covering the stair angle. Reach inside and draw a line, and you have the needed angle for all cuts, which may then be transferred (this is where a table saw is a delight) to the two-by-four frame top when it is ripped to width and angle.

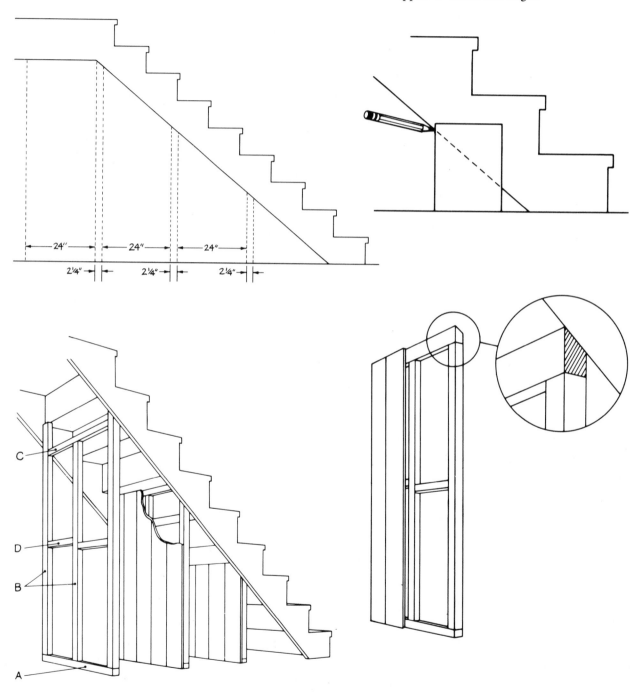

5-49 (Courtesy of the Western Wood Products Association)

Storage Bin

Assemble the bottom frame using 8d nails and wood glue, making sure it is square. Next, glue and nail the four two-by-two corner posts to the outside corners of two one-by-four bottom boards. Glue and nail the one-by-four bottom boards in place, with the bottom boards that have posts set so the posts are in the corners. Use 4d nails.

Glue and nail the top frame to the corner posts, 1½" below the tops of the posts using 8d nails. Apply the one-by-four sides with glue and 4d nails.

Turn the unit over, and attach the 2" casters with the screws provided with the casters. Make sure each caster doesn't extend past the outside edge of the box when it swivels.

Tabletop

To increase the utility of the bin, and to keep dust out, a tabletop is handy. Make the tabletop of one-by-twelves as shown.

Materials

- two 27" one-by-twelve top A
- two 22½" one-by-twelve cross braces B
- four 30" one-by-two edge trim C
- ½ lb 3d finishing nails
- wood glue
- clear finish

Assemble the one-by-twelves by spacing the one-by-two cross-braces 21¼" apart and equidistant from each end. Glue and nail in place using 3d nails. Then cut to size and glue and nail one-by-two edge trim to the table edges. The unit sits right on the bin, covering it, and making it useful as a laundry table or any number of other things.

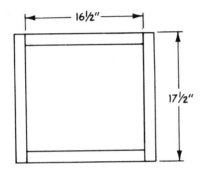

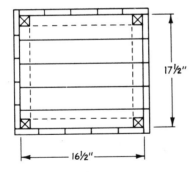

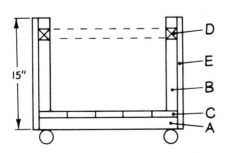

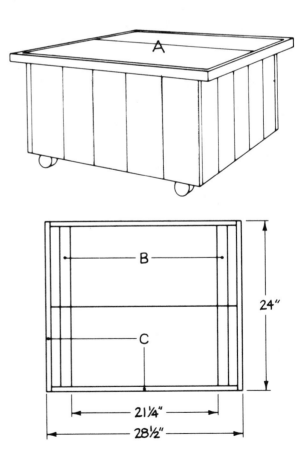

5–50 *(Courtesy of the Western Wood Products Association)*

Drawers

These simple drawers can serve innumerable storage purposes, and installation after construction is very easy.

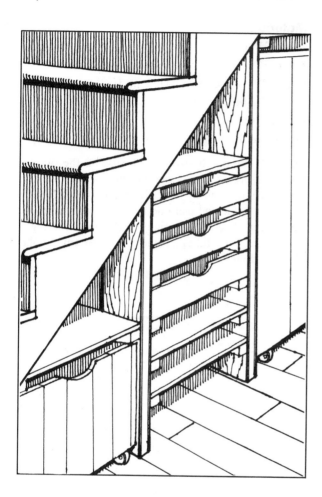

Cut pieces to size; then use a jigsaw or band saw to cut the handhole to size (make an arc over the space of 6″ wide by 2″ high). Glue and nail the sides to the front and back with 4d nails, keeping the unit square. Glue and nail the one-by-one drawer bottom supports in place using 3d nails. Position the supports ¼″ from bottom edges. Make a final check of square, and then glue and nail the ¼″-plywood bottom in place.

Position the two-by-two drawer glides 1″ inside the front edge of the dividers. Glue and nail in place using 6d nails. For the installation of a group of drawers, place drawer glides 7½″ apart vertically. If you apply a light coating of canning wax, beeswax, or candle wax, the drawers will slide more easily.

Materials

- two 22″ one-by-six drawer front and back A
- two 30″ one-by-six drawer front and back B
- two 22″ one-by-one (moulding stock) drawer supports C
- two 27″ one-by-one (sides) drawer supports
- ¼″ x 22″ x 28½″ plywood, waferboard or similar material, for drawer bottom D
- two 30″ two-by-two drawer glides E
- ½ lb 3d finishing nails
- ½ lb 4d finishing nails
- ½ lb 6d finishing nails
- wood glue
- clear or other finish

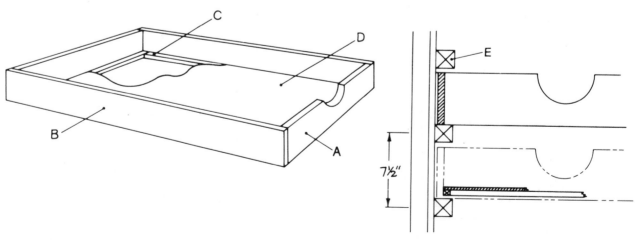

7½″

5–51 *(Courtesy of the Western Wood Products Association)*

Pull-Out Rolling Shelves

This unit may be arranged to suit many kinds of storage needs, from total shelving to the installation of a clothes rod. It is versatile and moves easily on its casters; I recommend getting top-quality casters, since this unit is moderately heavy when it is assembled and full of stored items.

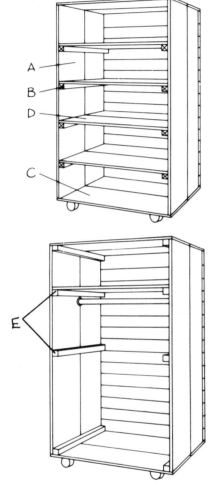

5–52 Pull-out rolling shelves. (*Courtesy of the Western Wood Products Association*)

Before starting construction, decide which unit you prefer; the shelving or the clothing storage. Assemble the sides for the shelving unit with the two-by-twos spaced as desired, or assemble sides for the clothes rod unit with nailing cleats at the top, bottom and middle of the sides. You can, if you like, add a shelf across the top.

Glue and nail the top and bottom to the assembled sides, making sure the unit stays square. Nail shelves (if it is a shelving unit) to the supports, keeping a close eye on squareness.

Place the unit face down on the floor, and check squareness by measuring diagonals; if the case is square, the diagonal measurements will be the same (double-check with a framing square or a large try square).

Either install the one-by-four back or the ¼″ plywood or hardboard back using glue and nails.

Install the casters; sand and finish. Your under-stairs storage is ready to use.

Materials

- four 60″ one-by-twelve sides A
- eight 22″ two-by-two shelf supports B
- six 22″ two-by-two nailing cleats for clothes storage (alternate spacing, as shown)
- four 36″ one-by-twelve top and bottom C
- eight 34½″ one-by-twelve shelves D
- seventeen 36″ one-by-twelve or ¼″ plywood or hardboard (I suggest the latter, as it reduces complexity and assembly time, as well as reducing weight) E
- clothes rod and brackets
- four 3″ swivelling casters
- ½ lb 3d finishing nails
- ½ lb 4d finishing nails
- ½ lb 6d finishing nails
- wood glue
- clear or other finish

6
Bedroom and Linens Storage

■ Raised-Panel Hope Chest

This chest is built of solid walnut except for the cedar lining and the floor, which may be of ½" hardwood plywood.

Hope chests traditionally are for girls and young women who are gathering linens and similar items in readiness for marriage; I made this one as a present for my youngest stepdaughter. There are other uses for such boxes, especially with a cedar lining.

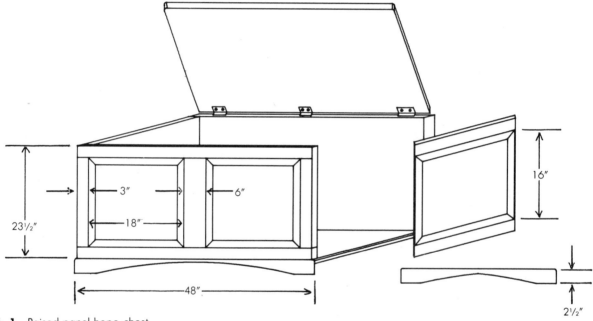

6-1 Raised-panel hope chest.

Materials

(All ¾" walnut unless otherwise specified.)
- four glued-up panels, 18½" x 16½" high
- one glued-up back, final size 24½" x 48"
- one glued-up top, final size 25½" x 50"
- one bottom, ½" oak or birch plywood, 47¼" x 23¼", or the equal in glued-up walnut
- six 3" x 18"
- one 6" x 18"
- two 4" x 48"
- four 4" x 24"
- two 2½" x 26"
- two 2½" x 50"
- 16 sq ft tongue and groove cedar lining

- 8 sq ft ½" cedar bottom lining
- three 3" brass hinges
- lock (optional)
- four casters (use casters of a size—1" or roller ball—to fit behind the small apron formed by the bottom edge trim pieces. You'll need blocking with the roller ball styles.)
- wood glue
- biscuits
- walnut stain
- satin tung oil or flat finish
- primer

Tools

- planer
- jointer
- table saw and dado blade set
- router and router table (minimum 1½ hp)
- panel raising bit set
- ½" straight bit
- large ogee or other decorative bit for moulding
- round-over bit for top edges
- lock mitre bit (optional)
- biscuit joiner

- mallet
- eight 24" bar clamps
- two or more four-way clamps
- two 6' bar clamps
- measuring tape
- square
- belt or reciprocating sander
- block or finishing sander
- 100- and 150-grit sandpaper
- 120-grit sanding belt or discs

The raised panels are glued up using biscuits, as are the top and back of the box, where no panels exist. If you prefer to have the entire box made of solid wood as I did, then go ahead and glue up a bottom of walnut, making sure to open that dado up to ¾" from the ½" presented.

Otherwise, the job is straightforward, resulting in a chest that is four feet long and two deep, and about the same height. The cedar lining cuts down on interior space only slightly, especially since I used tongue and groove cedar for the sides; the material is called closet liner and is only ⅜" thick. The bottom is done in local red cedar, planed to ½" thickness, so the overall loss is small.

6–2 Belt sander is used to remove ridges and other heavy mars.

Begin by planing all walnut stock to the same thickness; or have it done. Joint edges on at least one side of all stock.

Rip material to be glued up for panels, top and back, to the sizes that will come closest to giving finished sizes, plus an inch or two. Take care to align the material carefully, matching grain as closely as possible. Alternate growth rings on flat-sawn wood to reduce warping and cupping on large panels (the raised panels don't really qualify as large at about 16" x 18", but the back and top sure do).

Glue up panels using No. 10 biscuits. Use regular wood glue to make the joints; clamp and allow to dry at least overnight.

Use a belt or reciprocating sander to remove any imperfections and get a level surface. The reciprocating sander will give a smoother finish.

Finish the four panels that are to be raised to their final size. The final size should be 18½" by 16½" to allow a ¼" insert all around.

Size all of the stile and rail parts now. These are cut first so that you can make any needed adjustments in panel size (and in the size of other parts) as the assembly of the chest continues.

Set up the router table to cut the stiles and rails, and proceed to cut them. Setting up to cut stiles and rails means getting stock to exact length and width, with parallel sides and square ends. You will need a number of small pieces for test samples.

Set the cutters by eye first, and then use the samples to get the proper depth and height cuts. Use a mitre gauge to make short end of stock cuts, and, when the same cutter is used to cut all sides, make end cuts first. Move stock into the bit as fast as the cutter will take it.

If end-grain cuts are a real problem in rails (for example), make the end-grain cuts in wide stock. Here, rails are 3″ and 6″ wide, so you could possibly combine two or three 3″ rails, and cut the ends on a 7″ piece of stock that might then be trimmed to final 6″ size before cutting side grooves. This will eliminate splintering. The actual box design is simple, with the bottom set into either a ½″ (for plywood) rabbet or a ¾″ (for solid wood) rabbet. Ends are set into rabbets in the front and back edges, and all are glued in place.

Remember, when gluing up stiles and rails, that panels are not glued in place, except possibly for a touch of glue top and bottom to keep the panel centered.

If you do use the above idea, make sure your wider stock also has enough material in it to allow for kerfs—with standard blades, kerfs are almost exactly ⅛″.

6–5 Rabbets are cut after stiles, rails, and panels are assembled.

6–3 Stiles and rails are dry-assembled before the panels are finished.

6–6 Panels, stiles, and rails must be sanded carefully.

6–4 The edges of the floating raised panels are cut after stiles and rails are dry-assembled.

6–7 Arches in base pieces are laid out with a curved rule.

6–8 Each piece must be held square as it is assembled in rabbets and glue sets.

6–9 The main carcass is assembled, glued, and clamped.

6–10 Base pieces are attached; then the ball rollers on blocks are placed at each corner, with the rollers exposed about ½".

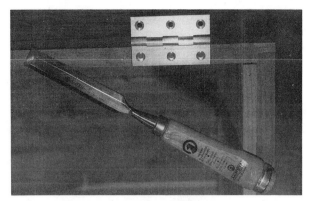

6–11 Hinges are mortised in with great care and a very sharp chisel.

6–12 Cedar lining is glued and clamped.

6–13 Hinges are installed, followed by the lid.

■ Bunk Bed Room Divider Bookshelves

This bunk bed design serves multiple purposes; though not strictly movable, it converts a room for two children into a much more useful space. It could be moved, however, if you move to a new house. This is not a small project; it takes six full panels of ¾" plywood, and a number of other items, plus, of course, the two mattresses.

6-14 Bunk bed/room divider. (*Courtesy of the American Plywood Association*)

Materials

- Six ¾" x 4' x 8' MDO or A-B interior plywood, oriented strand board, or waferboard
- four 1" x 6" x 77" lumber rails
- two 1" x 2" x 92" border trim
- one 1" x 2" x 38½" border trim
- one 1" x 2" x 41½" border trim
- six 1" x 2" x 10⅞" bookshelf trim
- four galvanized sheet metal angle clips, with screws

- one closet rod bracket for 1½" dowel
- 11' 1½"-diameter dowel for ladder rungs and guardrail
- twenty-four ⁵⁄₁₆" x 2" bolts with washers and nuts
- wood glue
- wood filler
- ½ lb 6d finishing nails
- one hundred No. 6 or No. 8 1¼" wood screws
- Paint

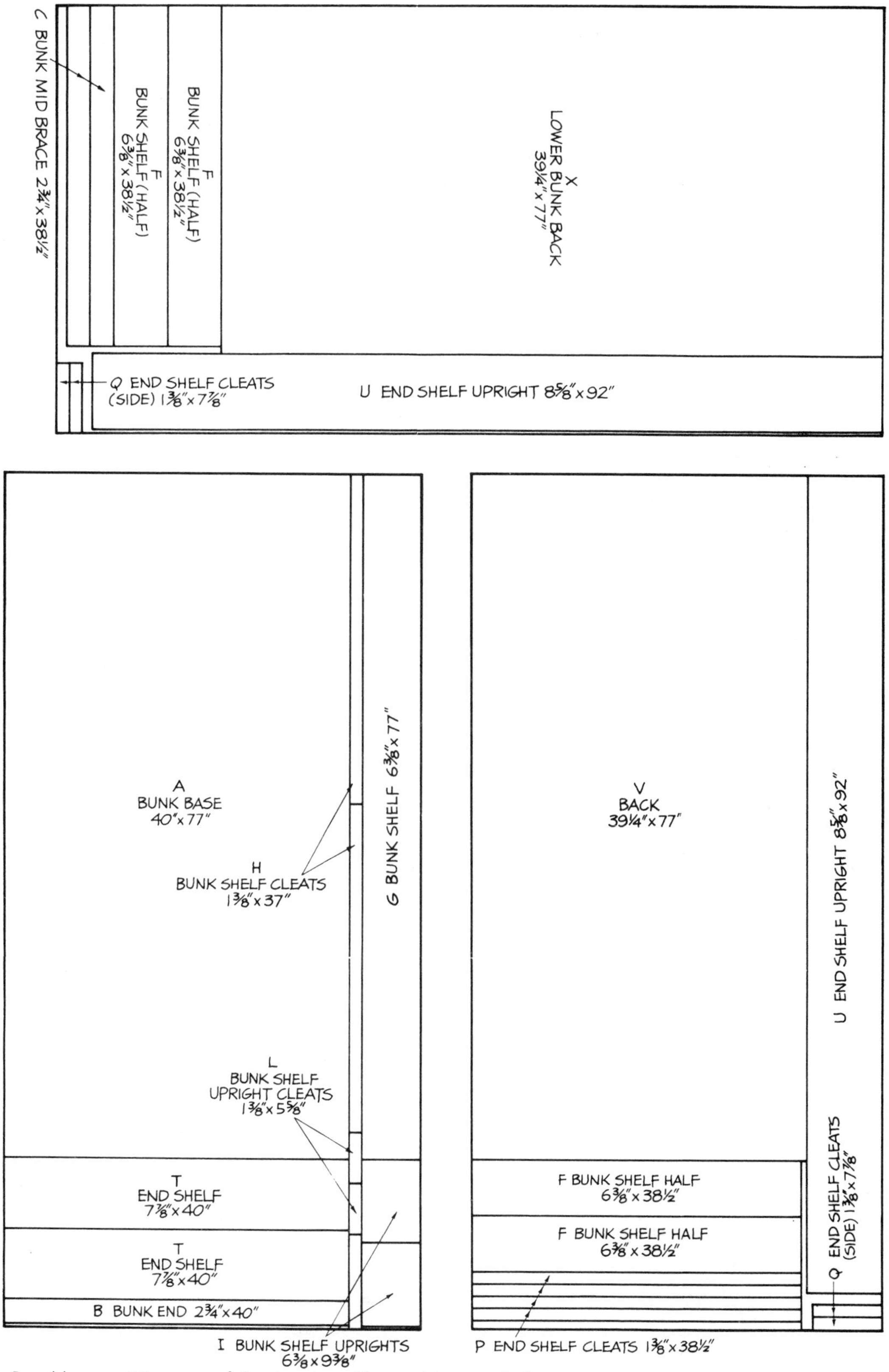
C BUNK MID BRACE 2¾"x38½"
F
BUNK SHELF (HALF)
6⅜"x38½"
F
BUNK SHELF (HALF)
6⅜"x38½"
X
LOWER BUNK BACK
39¼"x77"
Q END SHELF CLEATS
(SIDE) 1⅜"x7⅞"
U END SHELF UPRIGHT 8⅝"x92"
A
BUNK BASE
40"x77"
H
BUNK SHELF CLEATS
1⅜"x37"
G BUNK SHELF 6⅜"x77"
L
BUNK SHELF
UPRIGHT CLEATS
1⅜"x5⅝"
T
END SHELF
7⅞"x40"
T
END SHELF
7⅞"x40"
B BUNK END 2¾"x40"
I BUNK SHELF UPRIGHTS
6⅜x9⅜"
V
BACK
39¼"x77"
U END SHELF UPRIGHT 8⅝"x92"
F BUNK SHELF HALF
6⅜"x38½"
F BUNK SHELF HALF
6⅜"x38½"
Q END SHELF CLEATS
(SIDE) 1⅜"x7⅞"
P END SHELF CLEATS 1⅜"x38½"

6–15 Panel layout. (*Courtesy of the American Plywood Association*)

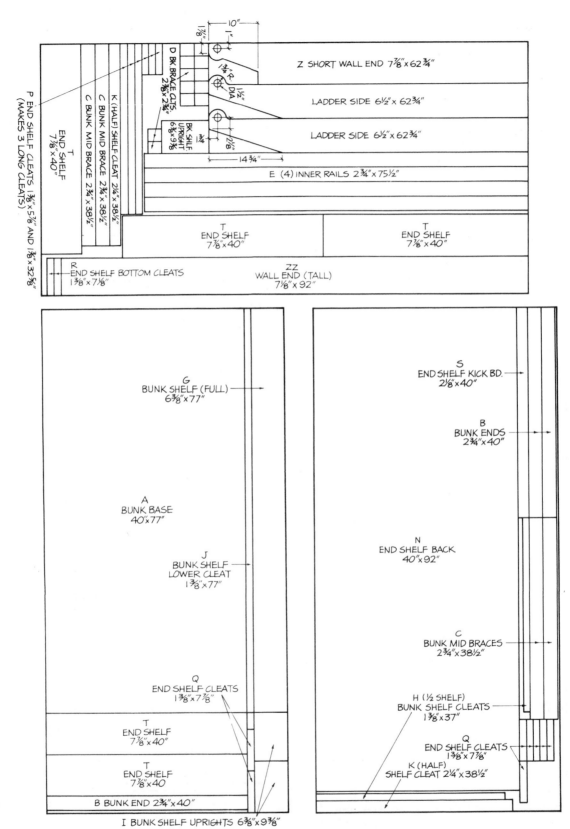

6-16 Panel layout. (*Courtesy of the American Plywood Association*)

Tools

- circular saw or table saw
- jigsaw
- drill
- $1/8''$ drill bit
- $5/16''$ drill bit for pilot holes, $1 1/2''$ drill bit for dowel holes; do NOT use a spade bit
- No. 2 Phillips driver bits
- screwdrivers
- claw hammer
- nail set
- square
- measuring tape
- finishing sander
- 100-grit sandpaper
- paintbrush

This is a straightforward assembly job; but it requires great care in layout, cutting, and later assembly. It's also a project of large size. It is, thus, not a beginner's project, and maybe not even a project for the intermediate, lone woodworker either.

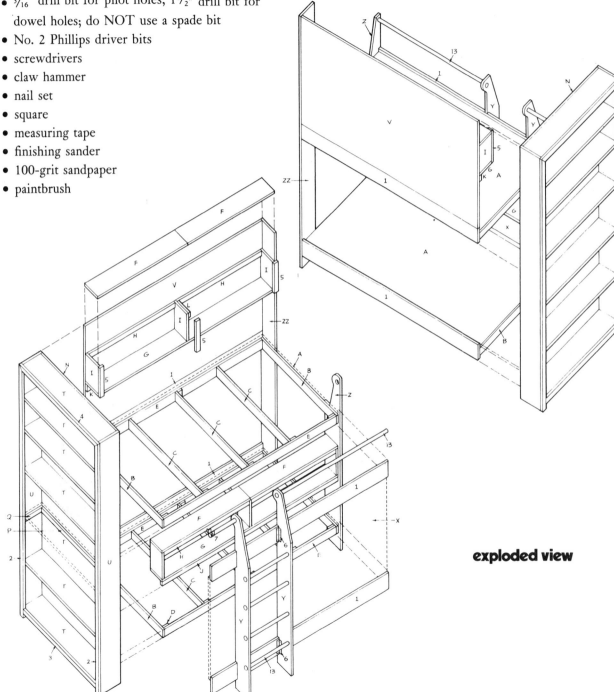

exploded view

6–17 Bunk bed/room divider. (*Courtesy of the American Plywood Association*)

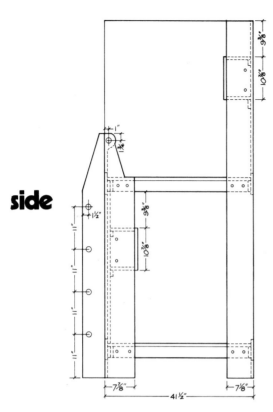

side

Begin with a single panel, using a compass or cardboard templates to mark any curved parts, and making sure to allow the standard 1/8″ kerf for cuts. Make cuts carefully, and go on to the next panel.

Assembly

Start the assembly with the lower bunk frame; then assemble the upper bunk frame, and add ends (you may wish to assemble the entire bookshelf unit first, too—it will work out easier that way). Keep an exceptionally careful eye on square all through this stage, because going even as little as 1/8″ out will throw off all of the later steps. As shown, the long bolts are used to assemble the bunk frames to the end pieces.

Continue assembly with the over-bunk shelves and bunk back panels. After that, drill the ladder uprights; assemble the ladder and place it.

Where the bolts are not used, use either glue and nails or glue and screws for assembly, setting all nails.

Finishing

Fill nail holes and plywood edges. After the filler dries, sand carefully, and finish in colors that will brighten children's outlooks.

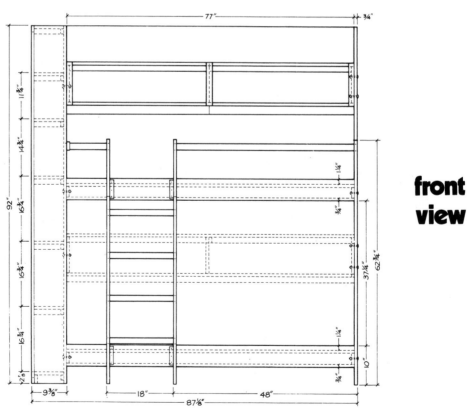

front view

6-18 Front and side views. (*Courtesy of the American Plywood Association*)

■ Stacking Storage Drawers

This version of movable storage is also very easy to make. The basic units are identical; so once set up, you can knock out as many as you need, and then stack them in the most useful configuration. In the configuration shown here, a group of six drawers is used to provide a dresser for a baby, with the larger units providing the base; the four smaller units stacked to configure the top as desired.

6–19 Stacking storage drawers. (*Courtesy of Georgia-Pacific Corporation*)

Tools

- circular saw or table saw
- dado blade (for cutting dadoes with table saw)
- router, ¾″ straight bit, edge guide
- 16-oz claw hammer and nail set
- drill, bits for handles
- four 24″ bar pipe clamps
- four 48″ bar or pipe clamps
- measuring tape and square
- finish sander
- 100- and 120- or 150-grit sandpaper

Materials

- two ¾″ x 4′ x 8′ hardwood plywood
- ⅛″ x 4′ x 4′ hardboard
- ½ lb 4d finish nails
- ¼ lb 2d finish nails
- wood glue
- eight handles, style as desired
- 50′ birch (or other species) hot-melt veneer edging
- stain, if desired
- satin or semi-gloss tung oil finish

Materials presented are for the configuration shown, and call for birch-faced hardwood plywood; you may use any face species you wish, or use an A or B face with paint.

Begin the project by laying out, in an economical manner, all pieces for the case backs on the sheets of plywood. Then continue by cutting all of the pieces to size, except for the case backs.

For the small cases, start with 18″ square tops and bottoms. Sides are 6½″ high by 18″ long (two per case). Cut the case backs from ⅛″ hardboard, each 18″ long by 8″ high. Cut the bottoms 17½″ long by 16⅜″ wide, with sides 5⅝″ by 17½″. Backs are 15⅝″ wide, while the fronts are 7¼″ by 17¼″.

Dado, or groove, the drawer sides and the back of the bottom piece for the drawer back. Set the grooves in ¾″ from the edges of the pieces; make the dado ⅜″ deep using a ¾″ setting on the dado blade set, or the ¾″ straight bit for the router.

To make the larger cases, the tops and bottoms are 3′ by 18″, with the sides 18″ by 8½″. The case back, of ⅛″ hardboard, is 36″ by 10″.

Cut drawer sides 17½″ by 7⅝″ high. Drawer bottoms are 34⅜″ wide by 17½″ long, while the drawer back is 33⅝″ wide. Cut the front to 35¼″ by 9¼″ high.

Grooves are cut just as for the smaller units, using the dado head or the ¾″ straight router bit, router, and edge guide.

For assembly, you will get the neatest job by making mitre cuts on edges that join; but to do such long mitres, you must have a table saw or radial-arm saw. The circular saw doesn't provide enough accuracy to do the job as it needs to be done.

Use the 4d finishing nails and wood glue to assemble each unit, clamping carefully after checking for square. Use just enough nails to make the assembly simpler, and to hold while glue is setting. Clamps are not essential for this project, but do ease the assembly; drive 2d nails into mitres so that the tips just project, and they'll help prevent the pieces from skidding as they're clamped. Finish nailing, and set the nails, after the clamps are in place and the edges are aligned and square.

Let the glue set overnight, and then remove the clamps. Measure for and drill holes for handles.

Sand carefully, first with 100-grit paper and then with finer paper. Use a tack cloth to remove dust, and apply, thinned by 50 percent, the first coat of finish. Let dry at least eight hours. If you're going to stain, now's the time, after the light sanding. Let stain dry at least twelve hours.

Sand lightly with 120- or 150-grit paper, and apply a full-strength coat. Finish with at least one more coat, allowing six to eight hours' drying time between coats. For best results, use at least four full-strength coats of tung oil—sanding, or steel-wooling (with 0000 steel wool) lightly between each coat.

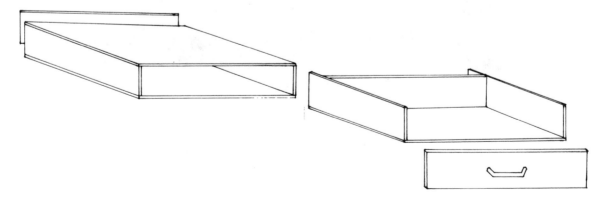

6–20 Stacking storage drawers. (*Courtesy of Georgia-Pacific Corporation*)

■ Bathroom Linen Storage

This fairly quick project is designed for use with linens, bath towels, and such; so it is suitable for a bathroom, a guest bedroom, or any area that could benefit from such storage. The storage shapes and sizes would be particularly useful in teenagers' bedrooms—able to serve many needs including linen storage, with space for a book or two.

Not only is this storage cabinet functional, it's attractive and easily built. All joints are butt joints, except for a couple of notch trims in the trim strips (cut those using a handsaw).

It's also easily reduced in one dimension if it proves too deep for your space (that 37+″ depth can be a lot for some areas). Simply subtract 10″, or 15″, from *all* 30″ measurements; that is, all material that measures 30″ to 38″ may be reduced by either 10″ or 15″ without changing other dimensions. Because storage is accessible from both sides, the wider units are very handy as long as space is available.

Of course, start by laying out the patterns on the plywood, making sure to leave at least ⅛″ for kerfs. Using a table saw, cut with the good face up. With the circular saw, cut with the good face down. For the handsaw or backsaw, cut with the good face up.

6–21 Bathroom storage. (*Courtesy of Georgia-Pacific Corporation*)

Tools

- circular saw or table saw
- handsaw or backsaw
- router, ⅜″ round-over bit
- mitre box
- 16-oz claw hammer
- nail set

- measuring tape
- square
- finishing sander
- 100-grit sandpaper
- tack cloth
- paintbrush

Assemble the ends, top, and bottom using 4d finishing nails and glue, and making sure the assembly stays square.

The dividers are positioned next; you may choose different spacing, but the ones shown here are placed 12″ and 20″ from the left side of the unit. That leaves 20″ for towel storage. Place dividers in 1⅛″ from the front edge. Secure the dividers with glue and 6d finishing nails.

Cut and place trim pieces as shown, using ¾″ or 1″ brads and wood glue.

The four supports are cut and secured into place with 4d nails and glue. These are flush with the front and rear edges.

To get rounded-over trim boards, a router is handy. Use a ⅜″ round-over bit to round the edges before or after cutting to length. Don't round the ends. Attach with 4d nails and glue. The tow trim boards without rounded edges are fitted so they're flush with the top of the unit and lapping over each support board. Nail and glue these into place.

Mitre and nail (with 4d nails) and glue the top trim boards. Next, notch the trim boards for the front and rear; make the notches 2½″ deep by ¾″ wide, so that the already placed trim strips are covered. Use glue and 4d nails to attach.

Set all nail heads and fill the holes with wood putty. Sand with 100-grit paper and coat with paint.

Materials

- two ¾″ x 32″ x 38″ plywood, B-C grade, top and bottom
- two ¾″ x 14″ x 37¼″ plywood, B-C, ends
- two ¾″ x 14″ x 35½″ plywood, B-C, dividers
- two ¾″ x 2½″ x 40½″ pine trim strips
- four ¾″ x 14″ half-round moulding, pine
- two ¾″ x 42″ half-round moulding, pine
- six ¾″ x 14″ x 1½″ rounded edge moulding
- four ¾″ x 14″ x 1½″ supports, pine
- box ¾″ or 1″ brads
- ½ lb 4d finishing nails
- ½ lb 6d finishing nails
- wood glue
- wood filler
- paint, as desired

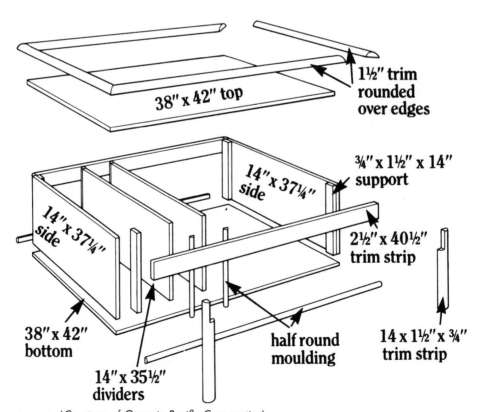

6–22 Bathroom storage. (*Courtesy of Georgia-Pacific Corporation*)

■ Desk That Grows

This desk set is not only fairly easily moved when empty, but its size can also be changed to suit the child for whom it is built. There is a 7½″ variability, for example, in seat and work surface height. The seat is moved up simply by removing it, upending the chair base and reinstalling the seat. The work surface moves up with a simple rearrangement of shelves and the drop-leaf desktop.

Best of all, the project takes only two panels of plywood, allowing you to go for the best quality and appearance. I suggest using an MDO plywood that is readily painted; youngsters seem to like bright colors more than they do a natural wood appearance. If the child for whom you're constructing the set feels otherwise, then it's not much more expensive to go to a top-quality oak- or birch-faced plywood, along with the appropriate iron-on veneer tape for covering the plywood edges.

6–23 Desk that grows. (*Courtesy of the American Plywood Association*)

Tools

- circular saw or table saw
- router, ¾″ straight bit and guide, or jig for dadoes (or dado blade set for table saw)
- jigsaw
- drill, ⅛″ bit for pilot holes, other bits as needed
- driver bit to fit screw heads
- square
- measuring tape
- finishing sander
- 100- or 120-grit sandpaper
- screwdriver
- claw hammer

Materials

- two ¾″ x 8′ x 4′ MDO or other plywood
- seventy-two No. 8 1¼″ wood screws for shelves, desk compartment, frame, chair back
- fifteen No. 8 1½″ wood screws for chair legs, fastening chair bottom to legs
- piano hinge, 34″ long, for desk top, plus screws
- two magnetic catch sets for desk closure
- 32″ small-link chain for desktop supports
- four eye screws for fastening chain
- wood filler or veneer edging tape
- wood glue
- enamel or clear finish

Begin by drawing all of the parts on the plywood, making sure to allow 1/8″ for kerfs. Use a compass, or cut shirt-cardboard templates, for the curves.

Lay all the vertical parts face down and draw the horizontal lines to locate the 3/8″ deep by 3/4″ dadoes.

Cut the dadoes with a router and 3/4″ bit and a dadoing jig, or with the table saw and a dado-blade set. With such long vertical pieces, the router is easier to use and control. Build a simple jig that has two long members just far enough apart to allow your router to slip

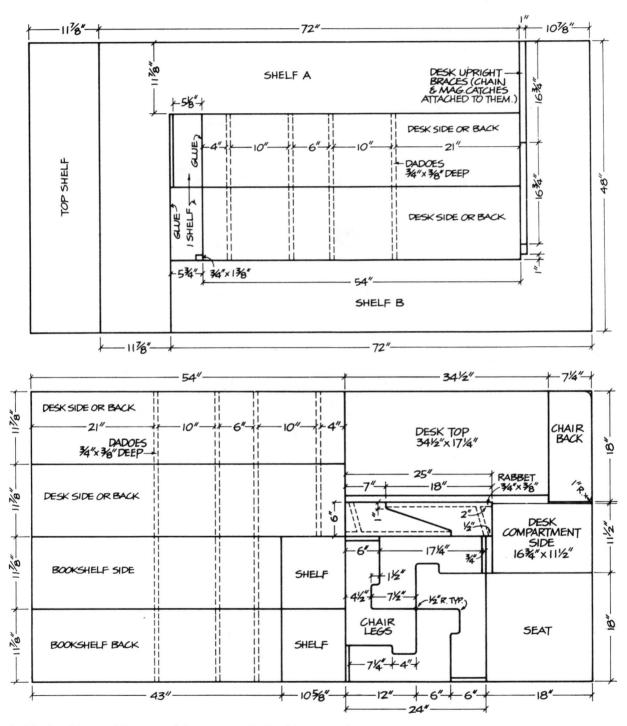

6-24 Panel layout. (*Courtesy of the American Plywood Association*)

along without wobbling from one side to the other. All the short members at the ends, at right angles, and screw and glue in place, maintaining the right angles. Overall, the long members must allow enough inside space for the widest dado to be cut (here about 11⅞″, but I recommend you make the jig 18″ to 24″ wide).

Drill screw holes through the dadoes, 2″ in from each edge on each part—make sure these distances are *exact* so you can later change the size of the project by interchanging parts.

For a paint finish, use wood putty on plywood edges, and sand smooth as you're sanding the rest of the project; do not fill until the project is assembled.

Assemble corner sections (vertical sides, and backs) and top shelf using glue and screws. Drill pilot holes for screws before doing the assembly. Next, install the piano hinge to join the desktop and shelf (this step may be left until finish is applied if you've gotten a piano hinge that won't accept paint, such as brass or chrome). Paint *all* parts.

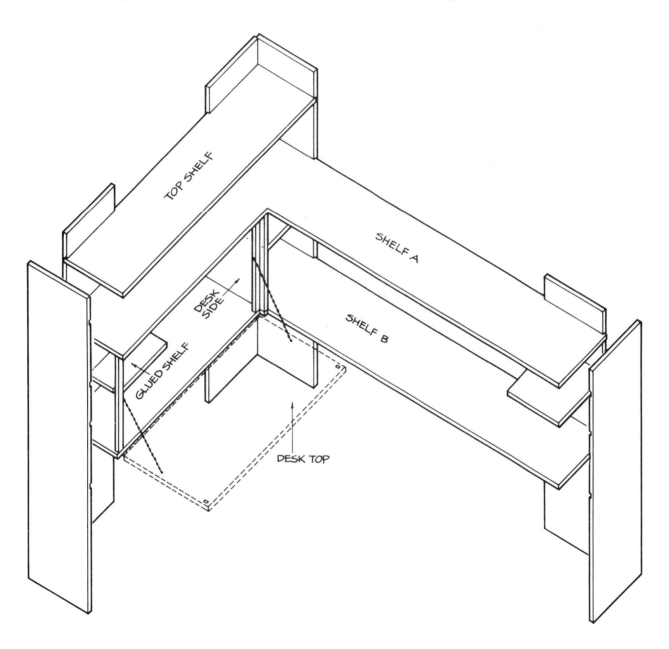

6–25 Desk that grows, child's version. (*Courtesy of the American Plywood Association*)

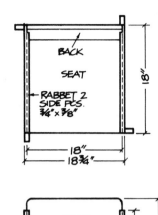

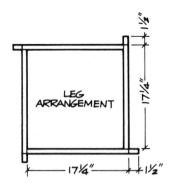

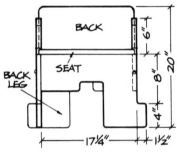

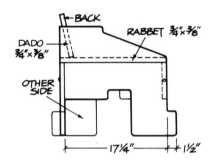

child seat

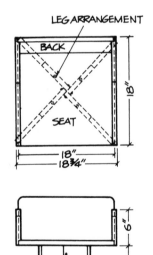

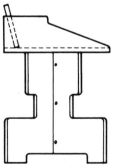

teen seat

6-26 Child seat and teen seat plans. (*Courtesy of the American Plywood Association*)

Install shelves in the desired arrangement, using *only* screws to fasten through previously drilled pilot holes.

Now, assemble 16¾″ by 11½″ desk compartment side panel, gluing and screwing it to the shelf. Two screws go into the shelf above the side panel, but glue is not used here, unless you wish the configuration to be permanent.

Install the front upright braces, and attach the desk support chains as in the drawings. Magnetic catches are installed on braces and strikers are installed to meet and match, but on the desktop.

Assemble the chair seat, then make dado cuts in the seat sides. The back is glued and screwed in place, as is the chair seat. The chair bottom is assembled at the desired height, using screws only. If you expect the chair to remain this size, then go ahead and use glue and screws for permanence.

Finish the chair seat and bottom, and mount the seat onto the bottom.

When you later change sizes, you'll need to fill the screw holes that are left and add touch-up paint or other finish.

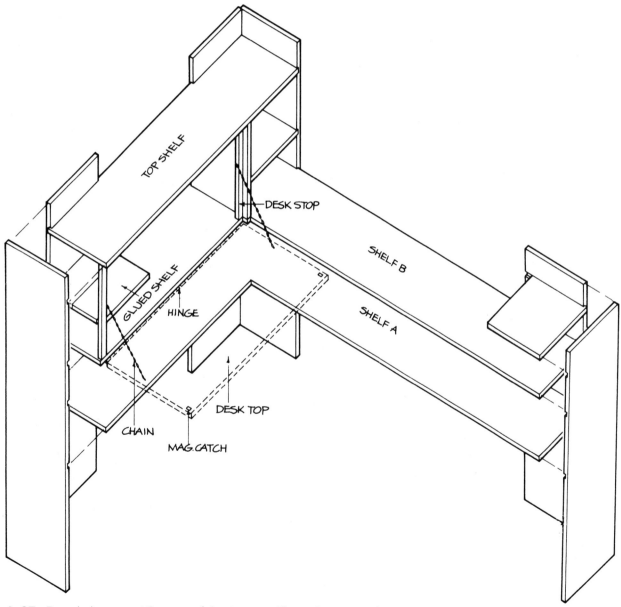

6-27 Teen desk version. (*Courtesy of the American Plywood Association*)

■ Toy or Linen Box

This plywood box is quickly built, sturdy, and of a size that is easily moved even when filled. You may add corner blocks and 1″ casters to ease around-the-room movement if you wish; but the rope handles should serve for most purposes.

Mark the plywood pieces, making sure to leave ⅛″ for kerfs. Cut the plywood pieces to size, and then cut ½″ by ⅜″ dadoes in the ends, front, and back 3″ up from the bottom edge. Mitre the ends, front, and back to fit. Drawings for two versions are given.

Mark the side and front raised design, allowing 4″ at each end on the front, and for the sides.

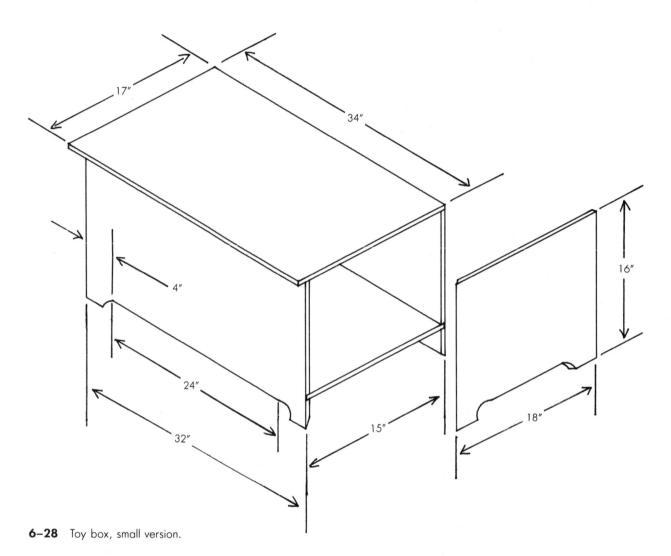

6–28 Toy box, small version.

Tools

- circular saw or table saw
- dado blade
- router (instead of dado set), ½″ straight bit and edge guide
- jigsaw or scroll saw
- drum sander
- 16-oz claw hammer
- nail set

- drill, ⅜″ drill bit for handle ropes
- four 24″ bar pipe clamps
- four 48″ bar or pipe clamps
- measuring tape
- square
- finishing sander
- 100- and 150-grit sandpaper
- tack cloth

Materials (small version)

- two 32" x 16" x ¾" plywood, A-C, front and back
- two 16" x 18" x ¾" plywood, A-C, ends
- one 17¼" x 31¼" x ½" B-C plywood, bottom
- one 17" x 34" x ¾" plywood, A-C, top
- paint or stain and clear finish
- wood filler (or veneer tape if stain and clear finish is to be used)
- ½ lb 4d finishing nails
- ¼ lb 2d finishing nails
- two 1½" x 3" hinges, or special toy box hinges that prevent too-rapid closing
- two 16" x ⅜" manila rope

Center a 24"-long line 2" up from the bottom of the front, and a 10" line on the sides. Join the lines with a compass set at a 2" radius. Use a jigsaw or scroll saw to cut the curves and the straight part. Sand with a drum sander in the curves.

Check the fit of the bottom, ends, and sides without glue. Assemble clamps and get them set within about 1" of finish clamping needs.

Spread glue in mitres and in dadoes, keeping dado glue spread fairly light. Assemble the parts, and clamp; glue, assemble, and clamp the back and both ends first. Insert the bottom, and then position the front. Use 4d finish nails on the corners, nailing carefully.

Measure for two ⅜" holes in each end, and back up behind the holes with scrap stock. Drill two ⅜" holes, 6" apart, in each end; center the 6" on the assembled end, about 10" up from the bottom of the plywood end panels.

Install the hinges and top.

Set nails and fill nail holes and edges with wood putty. Sand with 100-grit sandpaper. If you go for a clear finish, use a 150-grit sandpaper and veneer tape edging.

Remove the hinges, and paint or coat with stain and clear finish. Reinstall all of the hardware once the finish dries.

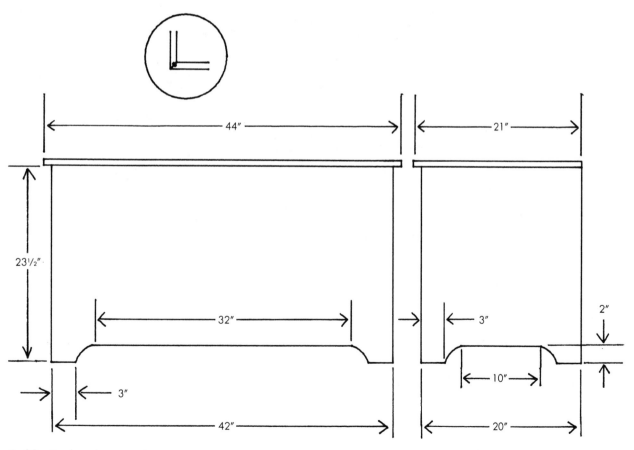

6–29 Toy box, large version.

■ Stagecoach Toy Box

This toy box can serve a number of purposes but is mobile enough to allow easy pickup of toys scattered through much of the house. Its good size (about 2' x 3' long, without the tongue) make it useful as a toy as well as a toy box—allowing children to add some Wild West fantasy to their playtime. The side door opens, the wheels roll, and there is a seat in front, on which one child may sit as the stagecoach "whip" or driver and another may ride shotgun.

To add to its good features, this project takes only a single sheet of ½" plywood! Any child will be absolutely delighted with this toy box.

6–30 Stagecoach toy box. (*Courtesy of the American Plywood Association*)

Materials

- one ½" x 4' x 8' MDO plywood
- two 1⁵⁄₁₆"-diameter dowels, 22" long (axles)
- one 1⁵⁄₁₆"-diameter dowel, 8" long (tongue)
- twelve ½" half-rounds, 1⅛" long (front wheel spokes)
- twelve ½" half-rounds, 2⅛" long (rear wheel spokes)
- two 1½" door hinges
- one metal door handle
- 6d finishing nails
- No. 6 1" wood screws
- wood glue
- wood putty
- latex paint or enamel

Begin by laying out the parts on the plywood sheet. Try to fit the drawing. Use a compass or cardboard templates to get curves and circles. Make sure to leave room for saw kerfs (about ⅛″), but be careful not to waste space on this project, as there is very little scrap wood from which you can recut parts. Cut parts carefully after checking the layout.

Glue and nail supports (O, P, Q) to sides (H, I). See the side view. Screw hinges to door (E), and then to side (H).

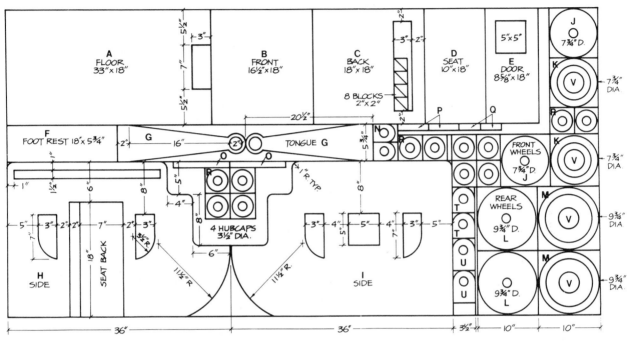

6-31 Panel layout. (*Courtesy of the American Plywood Association*)

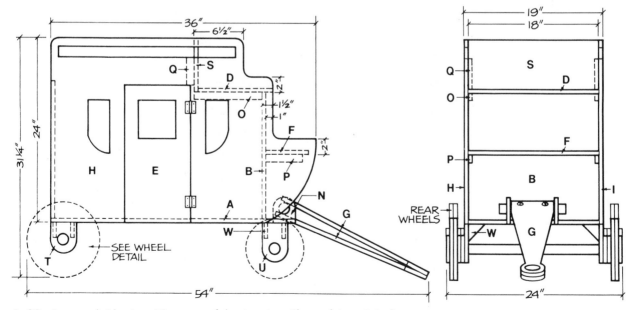

6-32 Front and side view. (*Courtesy of the American Plywood Association*)

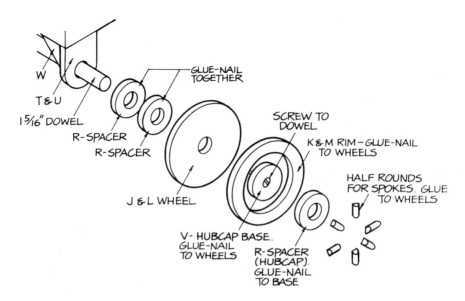

6-33 Wheels. *(Courtesy of the American Plywood Association)*

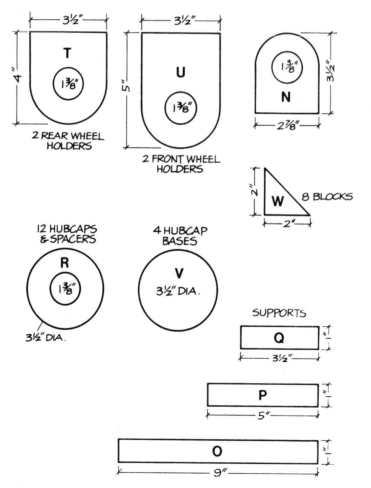

6-34 Details. *(Courtesy of the American Plywood Association)*

Next, begin assembling the sides, and floor, using glue and nails. Add the front and back, squaring the assembly where needed.

Assemble (glue and nail) set back (S), seat (D), and foot rest (F) to sides and to supports (O, P. Q). Glue and nail two corner blocks (W) to the rear wheel holders (T), and to the front wheel holders (U). Complete assembly to floor of the coach box.

Tools

- table or circular saw
- jigsaw
- claw hammer
- screwdrivers, No. 2 Phillips and $\frac{3}{16}''$, $\frac{1}{8}''$ straight
- drill, $\frac{1}{8}''$, $\frac{1}{2}''$ bits (for starting holes for jigsaw)
- No. 2 Phillips drive bits
- finishing sander
- 100-grit sandpaper
- paint brush

Assemble the wheels, and attach them to the axles. Glue and nail the tongue holders (N) to the floor, then screw the tongue parts (G) together at the handle end and at tongue dowel.

Sand with 120-grit paper, prime and paint. Use a flat or satin latex paint, and coat carefully. To add the lettering and decorative stripping shown in the photograph, start at your office supply store. Press-on letters in many styles and sizes are available, as is press-on striping. To keep the lettering and striping looking good over time, coat with a clear finish.

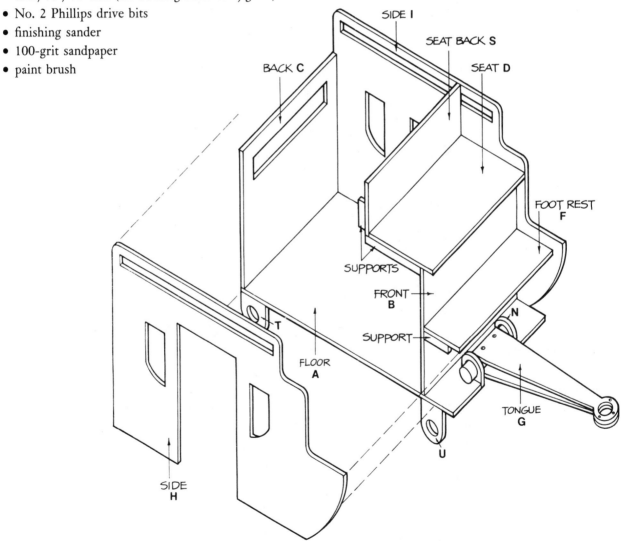

6–35 Stagecoach toy box. (*Courtesy of the American Plywood Association*)

■ Flip-Top Chest

This is another fast and simple project, of hardwood plywood this time. It provides easy storage for linens, towels and similar items in any room of the house, and may be placed on casters for easy mobility.

The sizes listed below for the plywood cutting include 1″ allowances for mitred corners on parts B, D, E, C, and for the undercarriage that makes this chest appear to float.

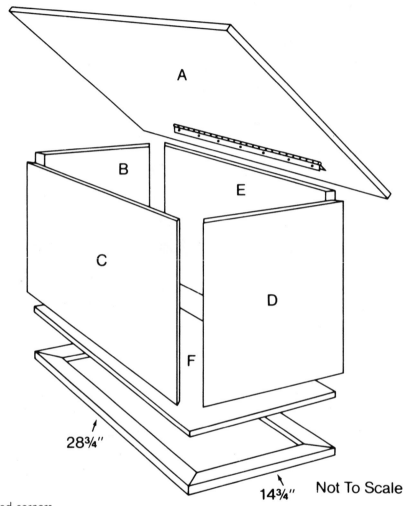

6–36 Flip-top chest, mitred corners.

Materials

- one ¾″ x 4′ x 8′ hardwood plywood
- one one-by-two x 6′ lumber to match plywood
- one one-by-two x 4′ lumber to match plywood
- one 31½″ piano hinge

12′ of wood veneer tape to match plywood

- two 16″ x ⅜″ manila rope
- 6d finishing nails
- twelve No. 6 1″ flathead wood screws
- wood glue

- wood filler to match wood grain
- tung oil finish
- tack cloth
- brush

Cut sizes

- A 24″ x 40″
- B 17″ x 15″
- C 31″ x 15″
- D 17″ x 15″
- E 31″ x 15″
- F 13½″ x 27½″

Bottom framing members are cut 28¾″ long (two) and 14¾″ long (two).

Cut to the stated size and then mitre to final size for the four pieces to be mitred. Assemble the mitred base unit first, using 6d finishing nails and glue. Next, check the fit of the sides—and front and back. Assemble one end and the front, and then do the same with the back and the opposite end. Use glue and 6d finishing nails to fasten.

Check square as you go, and, after 45 to 90 minutes, assemble the two L-shaped units; you may assemble them earlier, but the glue will not have set up. Nail starting about one inch in from the joint ends, and nail every four inches. If you're having trouble keeping the L shapes square, go ahead and do the four-side assembly quickly, so that adjustment is possible.

Once the box is assembled, insert the bottom and fasten in place with 6d finishing nails and glue. Nail as above.

Tools

- table saw
- claw hammer
- screwdriver for hinge screws
- drill, bit for hinge screw pilot holes, ³⁄₃₂″ bit for pilot holes to fasten floating base to bottom
- nail set
- square
- measuring tape
- 100- or 150-grit sandpaper
- finishing sander

Center the floating base and assemble that to the bottom, using 1″ wood screws and glue, placing the screws through the floating base.

Center the box on the underside of the top, and mark at the back edge, and at least two corners. Position the piano hinge in place and drill pilot holes. Install enough screws to check the fit and action of hinge.

Measure for two ³⁄₈″ holes in each end, and back up behind the holes with scrap stock. Drill two ³⁄₈″ holes, 6″ apart, in each end: center the 6″ on the assembled end, about 10″ up from the bottom of the plywood end panels.

Remove the hinge. Iron on veneer tape for exposed edges of top. Sand with 120- or 150-grit paper.

Finish, inside and out, with at least three coats of tung oil, thinning the first coat 50 percent. Wait at least six hours between coats.

If casters are to be used, install plate casters at the corners using ¾″ screws.

Install the rope handles, knotting carefully on the inside so they cannot pull through the holes. If pull-through seems apt to be a problem (it shouldn't), simply tie each knot around a ½″ x 3″ piece of dowel.

Reinstall the hinge, and place the finished chest where desired, from the living room to the bedroom to the bathroom.

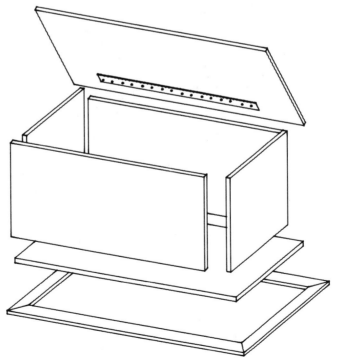

6–37 Flip-top chest, butt-joined corners.

■ Fort Bunker Beds

These bunk beds combine cubbyholes for storage and for climbing with comfortable sleeping space. The bunks-in-a-fort design provides storage for toys and hiding places for treasures. The cubbyholes provide lots of space for clothing, linens, sleeping bags and extra pillows. The boxes form the bed frame, stacked one upon the other in differing configurations, while shelving boards between the boxes provide trim and shelf space. The beds are standard 39″ x 75″ twin mattresses, with plywood forming the mattress platforms. Disassembly and relocation is readily accomplished with the removal of a few screws.

Overall, the project is designed to take a 5½″ by 8½″ floor area under an 8′ ceiling. The unit works well either as a room center or with the headboards against a wall.

There are as many ways and colors in which to finish this project as there are people who will build it. Try using white wiping stain over the solid woods, with bright colors used for accents on shelving and reveal boards.

This is not an easy project; so please review carefully all materials and tool needs. Keep a check on measurements and make corrections or allow for changes as you proceed. Take your time and read all instructions before starting.

6–38 Fort Bunker beds offer children ample sleeping space, and a great deal of storage room, plus plenty of opportunity for the imagination to roam. (*Courtesy of the Western Wood Products Association*)

Tools

- table saw, radial-arm saw, or circular saw
- router, edge guide, bits, as needed
- mitre box or power mitre saw
- electric drill, bits, to fit pilot hole needs, and a countersink for the flathead screws
- screwdriver and chisel
- tape measure and framing square
- brush and steel wool
- 100-grit sandpaper and finishing sander

Materials

(*Unless otherwise specified, pine, spruce, fir or hem-fir*)

Base Platform
- 175′ two-by-two
- 24′ one-by-three
- 51′ one-by-two
- 52′ one-by-twelve

Modules
- 200′ one-by-twelve

Reveal boards
- 68′ one-by-twelve

Upper Platform
- 80′ one-by-twelve
- 24′ two-by-two
- 45′ one-by-two
- 18′ one-by-three

Rafter

- 40′ two-by-four
- 8′ two-by-six
- 14″ x 16″ x ½″ Baltic plywood

Mattress Support

(Both below are ¾″ plywood, at least B-B Interior grade)

- one 40½″ x 76½″ (from a 4′ x 8′ panel)
- one 59½″ x 100½″ (from a 5′ x 10′ panel)

Further Materials

- flathead wood screws, as indicated: 1¼″; 1½″; 2″
- 1 lb 4d finish nails
- 1 lb 6d finish nails
- 3′ x ¼″ wood dowel
- four ½″ x 14″ threaded steel rods
- fifty-eight ⅜″ wood buttons
- four 7″ wood balls
- wood filler
- clear finish
- white or other wiping stain
- enamel

Start the project by cutting, and then notching as shown, the two-by-two framing for the base platform. Cut six two-by-twos to 100½″ length, and cut another five to 64½″ length (if good, straight two-by-twos are available and transportable, 14′ lengths are the best for this job, as each 14′ two-by-two will make one 100½″ and one 64½″, leaving less than 3″ of total waste). Notches are placed as shown in the drawings, and are ¾″ deep.

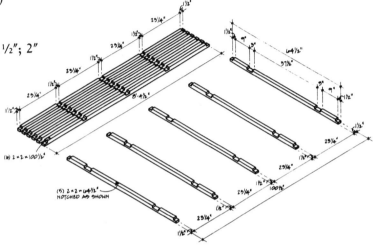

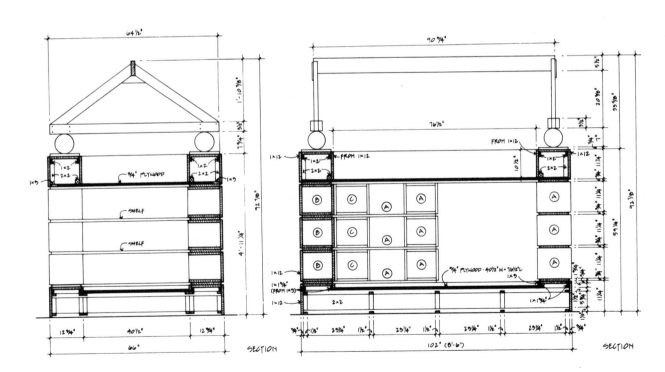

6-39 *(Courtesy of the Western Wood Products Association)*

The Frame

Put the frame together edge-gluing the doubled two-by-twos for greatest strength. As you go through the next steps, keep a check on the squareness of the frame. Use glue and a single 1¼″ screw per joint to secure the frame. Screws must be set off-center, and countersunk, or the next step won't work correctly.

Thirty two-by-two posts, each 5¾″ long, are now cut, and installed on the frame, using 3″ screws from the underside of the frame.

Construct a second frame section identical to the bottom frame section, and position it on the posts, driving 3″ screws in from the top.

Set the frame up on four small tables or other stands, making it easier to work on; make sure the tables are level so that the base is level when set on them.

Cut two one-by-twelves to 102″ long, with corners mitred. Cut two more to 66″ long, again with corners mitred. Glue the one-by-twelves to the outside of the frame and at the mitred corners. Nail in place using 2″ nails, doing the nailing from the inside of the frame.

Cut two one-by-threes to 100½″ and two to 40½″, and place as shown, gluing and clamping in place. Make sure the inside face of the long one-by-three aligns with the joint of the doubled two-by-two below it (see Detail C). Glue the short one-by-threes in place, end-nailing them to the long one-by-threes.

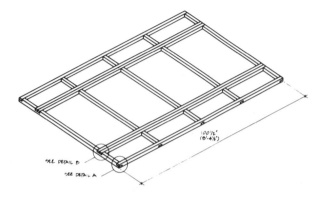

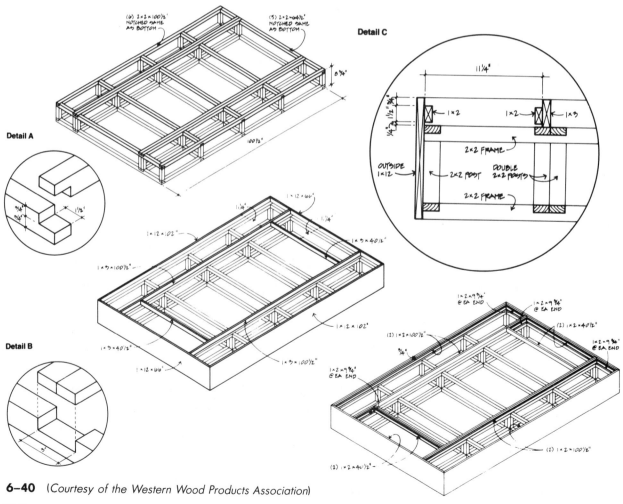

6–40 (Courtesy of the Western Wood Products Association)

Cut four one-by-twos to 100½″ lengths, plus four more at 40½″ lengths. Next, cut four one-by-twos to 9¾″ lengths. Glue and nail the one-by-two ledgers to the frame, allowing ¾″ at the top and ¼″ space at the bottom.

Next, cut two one-by-twelves to 100½″ and two to 40½″. Glue and clamp the one-by-twelves to the one-by-two ledgers.

Cut the 40½″ by 76½″ plywood panel, and drill ¾″ finger holes in each corner of the panel so it can be readily moved.

Cut one-by-twelve boards; one 38¼″ long, one 64½″ long, one 49½″ long, and one 11¼″ long.

At this point, you must decide whether or not you wish to screw everything together before you finish the unit. Finishing each module by itself, before assembling the final unit, may give a more interesting look, and make finishing easier, because you can use different stains or colors of enamel without worrying about slopping it on a to-be-stained, or already-stained, piece.

The reveal boards attach as shown, with 1½″ screws.

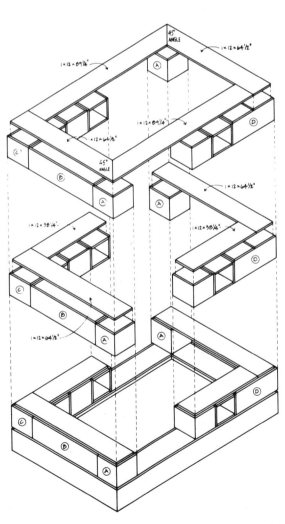

6-41 *(Courtesy of the Western Wood Products Association)*

Module A

Box modules A are built now, and you need eighteen of them. Cut thirty-six ¾" by 11¼" by 12" (one-by-twelve-by-twelve). Next, cut and mitre one side edge of each of thirty-six ¾" by 11¼" by 12¾" (one-by-twelve by 12¾") pieces. Mitre two side edges of eighteen one-by-twelve by 12¾" (same base size as preceding thirty-six boards). Keep the wood grain running in the direction shown, if at all possible.

Assembly is identical for all eighteen boxes. Assemble using 1½" nails and glue; try to place the nails on sides where they are not going to be seen. Keep a check on square as you assemble *each* box.

Module B

You need only three rectangular Module B units. Cut six 39"-long one-by-twelves, and six 40½"-long one-by-twelves. Cut six 11¼" one-by-twelves for ends (¾" x 12" x 11¼" real measurements). Assemble the modules with the ends and 39" lengths fitted inside the 40½"-long lengths, using 1½" nails and glue. Keep boxes square as you're fastening them.

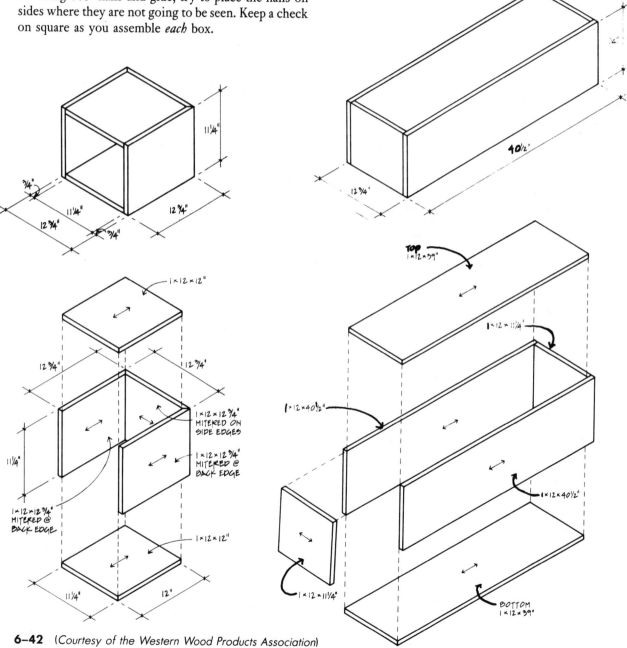

6-42 (Courtesy of the Western Wood Products Association)

Module C

Module C, of which you need three, takes three 12″ one-by-twelves, two 12¾″ one-by-twelves, one 25½″ one-by-twelve, and one 12¼″ one-by-twelve. You need to chisel or rout or otherwise cut a ¼″-deep by ¾″-wide groove 12¾″ from one end, and 12″ from the other on the 25½″-long board.

Assemble as with the other modules, noting that the only mitre joint on this one is the back joint. All other joints are butt joints. Use 1½″ nails and glue.

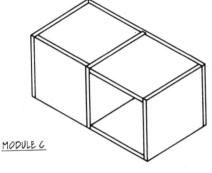

MODULE C

Module D

Module D again is a triplet, so you need to triple all pieces. The back is again a 25½″ one-by-twelve piece, with a dado centered as is the one in Module C. You also need two 12″ one-by-twelve pieces, and four 12¾″ one-by-twelve pieces.

Assemble as shown in the drawing, noting this time that *all* joints are butt joints. Use 1½″ nails and glue.

Reveal boards are cut now, with two 64½″ one-by-twelves and two 38¼″ one-by-twelves. Attachment is from the top, with two 1¼″ screws per board. The next tier of modules takes identical reveal board sizes, but the final level takes two 89¼″ one-by-twelves with one end mitred and two 64½″ one-by-twelves with one end mitred: These meet at the mitred ends over A modules.

To reduce the problems with setting up and mitring 11¼″-wide boards (the actual width of a one-by-twelve), for the shorter boards, the inside length is 53¼″ and for the longer boards it is 78″. Again, attachment is from the top with 1¼″-long screws.

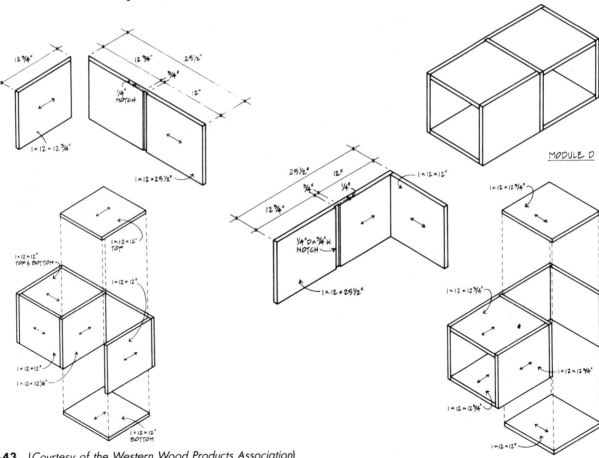

6–43 (*Courtesy of the Western Wood Products Association*)

Upper Platform

The upper platform is cut to 100½″ by 59½″, after which a 100½″-long one-by-three is glued and clamped along each side.

Your next task is cutting one-by-two ledgers to length, two each, as follows: 100½″; 63″; 79½″; 42″. Place the ledgers ¾″ below the top on the inside of the outer frame, and the same on the outside of the inner frame, gluing and nailing in place with 1¼″ nails.

Ball Assemblies

Cut two one-by-twelves to 78″ lengths and two to 64½″ lengths, and place as shown, gluing them in place. Drill 1½″-diameter corner holes for the wood ball assemblies.

Cut four two-by-fours to 10″ long, and shape as shown in the drawing. Drill a 9/16″ hole in the center of the step on each piece. Drill a matching hole in each 7″ ball if yours are not predrilled.

If you're unable to locate 7″ wood balls, use 7″ cubes of your own construction, laminating four pieces of 7″ two-by-eights and trimming to final size. Cut four 11¼″ squares from one-by-twelve stock, and drill 9/16″ holes in the centers. Put a nut on the top of a ½″ by 14″ threaded rod and insert the rod through the two-by-four, the ball, and the one-by-twelve base. Attach a nut to the bottom of the rod and tighten (do not adjust the top of the nut, which must be flush with the top of the rod—make all adjustments, and tighten, on the lower nut only).

Position the ball assemblies at the corners so that the end of the threaded rod drops into the holes in the top frame.

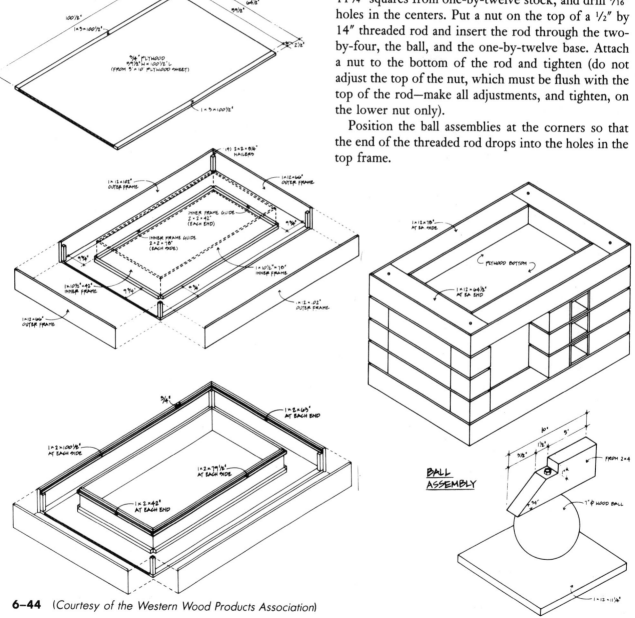

6-44 (*Courtesy of the Western Wood Products Association*)

Rafter

To make the rafter, cut rafter joists from four two-by-fours, 64½″ long. Then cut four 40″ two-by-four rafters with 34 degree angle top cuts, as shown. Mark the angle at the top, and cut. Then measure down 38″ and mark the 124 degree angle, and cut as shown. Check 3½″ and 1¼″ dimensions before cutting the second angle, and reset if necessary.

Assemble end rafters using two two-by-four joists for the base. Lace a two-by-six block between the end rafters at the top. Line up lower edges and fasten the joists to the rafters with two 2″ screws on each side. Counterbore screws ¼″ and install ⅜″ wood buttons.

Cut rafter gussets from Baltic birch plywood (Detail K), after cutting a two-by-six ridge rafter to 90¾″ long, and setting it in place between the end rafters. Attach the gusset to the ridge and end rafters with glue and five 1½″ screws per end. Counterbore screws ¼″ and finish off with ⅜″ wood buttons.

Final Assembly

Lift the top frame into position on top of the ball assembly. Attach the frame to the ball assembly with two 2″ screws on each side. Attach the ball assembly to the bed with four 2″ screws in each one-by-twelve base. Counterbore all of these screws and cap off with ⅜″ wood buttons.

If you've done most of your finishing as you've gone along, the unit is now ready for use, after the mattresses are added.

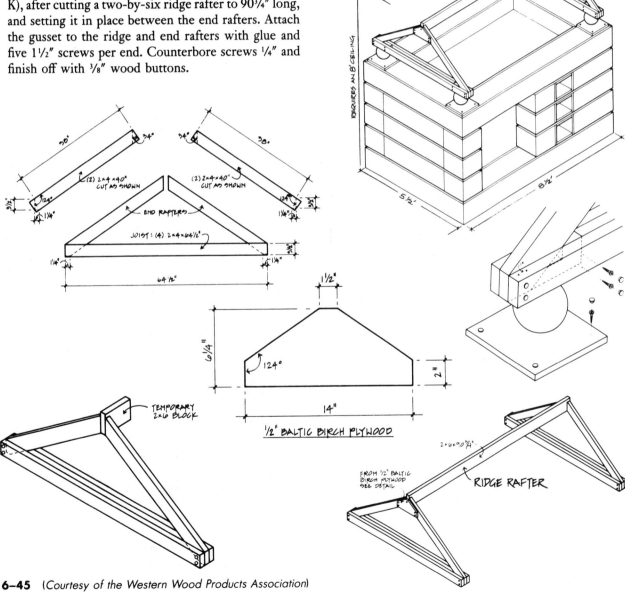

6–45 (Courtesy of the Western Wood Products Association)

■ Modular Storage System

If you have children, you know what a problem toy storage is; if you don't know yet, you will!

The modules described here work exceptionally well with everything from teddy bears and other stuffed toys to puzzles and dolls and balls and most other games, and, of course, the plethora of oversize books that most children quickly accumulate. As the children grow and the coloring books and stuffed an-imals are replaced with other items, these modules continue to remain useful with just some minor rearranging, and possibly an additional unit or two.

There is a further benefit; the modules are designed to aid children in using their imaginations to let the units serve as props for play. The units might become a kitchen or a bookstore—or a fort, or any number of imaginary play supports. The unit is designed for ease of assembly, with four basic modules that may be changed slightly to suit differing conditions.

6–46 Kid-size modular storage system. (*Courtesy of the Western Wood Products Association*)

Materials

(Unless otherwise specified, all wood is pine, spruce, fir or hem-fir.)

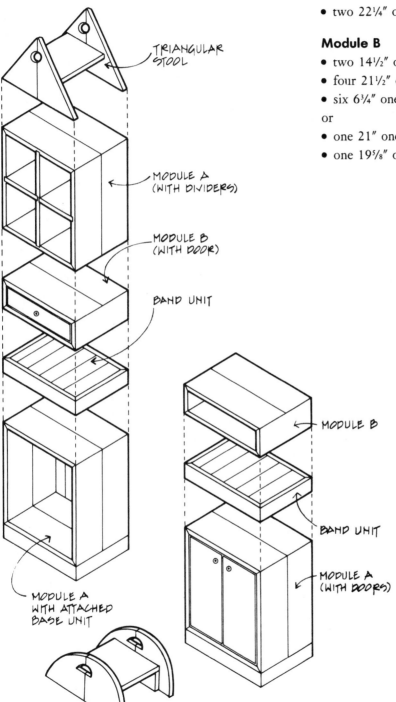

Module A
- four 24″ one-by-eight, sides
- four 21½″ one-by-eight, top and bottom
- six 23½″ one-by-four, back
- two 22¼″ one-by-twelve, doors

Module B
- two 14½″ one-by-eight, sides
- four 21½″ one-by-eight, top and bottom
- six 6¾″ one-by-four, back

or

- one 21″ one-by-eight
- one 19⅝″ one-by-eight, door

Base unit
- two 21½″ one-by-three, sides
- two 14½″ one-by-three, sides
- two 14½″ one-by-three, blocking
- two 20″ one-by-three, blocking
- six 13″ one-by-four, decking

Band unit
- two 21½″ one-by-three, sides
- two 14½″ one-by-three, sides
- two 14½″ one-by-three, blocking
- two 20″ one-by-three, blocking
- six 13″ one-by-four, decking

Dividers
- two 23″ one-by-eight vertical
- four 10⅛″ one-by-eight horizontal

Triangle/stool
- two 30″ one-by-twelve, ends
- one 13″ one-by-twelve, seat
- two 13″ one-by-six, seat supports

Half circle/stool
- two 22″ one-by-twelve, ends
- one 13″ one-by-twelve, seat
- one 13″ one-by-three, seat
- two 13¾″ one-by-six, seat support

6–47 Kid-size modular storage system. (*Courtesy of the Western Wood Products Association*)

Module A

Edge-glue and clamp one-by-eights to make the sides for module A, and then repeat the process to make the backs (overall, you need two 96″ one-by-eights. When the glue sets, cut pieces to length.

Assemble module A after mitring the edges of the sides, top, and bottom, and rabbeting the back edge for the back insertion. Rabbets are ½″ wide by ¾″ deep to accept nominal 1″ back boards (actual measurement will be ¾″); you may use the table saw and a dado head to make this rabbet cut—or two passes with a straight blade, instead of using the router.

Apply glue to the mitred corners and assemble with four 4d nails per corner. Check the corners with a framing square or a try square; with box construction of this type, it's important to keep a constant check on square and to make needed corrections before the glue sets hard. Predrill nail holes and nail from both sides of the corners. Use a drill bit that is slightly smaller than the nail diameter. (For a real time saver, locate a finishing nailer, compressed-air type, and use that to do your nailing. It saves time predrilling and usually eliminates any need to countersink the nails so you can apply wood filler to cover the nail heads.)

Run glue in the rabbet joint for the back, and then edge-glue one-by-fours and place them, using two 4d nails per board at each end and four nails per side to hold them in place. Predrill nail holes if you're not using an air nailer.

Set all nails and fill the nail holes.

Tools

- table saw, radial-arm saw, or circular saw
- 12- or 10-point crosscut saw
- mitre box or power mitre saw (optional)
- jigsaw
- router, bits (either a rabbeting bit, or a straight bit; if you use a straight bit for rabbeting backs, you'll also need an edge guide to fit your router)
- electric drill, bits, to fit screws as pilot bits, plus a 1¼″ or 1½″ bit to drill pull holes
- countersink
- bar clamps (you need at least two 30″ and two 24″, but four of each is best)
- screwdriver
- chisel
- tape measure
- framing square
- brush
- steel wood
- 100-grit sandpaper
- finishing sander

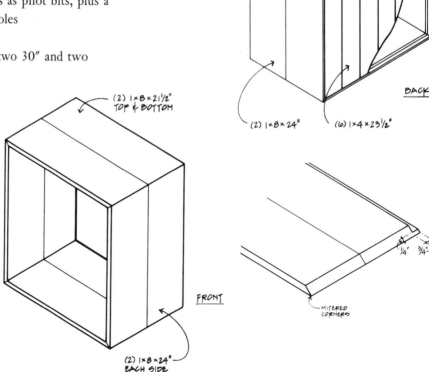

6–48 Kid-size storage modules. (*Courtesy of the Western Wood Products Association*)

Module B

To build module B edge-glue and clamp more one-by-eights just as you did for module A. When the glue sets, cut to length and mitre the ends. For the sides, the mitres are made with the grain of the wood. Cut the same depth rabbet in the backs of the boards for the sides, top, and bottom. I suggest making the rabbet before cutting the mitres if you're using a router and a piloted bit for rabbeting.

Predrill nail holes and assemble with 4d finishing nails in each corner, as per module A. Again, keep a check on corners using a framing or try square.

The back is made of one-by-fours cut to length and glued and nailed in place, as in Module A.

Base Unit

The base unit goes together easily with all four sides, of one-by-three, cut to the proper lengths. Ends are mitred and nailed using two 4d nails per corner along with glue. Keep square corners, and predrill nail holes if you're not using an air nailer. Blocking is cut from ripped down one-by-three (to 1¾″ width) glued and nailed, with 3d nails, inside the frame, so that the one-by-four decking is readily fastened right in place, using 4d nails and wood glue. The base unit is attached to module A by turning module A upside down and attaching the base unit to the module's bottom with four 1¼″ countersunk screws.

Band Unit

The band unit also goes together easily. Cut one-by-threes for the frame to size, and mitre the corners; assemble as with the base unit. Blocking is cut from one-by-two to a 1″ side and is centered inside the frame allowing installation of ¾″-thick decking on both sides of the band unit. Keep corners square, and use 3d nails to glue and nail the blocking in place.

Cut the dozen one-by-fours for decking to length, and place on both sides of the band unit, using glue and 4d nails.

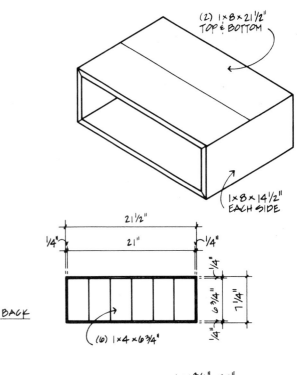

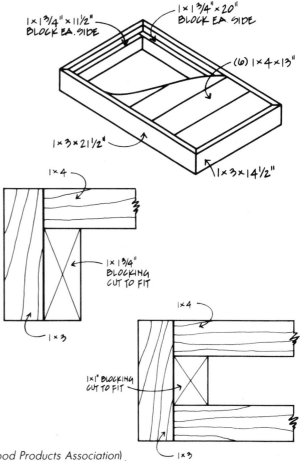

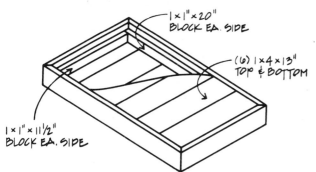

6–49 Kid-size storage modules. (*Courtesy of the Western Wood Products Association*)

Doors

Returning to module A, we find one important change: doors. Doors are made from two lengths of one-by-twelve, ripped to 9¹³/₁₆″ wide, and hinged in place, as shown. Install one leaf of the hinge to the inside of the module. Shim the door into place (doubled shirt cardboards make wonderful ⅛″ door shims). Install one leaf of the hinge to the door. You can drill holes for hand pulls or install commercial units. You may wish to place a 3″ one-by-one stop block top and bottom to keep doors from swinging inwards; a similar result may be had by running a stop strip up the back inside edge *of one door*, leaving a ½″ to 1″ overlap, or by using self-closing hinges.

Doors for module B are cut from a one-by-eight, ripped to 5⅜″, with the hinges mounted at the bottom. Use a magnetic latch or a stop block to keep the door from being pushed the wrong way.

Further Materials

- two hinges per door, invisible preferred
- magnetic latch (or get hinges that are the self-closing type)
- 1 lb 3d finishing nails
- 1 lb 4d finishing nails
- 1¼″ flathead screws
- drawer pulls (optional)
- wood glue
- clear or other finish

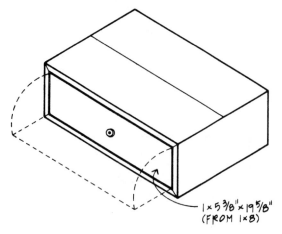

1 × 5⅜″ × 19⅝″
(FROM 1 × 8)

MODULE B WITH DOOR

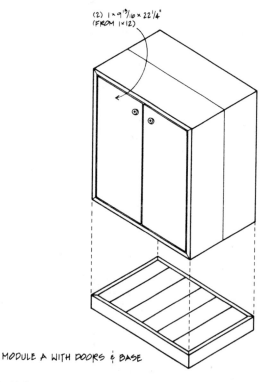

(2) 1 × 9¹³/₁₆ × 22¼″
(FROM 1 × 12)

MODULE A WITH DOORS & BASE

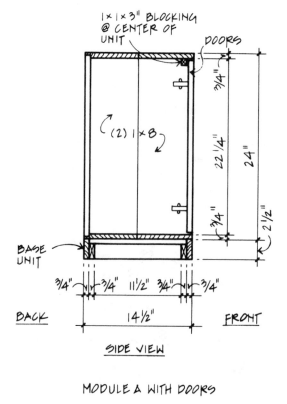

1 × 1 × 3″ BLOCKING @ CENTER OF UNIT

DOORS

(2) 1 × 8

¾″

22¼″

24″

¾″

2½″

BASE UNIT

¾″ ¾″ 11½″ ¾″ ¾″

BACK

14½″

FRONT

SIDE VIEW

MODULE A WITH DOORS

6–50 Kid-size storage modules. (*Courtesy of the Western Wood Products Association*)

Dividers

Dividers are installed into dado joints made in the top and bottom and sides of the unit. Cut the dadoes *before* assembling the storage module. Make all dadoes ¾″ wide by ¼″ deep.

Make dividers by edge-gluing 4′ lengths of one-by-eight, and then ripping the resulting board to 13¾″ wide. Cut to the correct lengths, and cut dadoes on both sides of the middle divider (unless you only want a single divider). Apply glue in the top and bottom dado joints and slide the vertical divider in place. Nail in place using 3d nails from the outside top and bottom into predrilled holes. Next, add glue to the dadoes in the vertical divider and in the sides, and slip in the dividers, nailing from the outside.

Set all nails and fill the nail holes.

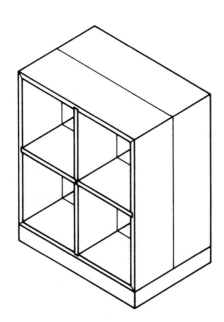

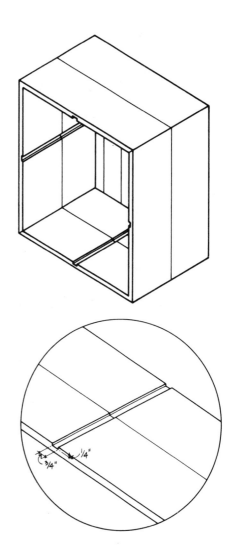

6–51 Dividers. (*Courtesy of the Western Wood Products Association*)

Triangle-Stool Unit

Making the triangle-stool unit requires edge-clamping of two 30″ lengths of one-by-twelve. When the glue sets, cut two triangles, as shown. Cut or drill (start with a ½″ drill hole and use the jigsaw to cut; but make sure to use masking or duct tape on the topside of the board to reduce splintering) the 2½″ holes at the peaks. Round triangle corners to a radius at least as large as a quarter.

Cut the seat from one-by-twelve and its support from one-by-six. Glue and nail in place using 4d nails and starting with the support.

Half-Circle Stool

The half-circle stool is made with two more lengths of one-by-twelve edge-glued and clamped together.

Mark the two semicircles and cut with a jigsaw or band saw (a band saw gives smoother cuts and is really easier to control, if one is available). Mark and cut two handholds to the indicated size, using a ½″ drill bit and a jigsaw.

Cut seat and supports to sizes shown, edge-gluing a one-by-twelve and a one-by-three to form the seat; install using one-by-six seat supports, glue, and 4d finishing nails.

Finishing

Sand to at least 120-grit sandpaper finish all over; stain (if desired) and coat with finish. Recently I've used several brands of water-based poly finishes, and I'm delighted with the results over unstained and stained woods.

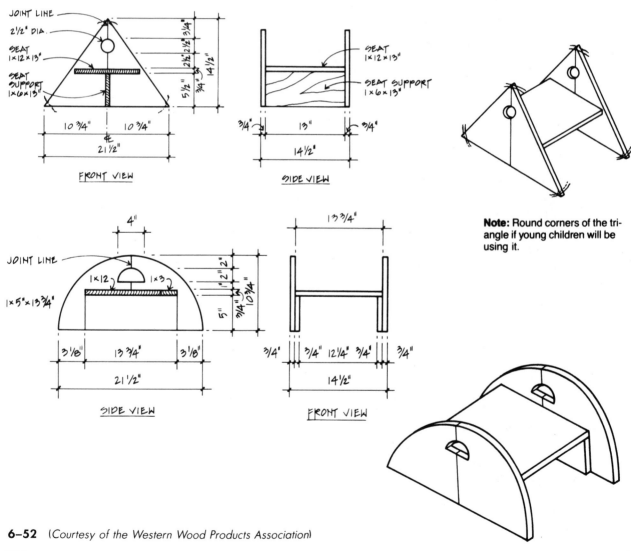

Note: Round corners of the triangle if young children will be using it.

6–52 *(Courtesy of the Western Wood Products Association)*

APPENDIX

■ Softwood Lumber Grades

The chart below does not take into account framing lumber grades; such grades are not generally applicable to small storage project construction, so are not covered. Such types as studs, structural joists, and planks are also omitted.

Adapted from chart by the Southern Forest Products Association

Product	Grade	Character
Finish	B&B	Highest grade, generally clear, limited number of pin knots allowed. Natural or stain finish. Good for storage projects that need fine appearance.
	C	Excellent for paint, or natural with lower needs. Limited number surface checks and small, tight knots allowed. Super general project grade.
	C&Btr	Combination of above 2 grades. Again, excellent for many storage projects.
	D	Economical, serviceable for natural or painted finish. Requires a sharp eye, but will give good storage projects.
Boards S4S	1	High quality, good appearance. Sound and tight-knotted, largest hole permitted $\frac{1}{16}''$. Forms, shelving, crating. Excellent for storage projects.
	2	High-quality sheathing. Tight knots, mostly free of holes. Good for some storage projects.
	3	Good, serviceable sheathing. May be, but not likely to be, good for storage projects.
	4	Pieces like No. 3, but below, with usable lengths at least 24″. A useful grade for our purposes, if care is used in picking boards.

Appearance grades are classed as Superior, Prime, E, and boards as No. 1 Common, down through No. 5 Common, with framing lumber starting at Select Structural No. 1, to SS No. 2, SS No. 3 (and the same for Structural joists and planks, as well as Timbers). Studs are classed as Studs.

With smaller projects such as boxes, it's a good idea to check out lumber at the lumberyard; find a yard that lets you choose your own lumber, piece by piece. For smaller projects, such selection is a nice way to match grain; for a series of projects your choices save lots of time and money.

Members of the American Plywood Association use uniform softwood plywood grading standards. Face grades vary from A to C, for our project purposes.

A is a sanded panel face, for painting or staining, with A-A grade, in Interior or Exterior plywood, made with minimum D interior filler plies on the Interior grade and C on the Exterior, best for uses where both faces will show. A-B has a second face not as good as the A face, but smooth enough for painting. With A-C only an Exterior type is made; A-D is only made in Interior grade.

B grades are classed like A grades, with a less attractive face ply. B grades are fine for uses where surfaces will be painted or covered with other materials, and serve very well under plastic laminates.

C grades are often unsanded, and have open spots in the face (C-C Plugged has most of those openings filled: it is Underlayment grade). C grades are of little use in storage project making.

Oriented strand board (OSB) is made from mechanically aligned wood strands bonded with resins, under heat and pressure. The strands are in layers, at right angles to each other. OSB may be a single panel, or the center layer in other panels.

Waferboard is a similar product, made from wood wafers instead of strands. The wafers are not directionally oriented. Waferboard and OSB might serve as the bottom or backing in storage projects.

Veneer grade N offers a natural-finish veneer, and may be ordered as all heartwood or all sapwood. Factory repairs are limited to six per panel, and must be parallel to the grain, matched for grain and color. This is the top grade of softwood plywood.

Face species for plywood is important only in how it affects your finish. Rotary-cut plywood isn't pretty

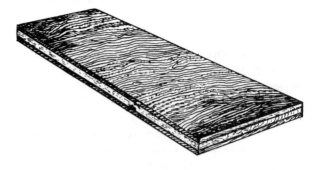

when stained, so a painted surface is usually best. If a natural finish is desired, low-grade solid pine is no more expensive than pine-faced plywood.

Plywood is laid up in odd-numbered plies, with 1/8″ and 1/4″ sheets having three plies, 3/8″ and 1/2″ thicknesses having five plies, and so on. Each ply changes thickness as plywood thickness changes. There are seldom more than seven plies, though some top grades have as many as 15. Sheets, or panels, are available in 4′ widths with lengths ranging from 8′ to 12′—some may be special-ordered longer. Most lumberyards offer smaller, easier to work, panels down to as small as 2′ by 2′. Mail order outfits cater to those of us who use pieces with the longest dimension being 48″ (shipping costs get out of hand if the panel is longer).

Various wood species are used for softwood plywood interior plies; some softwood, some hardwood (though usually aspen, the softer maples, cottonwood, basswood and similar hardwoods, some may actually be beech, birch, sugar [hard or rock] maple, lauan, and sweetgum when use is hardwood). The lower the group number—there are five—the stiffer and stronger the plywood, so look for Group 1 or 2 when strength and stiffness is important.

Index